# EDUCATION STATUS IN INDIA

# EDUCATION STATUS IN INDIA

*Editor*

M.L. Dhawan

ISHA BOOKS
DELHI-110 033

*Education Status in India*

Rs. 750

ISBN: 81-8205-160-6



Published in 2005 in India by
Isha Books, D-43, Prithviraj Road,
Adarsh Nagar, Delhi-110 033

*Laser Typesetting at*: Shree Vaishnavi Creations, Delhi
*Printed at*: Mehra Offset Press, Delhi

# PREFACE

India is famous for its glorious culture from the time immemorial. A well structured system of education was prevailed in India from the remote past. Ancient records of the Indian tradition testify to the search of the *rishis* and sages for higher knowledge, and their discoveries have been continuously transmitted to posterity and kept alive through its long history, marked by periods of expansion, specialization, decline and renewal. Although the ancient education system mainly served the interests of people belonging to the upper classes of the society, it also respected the social plurality and cultural diversity of the region. Gurugrhas, ashramas and Buddhist viharas served as centres of education. That secular subjects were taught along with religious studies are clear from the books that have come down to us.

The rulers of medieval age encouraged the spread of education, scholastic or elementary, to fulfil their religious obligations. To maintain the educational establishments the rulers granted rent-free lands as endowments to pious men of learning who gave instructions to others as a matter of their duty. Domestic instructions were also arranged by wealthy people in their localities through private tutors engaged by them. System of education was closely associated with religious instructions.

The traditional system of education developed in medieval period gradually declined with the advent of colonial rule. The education system of India undergone remarkable changes during this period. Initially, the government of the English east

India company did not consider promoting education among Indians as a part of its duty or obligation. A change, however, came in 1813 at the time of the renewal of the Company's Charter, when a minimum of one lakh rupees were sanctioned annually for the education of Indians. The Charles wood's education despatch of 1854 proposed the creation of separate departments for the administration of education in each province, the founding of the Universities of Calcutta, Bombay and Madras in 1857, and the introduction of a system of Grants-in-Aid. It also laid the basis of the future educational policies adopted by the government. The Christian missionaries also played a significant role in development of education.

However, prior to independence, the growth of institutions of education in India was very slow and diversification in areas of studies was very limited. After independence, the number of institutions has increased significantly. Despite serious handicaps of means and resources, the country has built up during the last 55 years a very large system of education and has created a vast body of men and women equipped with a high order of scientific and technological capabilities, robust humanist and philosophical thought, and creativity. This massive development has been guided by a process of planning and recommendations of several national commissions set up by the Government of India.

Pursuit of integral knowledge and liberation, which has been a constant endeavour of Indian culture, is also the central objective of education. Education is also visualised as an evolutionary force so that each individual is enabled to evolve from purely material consciousness towards superior planes of intellectual and spiritual consciousness. The educational system also aims at promoting environmental protection, universal peace, and international cooperation; and since harmony and unity in external space can best be realised through internal purification and perfection, the educational system endeavours to promote harmonious relationship between both the inner and outer dimensions of the individual, environment and the cosmos. Though riddled with explosion in the growth of population, a large illiterate population and problems of economic poverty affecting one-third of the people, modern India is still set to forge a bright future and to contribute significantly to the higher goals of world peace, human unity and universal welfare.

The present volume comprehensively analyses the status of education in India from ancient period to present day. The development, issues and challenges of Indian education system are described in an elegant style. All landmarks in the history of Indian education are highlighted. The book will serve as a highly valuable reference tool for all who interested to know about the education system of India.

***Editor***

# Contents

# 1

# INTRODUCTION

The first seperate department for education was created in 1910 to look after the education in India. But it was after India achieved its Independence on 15th August 1947. A full fledged Ministry of Education was established on 29th August 1947. The nomenclature and responsibilities of the Education Department has undergone some changes since Independence. The present Department of Education is one of the four constitutent departments of the Ministry of Human Resource Development which was created on 26th September, 1985.

## A NEW POLICY FOR EDUCATION

Education was given high priority after India gained independence in 1947. The new Constitution called on the State to provide free and compulsory primary education and gave the federal government the responsibility for maintaining standards in higher and technical education. By a subsequent amendment to the Constitution education was also declared to be a concern of the provincial governments. India opted for a planned economy, and each five-year plan indicates the directions for educational development.

Dramatic expansion of education has taken place since independence. The number of primary schools has tripled and enrolment has increased from about 30 per cent to 80 percent. The increase in the enrolment of girls at primary level has been particularly impressive, from 17.7 per cent in 1950-1951 to 64.6 per cent in 1986-1987.

Increase in enrollments has been even more spectacular in secondary education, and the number of schoolteachers has risen from 750,000 to 3.7 million. In higher and professional education, the number of institutions and enrolments has increased eightfold and in technical education about tenfold.

In 1964, the government of India appointed a commission to advise on the national pattern of education and on the general principles and policies for educational development. Four years later, an education policy formulated on the basis of the commission's recommendations called for a transformation of the education system which would relate it more closely to the life of the people; a continuous effort to expand educational opportunity; a sustained and intensive effort to raise the quality of education at all stages; an emphasis on the development of science and technology; and the cultivation of moral and social values.

The most remarkable change which took place after the adoption of the 1968 Education Policy was the establishment of a common structure of education. This consisted of ten years of common schooling for all children, followed by two years of higher secondary education and a three-year degree course.

In 1985, the Central Government again reviewed the educational situation and decided to initiate a new National Policy on Education, which was debated extensively by students, teachers and people in all walks of life before it was passed by the two Houses of Parliament in February 1986. A detailed Programme of Action was completed a few months later to ensure that the policy would be implemented without delay.

The1986 education policy envisages a national system which will take determined action to bring about universal primary education an promote the spread of adult literacy, thereby helping to reduce inequalities. The education system will be based on a national curricular framework which contains a common core as well as components specific to each region. The core will cut across subject areas and will be designed to promote such values as India's common cultural heritage, egalitarianism, democracy and secularism, equality of the sexes, protection of the environment, observance of the small family norm, and the scientific approach. Pace-setting schools called Navodaya Vidyalayas will provide quality education to particularly gifted chil&en, irrespective of their families' means, and will promote excellence as well as equity and social justice.

The 1986 policy also emphasizes the need to raise the level of investment in education from about 4 per cent of national income in 1986 to 6 per cent by 1990 and even higher thereafter. Soon after assuming office in 1984, Prime Minister Rajiv Gandhi announced his decision to launch a National Literacy Mission (NLM) to bring functional literacy to some 80 million illiterate people in the 15 to 35 age group.

The teaching of functional literacy is designed to achieve a variety of goals, including selfreliance in literacy and numeracy; the development of awareness among the poor and the illiterate of the causes of their deprivation; the acquisition of skills to improve economic status and general well-being; understanding of the values of national integration; conservation of the environment; women's equality; and the small family norm. NLM also stresses the importance of post-literacy and continuing education. A number of important initiatives have been taken as a result of the new national policy on education:

— A nationwide programme for the improvement of primary education facilities, including reorganization of teacher training, is now under way.

— New curricula have been written for primary and secondary education and new textbooks and teaching materials have been prepared.

— Special programmes have been launched to improve science teaching, introduce computer literacy and promote awareness of environmental issues.

— By 1988, 256 Navodaya Vidyalayas had been established.

— Approximately 500,000 students and 500 voluntary agencies were involved in the National Literacy Mission in 1987-1988. Several districts and big cities such as Delhi, Bombay, Bangalore, Madras and Ahmedabad are launching campaigns to eradicate illiteracy by the end of 1990.

## EDUCATION AND SOCIETY

Historically, Indian education has been elitist. Traditional Hindu education was tailored to the needs of Brahman boys who were taught to read and write by a Brahman teacher. During Mughal rule, Muslim education was similarly elitist, although its orientation reflected economic factors rather than those of caste background. Under British company and crown rule, official education policies reinforced the preexisting elitist tendencies of South Asian education. By tying entrance and advancement in government service to academic education, colonial rule contributed to the legacy of an education system geared to preserving the position and prerogatives of the more privileged. Education served as a "gatekeeper," permitting an avenue of upward mobility to those few able to muster sufficient resources.

Even the efforts of the nationalistic Indian National Congress faltered in the face of the entrenched interests defending the existing system of education. Early in the 1900s, the Congress called for national education, placing an emphasis on technical and vocational training. In 1920 the Congress initiated a boycott of government-aided and government-controlled schools; it founded several "national" schools and colleges, but to little avail. The rewards of British-style education were so great that the boycott was largely ignored, and the Congress schools temporarily disappeared.

Postprimary education has traditionally catered to the interests of the higher and upwardly mobile castes. Despite substantial increases in the spread of middle schools and high schools' growth in enrollment, secondary schooling is necessary for those bent on social status and mobility through acquisition of an office job.

In the nineteenth century, postprimary students were disproportionately Brahmans; their traditional concern with learning gave them an advantage under British education policies. By the early twentieth century, several powerful cultivator castes had realized the advantages of education as a passport to political power and had organized to acquire formal learning. "Backward" castes who had acquired some wealth took advantage of their status to secure educational privilege. In the mid-1980s, the vast majority of students making it through middle school to high school continued to be from high-level castes and middle- to upper-class families living in urban areas. A region's three or four most powerful castes typically dominated the school system. In addition, the widespread role of private education and the payment of fees even at government-run schools discriminated against the poor.

The goals of the 1986 National Policy on Education demanded vastly increased enrollment. In order to have attained universal elementary education in 1995, the 1981 enrollment level of 72.7 million would have had to increase to 160 million in 1995. Although the seventh plan suggested the adoption of new education methods to meet these goals, such as the promotion of television and correspondence courses and open school systems, the actual extended coverage of children was not very great.

Many critics of India's education policy argue that total school enrollment is not actually a goal of the government considering the extent of society's vested interest in child labor. In this context, education can be seen as a tool that one social class uses to prevent the rise of another. Middle-class Indians frequently distinguish between the children of the poor as "hands," or children who must be taught to work, and their own children as "minds," or children who must be taught to learn.

The upgraded curriculum with increased requirements in English and in the sciences appears to be causing difficulties for many children. Although all the states have recognized that curriculum reform is needed, no comprehensive plan to link curricular changes with new ways of teaching, learning, teacher training, and examination methods has been implemented.

The government instituted an important program for improving physical facilities through a phased drive in all primary schools in the country called Operation Blackboard. Under Operation Blackboard, Rs1 billion was allocated—but not spent—in 1987 to pay for basic amenities for village schools, such as toys and games, classroom materials, blackboards, and maps. This financial allotment averaged Rs2,200 for each government-run primary school. Additional goals of Operation Blackboard included construction of classrooms that would be usable in all weather, and an additional teacher, preferably a woman, in all single-teacher schools.

The nonformal education system implemented in 1979 was the major government effort to educate dropouts and other unenrolled children. Special emphasis was given to the nonformal education system in the nine states regarded by the government as having deficient education systems: Andhra Pradesh, Assam, Bihar, Jammu and Kashmir, Madhya Pradesh, Orissa, Rajasthan, Uttar Pradesh, and West Bengal. A large number of children who resided in these states could not attend formal schools because they were employed, either with or without wages. Seventy-five percent of the country's children who were not enrolled in school resided in these states in the 1980s.

The 1986 National Policy on Education gave new impetus to the nonformal education system. Revised and expanded programs focused on involving voluntary organizations and training talented and dedicated young men and women in local communities as instructors. The results of a late 1980s integrated pilot project for nonformal and adult education for women and girls in the Lucknow district of Uttar Pradesh provide important data for analyzing recent implementation trends and initial results of both the nonformal education system and adult education in India. Under this project, 300 centers were opened in rural parts of the district with the approval of the Department of Education, the central government, and the state government of Uttar Pradesh with financial and advisory support from the United Nations Educational, Scientific, and Cultural Organization (UNESCO).

Because of the shortage of women teachers in rural areas of Uttar Pradesh, in the pilot project nonformal education for girls aged six to fourteen was integrated with the adult education program for women aged fifteen to thirty-five, so that the same staff and infrastructure could be used. Most of the families of the project participants were in subsistence farming or engaged as farmhands, clerical workers, and petty merchants. Often the brothers of female participants attended a formal school situated about one or two kilometers from their homes. Most of the 300 instructors for the 300 centers were young women between the ages of eighteen and thirty-five. Each center averaged twenty-five women and twenty girl participants.

The physical facilities of the centers varied from village to village. Classes might be held on the balcony of a brick house, within a temple, in a room of a mud-walled house, or under open thatch-roof structures. Besides focusing on the acquisition of literacy skills, the project increased participant motivation by also offering instruction in household work, such as sewing, knitting, and preserving food.

In 1987 a UNESCO mission to evaluate progress in this project in the areas of functional literacy, vocational skills, and civic awareness observed that randomly chosen participants in both nonformal and adult education classes effectively demonstrated their reading and writing skills at appropriate levels. As a result of many such local programs, literacy rates improved between 1981 and 1991. Male literacy increased from 56.5 percent in 1981 to 64.2 percent in 1991 while women's literacy rate increased from 29.9 percent in 1981 to 39.2 percent in 1991.

Understanding India's health care and education systems contributes to the larger understanding of this complex nation's diverse society. General trends and averages concerning social conditions on a national level may not adequately describe how human activity is expressed spatially and temporally in specific areas. The great variations in local environmental and social conditions require that national and state or union territory programs aimed at improving the quality of life not adhere too strictly to any one standard plan.

Local climate, topography, and drainage patterns all need to be considered in terms of how they relate to local forms of land use and ethnic and linguistic groupings. Increasing urbanization in India also complicates efforts at monitoring local conditions. Only with the full support and understanding of India's many rural and urban residents will new ways of focusing India's immense human resources toward the goals of developing and conserving renewable natural resources, limiting population growth, providing increased health care, and achieving education for all be successful.

Education has been in prime focus throughout India's development plans. Its importance can be gauged from the fact that it is included as a part of the Directive Principles of State Policy in the Constitution, which states that " the State shall endeavour to provide within a period of ten years from the commencement of this Constitution, for free and compulsory education for all children until they complete the age of fourteen years".

Educational policy and progress are reviewed in the light of the goal of national development and priorities set from time to time. The National Policy on Educatuion was formulated in 1982, and was later updated in 1992, where specific responsibilities for organising, implementing and financing its proposals were assigned. The total budgetary expenditure on

Education by the Education Departments of the Centre and States has increased from Rs. 644.6 millions in 1951-52 to Rs. 300,000 millions in 1995-96. There are, at present 130 plan schemes in the Department with a total Eighth Plan outlay of Rs. 74430 Millions.

The state of political and economic affairs too are responsible for determinig the educational policy. For example, in the second five year plan (1956-60) when heavy industries became the basic industries, the socialistic education was given and was put emphasis on conversion of basic education and secondary and higher educations. Also, when India saw the economic crisis and the school attendance rate fell in 1960's a big reconsideration on the whole education was done establishing the advisory committee including foreigners.

Today the system which was decided by the international conference party is revolved. It has 10-2-3 system and in some states it has 5-3-2 system or 4-3-3 system. The elemtary education is divided into the first term and the latter term. The secondary education is divided to the first term and the latter term, and the first term is for studying the extention of elementary education and the latter term is divided into the college entering course and vocational education course to study. It is the characteristic that scientific education and talent education are done. The rate of the students to enter the first term is 24.6%. For the higher education, 137 higher educational systems aim at the improvement of the qualities of education and research in scientific technology

## ROLE OF UN

Impressive gains have been made in education, yet the goal of universalisation of primary education is still elusive. While 95 per cent of villages have a primary school within walking distance, some 69 million children between the ages of 6-14 years are out of school. UNDP's focus is on enhancing the capacities of communities and teachers to support improvement of the quality of primary education.

UNDP's approach to the problem of out-of-school children, proposes that all such children be included into the schooling system irrespective of whether they work in agriculture, in industry or at home. In the Indian context, many commentators and development agencies have sought to distinguish between children who work at home, in agriculture or in assisting petty family business from those who work outside the home for a wage. For UNDP there is no such distinction because in both cases, the children's Constitutional right to education is denied. Moreover, since it is primarily girl children who work at home assisting their mothers in the household tasks of looking after younger siblings, cooking, cleaning, washing etc., such a distinction would discriminate against female children.

### *School Health Programme*

Two initiatives with somewhat varying strategies and emphasis are being simultaneously undertaken under this pilot programme

- *Urban School Health Initiative*: Assisted by a local health NGO, this pilot initiative focuses on building capacities of school teachers, Parent Teacher Associations (PTAs) and Government health personnel in select clusters, and has helped to develop a common perspective and understanding of the health of children. The intervention supports training of one teacher from each class to do the initial screening of children in her/his class. PTAs are playing a critical role not only in monitoring the programme interventions but also in carrying the issues of hygiene and sanitation into their own neighbourhoods.
- *Initiative for Learning Disabilities*: With technical backstopping and assistance in networking from the Society for Rehabilitation of Cognitive and Communicative Disorders, this initiative builds on the experience of Government's District Primary Education Programme (DPEP) in community mobilisation for advocacy on issues of learning disabilities. Educated youth in the community

are being identified and trained along with school teachers and Primary Health Care (PHC) doctors and other health personnel to assist in screening children, providing ongoing support for children with mild learning disabilities and in maintaining a record of the progress of each child.

### *UN Support for the Community-based Primary Education*

Five UN organisations – UNDP, UNICEF, UNFPA, UNESCO and ILO – are participating in the programme with their five nodal Ministries and nine State Departments. The programme is a vehicle for channeling UN System support for the ongoing efforts of the Government of India towards Universalisation of Primary Education (UPE).

The programme is helping to enhance and sustain community participation in effective school management and the protection of child rights. Support is also being provided for improving performance of teachers in the use of interactive, child-centred and gender-sensitive methods of teaching in multi-grade classrooms, and to redress social constraints which affect attendance and performance of school-age children, mainly girls, in selected areas. The focus is on addressing the educational needs of working children, children with disabilities and adolescent girls.

Primary schools in selected areas are being transformed into *empowered community schools* through reflection, analysis and learning from shared experiences. The programme is being piloted in select districts with high concentrations of tribal populations, low female literacy, low economic status, contiguity, visible UN presence and educational backwardness in nine states – Andhra Pradesh, Chattisgarh, Jharkhand, Karnataka, Maharashtra, Madhya Pradesh, Orissa, Rajasthan and Uttar Pradesh. The interventions are location-specific and respond to situational variations.

## FREE AND COMPULSORY ELEMENTARY EDUCATION

In a milieu of increasing deprivation, the absence of clarity on the questions of legal liability and quality renders meaningless the constitutional amendment on free and compulsory elementary education. For primary education in India, these have been the best of times. Arguably, these have also been the worst of times. The elevation of elementary education to the status of a justiciable fundamental right does not explain how such a move would reverse the conditions that prevented the universalisation of elementary education in the last 51 years of operation of the Indian Constitution. In the absence of sustained raising of the issue, this elevation may, in fact, increase the powers of the executive to take away from the poor the entitlement to meaningful education.

In the bureaucratic rush to educate anyhow, the substantive debates around issues such as curriculum, pedagogy, teacher orientation and appropriate institutional arrangements are likely to be rendered irrelevant. Debates on the relationship of education to issues such as poverty, food and child labour too are likely to meet a similar fate. Etched into the Constitution at the time of its inception as a Directive Principle of State Policy, Article 45 was the only Article that had a deadline attached to it. Universal elementary education (UEE) had to be achieved within 10 years of the operationalisation of the Constitution, that is, by 1960. This deadline was extended 10 years at a time, up to 2000. The 1990s saw increased attention to education and literacy. At the Jomtien Conference on Education For All, held in 1989, this issue received the focussed attention of international aid agencies as well. Meanwhile, failures in the realisation of the goals of development were instrumental in inducing a change within the development discourse, from the language of policy to the language of rights.

The shift from the language of policy to the language of rights occurred in the 1980s, but the ground for this shift was already under preparation in the 1970s. The failure of economic development as a policy in the Third World countries was all too apparent in the early 1970s. The shift in the field of education of the deprived, especially adults - from social education and skill training amongst the farmers in the 1960s to the conscientisation of the masses in the 1970s and to their empowerment to fight for their own rights in the 1980s and 1990s - is all too well known.

In addition, the emergence of women's movements, autonomous and party-affiliated, compelled the government to give attention to women's development based on this philosophy. Women's development programmes created a bizarre situation wherein the state, instead of ensuring the implementation of policies such as the payment of minimum wages, equal pay for equal work and so on, taught women to wage struggles for such rights against the establishment. With the failures of structural adjustment policies in Africa and Latin America, there was a loss of faith in the executive arm of the government.

International development opinion made a noticeable shift towards the human development paradigm with an inclination towards rights. According to this paradigm, every human being is entitled to a basic set of rights. Rights empower people whereas policies are instruments of the government: this was the implicit belief of the rights-based approach to development. However, the immediate motivation for this change of status for UEE from policy to right came from a Supreme Court verdict in the early 1990s.

The Supreme Court observed in the Mohini Jain case in 1992 that the Directive Principles, which are fundamental in the governance of the country cannot be read separately from the Fundamental Rights. The more notable part of the judgment was its insistence that the right to education be read as an integral part of the right to life guaranteed under Article 21, Part III. Interpreted in an extended sense, the right to life implies a life worthy of living, which can hardly be conceptualised without giving a significant place in it to education.

The new constitutional amendment seeks to make elementary education free and compulsory for children in the age group of six to 14 years. The ambit of meanings of the key terms "free" and "compulsory" is to be explicated by subsequent legislation, a Central law serving as a framework for a plethora of State laws. Commentators have been quick to point out that the crucial age segment of zero to six has been left out, and that there is no state commitment to quality.

In addition, there is the important issue of deciding as to whose legal liability it is if the child does not go to school once the state has made the provision for free schooling. We must remember that terms such as "free" and "compulsory" are not new policy gestures. There already exists in many States a record of legislation that makes education free and compulsory. In Travancore, now part of Kerala, primary education was made "free" in 1904 and "compulsory" in 1945. Compulsory education Acts were also passed in the States of Madhya Bharat; Bihar and the United Provinces.

Many States have also taken substantial measures to enhance the scope of public instruction. There are measures such as freeships for the socially disadvantaged sections; where there is a fee, it is minimal. Similarly textbooks and uniforms are provided free of cost to the weaker sections and in some cases to girls. According to the Sixth All India Educational Survey, of the 5,70,455 primary schools in the country, 29.96 per cent gave free uniforms to pupils. In Tamil Nadu, 95 per cent of primary schools have implemented the scheme of supply of free uniforms, and free textbooks are distributed in 54.56 per cent of the primary schools. Mid-day meal programmes have been in operation in many States, at least intermittently. It is important to ask why, despite all these measures, poor households bear a major share of the expense of sending children to school.

According to the estimates presented in National Sample Survey (NSS) 52nd round, 1995-96, and National Council for Applied Economic Research (NCAER), 1994 household surveys, these households bear 38-43 per cent of the visible cost of sending children to government schools where significant measures like freeships already exist. This estimate excludes the opportunity costs borne by the household, which are difficult to quantify.

The only new dimension to this issue would be the enhanced force of the state to coerce children into attending any manner of schools, including the ones staffed by para-teachers working in ramshackle classrooms that overflow with children. It is important to remember that the right to education has come at a time when the poorest sections of society face exclusion from the production process itself. Increasing unemployment, casualisation and large-scale retrenchment of labour and suicide by indebted farmers - at times by consuming the same poison that is supposed to save their crops and bring prosperity - form the context in which this constitutional amendment has been made.

Between 1997 and 2000, there have been 1,826 cases of suicide in Anantapur district of Andhra Pradesh alone. Out of this, as many as 868 people killed themselves by consuming Monocrotophos, the pesticide supplied free to the farmers by the Andhra Pradesh government. Given the slowdown in agricultural growth, the rising food prices, a decline in investment in rural infrastructure and reduced employment opportunities, a rise in rural poverty is not surprising.

Hunger deaths amidst overflowing granaries and suicide by farmers across the States were the starkly visible signs of growing deprivation and helplessness during the past decade of reforms. Parts of India have also been reeling under drought. In this grim situation, it is worth asking what kind of measures will make the newly legislated right an enforceable policy.

One gets an inkling of a future scenario from a report that appeared in The Hindu. It showed the Andhra Pradesh Chief Minister's view on who should bear the responsibility for children's absence from school: "...The Chief Minister referred to a Supreme Court order to the Government of India in this regard, and said the State government would amend existing laws to enable compulsory education. It was proposed to introduce deterrent punishment and other disincentives to those who declined to send their children to school." In addition, the Chief Minister made an erring parent, who did not send his child to school, tell the audience that what he did was an offence. In fact, punishing parents has been one of the central issues in the States legislation, and the National Alliance for Fundamental Right to Education (NAFRE) claims that a large number of parents have indeed been persecuted.

One can guess from such views what manner of accountability the new Act is expected to promote. It seems there will be a new emphasis on the myth that it is the ignorant who are responsible for perpetuating ignorance. It is the parents who will be seen as having committed a cognisable offence by not sending their child to school. Where will the parents lodge their complaint about the poor quality of schooling? Where will they find a forum to protest against discriminatory policies such as the recruitment of para-teachers for schools that serve the poor? DESPITE the noticeable silence in the amendment with regard to a commitment to quality, the freezing of the contested terrain of education as a legal entity is likely to reinforce a particular turn towards teaching as an evidence-based activity.

Teaching functionaries in government schools, wary of the legal action that they may become liable to, may shun efforts towards creative pedagogy. In debates on education, empirical testing for outcomes is likely to triumph over the more qualitative process-based approaches. The former may stand the scrutiny of courts better. If a poor person were to approach the court saying that the provision of a para-teacher meant downgrading of quality, a denial of the right to quality, what manner of evidence would the courts admit on quality issues? The new policy of defining curricular goals in terms of 'minimum levels of learning' hints at the direction in which school education is being pushed.

The earlier concern for overall development is being replaced by a preference for behaviouristic, necessarily superficial, symptoms of learning. To conclude, one must note the view taken by the National Human Rights Commission (NHRC) in response to a petition submitted by Janaki Rajan, Kumkum Roy, Ashwini Cariappa and Sanaya Nariman. These petitioners argued that the right to education would become meaningless if the curriculum was used for the propagation of communalism and if the basic infrastructure remained poor and inadequate.

In its response, the NHRC has said that the right to education can only be safeguarded by a democratically oriented system that is capable of providing education of a certain quality. The Commission has merged the issues of equality and quality, paving the way for a fresh debate on provision of education. The notice served to the Human Resource Development Ministry and others argues that the status of education as a fundamental right extends to the character and the quality of the education provided.

## UNIVERSAL PRIMARY EDUCATION IN INDIA

In a nation as sprawling and diverse as India, offering even a few years of education to all boys and girls is a daunting prospect, but one that the government is confronting with the aid of the international community.

Initiated in the early 1990s, the District Primary Education Program (DPEP) was designed to facilitate India's efforts to achieve universal primary education and it has since become the world's largest education program, reaching 60 million children.

While the World Bank is the single largest contributor to this initiative, having provided $1.2 billion, the program is also supported by many other donors, including the European Commission, UNICEF and the governments of the Netherlands and Sweden. Spread over 271 districts in 18 states in India, the program operates where female literacy levels are below the national average.

The focus of DPEP is children between the ages of six and 14, and its target is to provide at least four or five years of quality primary education. The project also aims to reduce the number of school dropouts and improve the overall quality of primary education. In addition to girls who were formerly prevented from attending school, the beneficiaries include children with mild to moderate disabilities, and working children.

Enrollment in general has increased, and in a three-year period enrollment of girls increased to 43 percent from 38 percent. The recently instituted national education program is using DPEP as a blueprint for its overarching aim of delivering universal primary education across India.

The Centre is unlikely to allocate additional funds to the primary education department for the Sarva Siksha Abhiyan and the mid-day meal scheme during the current fiscal, though it is expected to collect nearly Rs 5,000 crore through the education cess. The funds are not expected to be allocated to the two schemes due to low absorptive capacity of the primary education sector, senior human resources development ministry officials said.

## PRIVATE SCHOOLING IN RURAL INDIA

Schools in India come in three basic forms – Government schools, Private Aided (PA) schools (almost fully government financed but privately managed), and Private Unaided (PUA) schools. A very large increase in the number of and enrollment in PUA schools at the primary school level has been noted in recent years. This is in stark contrast to earlier trends, where PUA schools were important only at the secondary education level.

A deterioration of the "public" school system (including a decline in the quality of PA schools, which tend to be very similar in most respects to government schools) has caused PUA schools to emerge even in areas that already had government of PA schools. There are also, however, found to be enormous variations in PUA fees, which enables some poor households to send at least one of their children to such schools.

## SECONDARY EDUCATION

The Secondary Education which serves as a bridge between primary and higher education is expected to prepare young persons between the age group 14-18 in the world of work and entry into higher education. The Secondary Education starts with classes 9-10 leading to higher secondary classes 11 and 12. The relevant children population at the secondary and senior secondary level, as projected in 1996-97 by NSSO has been estimated at 9.66 crores. Against this population, the enrolment figures of the 1997-98 shows that only 2.70 crores attending schools. Thus, two-third of the eligible population remains out of the school system. To accommodate the children in schools at secondary level, we have at present 1.10 lakhs institutions (1998-99). With the emphasis on universalisation of elementary education and programmes like District Primary Education Programme, the enrolment is bound to increase and once this universalisation takes place, we may require more than two lakhs institutions at the secondary level to accommodate them.

The Secondary education is supported by the following organisations under the administrative control of the Union Department of Education:

— National Council of Educational Research and Training (NCERT)

— Central Board of Secondary Education (CBSE)

— National Institute of Open Schooling (NIOS)

— Kendriya Vidyalaya Sangathan (KVS)

— Navodaya Vidyalaya Samiti (NVS)

— Central Tibetan Schools Administration (CTSA)
— Central Institute of Education Technology
— State Institute of Education Technology ( AP, Bihar, Gujarat, Kerala, Maharashtra, Orissa, UP)

### *National Council of Educational Research and Training (NCERT)*

The NCERT was established in 1961. It functions as a resource centre in the field of school education and teacher education. The NCERT undertakes programmes related to research, development and training extension and dissemination of educational innovations etc., through various constituent Departments at the headquarters in New Delhi and 11 Field Officers all over the country. Publication of school textbooks and other educational material like teachers' guides/manuals etc. are its major functions. The NCERT undertakes time bound projects in Pre-School Education, Education for Girls and Education for SC/STs. The NCERT has following constituent units in the field: (i) RIE at Bhubaneshwar, Ajmer, Mysore, Bhopal (ii) CIET (iii) NIE (iv) PSSCIVE, Bhopal. A fifth RIE is proposed at Shillong.

Central Institute of Education Technology (CIET) is an important unit of NCERT which is engaged in the production of satellite based audio and video programmes for Elementary and Secondary levels which are aired on All India Radio, and Doordarshan. CIET also coordinates programme production activities of the six States Institute of Education Technology at Patna, Lucknow, Ahmedabad, Hyderabad, Pune,and Bhubaneshwar.

### *Central Board of Secondary Education (CBSE)*

The Central Board of Secondary Education was set up by a special Resolution of the Government of India in 1929 with a specific responsibility of raising the standard of Secondary

Education and making the services of the Board available to various educational institutions in the country. It is a self-financing institute that manages all the financial requirement out of its own funds generated through collection of fees and sale of material brought out by the Board.

The Board is headed by its Chairman, who controls all the functions of the Board and heads all the committees constituted for the purpose. The Board has seven committees, namely, Finance, Curriculum, Examination, Result, Affiliation, Committee for Private Candidates and Committees of Courses. The Chairman is also the Head of the Governing Body who governs and gives advices on different matters of the Boards from time to time. The Education Secretary is the Controlling Authority of the Board.

The Board has six regional offices at Ajmer, Chandigarh, Chennai, Allahabad, Guwahati and Delhi to ensure better communication and services to different agencies and schools affiliated in various parts of the country. The number of schools affiliated to CBSE has gone up phenomenally from 309 in 1962 to more than 6700 in 2003.

### *National Institute of Open Schooling (NIOS)*

National Institute of Open Schooling (earlier known as National Open School) was established in November 1989 as an autonomous registered society. Since October 1990, through a Resolution NIOS has been vested with authority to examine and certify students registered with it, up to pre-degree courses.

Admissions are held thrice a year during May and November (Direct Admission) and in July (through Accredited Institutions). Currently National Institute of Open Schooling has more than 14 Lakh students on its rolls from almost every State and Union Territory of India and abroad. The NIOS provides the following programmes:

— Foundation Course

— Secondary Education Course

— Senior Secondary Education Course

— Vocational Education Programme

— Life Enrichment Programme

— Open Basic Education for Universal Elementary Education (UEE)

NIOS conducts examinations twice a year during March/April and September/October. Candidates are allowed to appear in one, two or more subjects and credits are accumulated till the certification criteria are fulfilled. A candidate can avail as many as nine chances to appear in public examinations.

NIOS serves its clients through a network of study centres all over the country. These centres provide individualised support to its learners to facilitate the learning processes. At present there are about 2500 Study Centres catering to about fourteen lakh students all over the country and abroad. These study centres are also known as Accredited Institutions (AIs), Accredited Vocational Institutions (AVIs) and Open Basic Education(OBEs).

### *Kendriya Vidyalaya Sangathan (KVS)*

Kendriya Vidyalaya Sangathan is an autonomous organisation established in 1965 with the primary objective of setting up and monitoring Kendriya Vidyalayas. The Kendriya Vidyalayas have a four fold mission, namely:

— To cater to the educational needs of children of transferable Central Government employees including Defence and Para-military personnel by providing a common programme of education.

— To pursue excellence and set the pace in the field of school education.

— To initiate and promote experimentation and innovations in education in collaboration with other bodies like the Central Board of Secondary Education (CBSE) and the National Council of Educational Research and Training (NCERT) etc.

— To develop the spirit of national integration and create a sense of 'Indianness' among children.

In pursuance of the above objectives, the Kendirya Vidyalayas have been set up with the following features:

— Common text books and bilingual medium of instruction.

— Affiliation to the CBSE.

— Co-education and composite system.

— Teaching of Sanskrit from class V to IX. Students also study Sanskrit as an additional optional subject in Class X and as an elective of +2 stage.

— Preference in admission to children whose parents had the higher number of transfers during the previous years.

— Maintenance of an appropriate teacher-pupil ratio to ensure quality of teaching.

— Waiver of tuition fees for boys up to class VIII for girls and for Scheduled Caste/Scheduled Tribe students, besides the children of the employees of the Kendriya Vidyalaya Sangathan (KVS) up to class XII.

Kendriya Vidyalayas are opened in the Civil Sector on the recommendation of various Ministries/Departments of Central Government/State Government or the Central Government Employees Welfare Co-ordination Committee. The number of schools in this sector are more or less frozen with a view not to increase the non-plan expenditure. Some Kendriya Vidyalayas are opened on the recommendations of the Ministry of Defence in the Defence Sector for which the expenditure is met by the Ministry of Defence. Kendriya Vidyalayas are also opened in the Institutes of higher learning and project sectors where the recurring and non-recurring expenditure are fully met by the sponsoring project authorities.

In order to meet the ever-increasing demands from the target groups (Civil and Defence Sectors), the Government had approved in May 1993 opening of up to 20 Vidyalayas each year during the period 1993-94 to 1997-98 and as many as may be practicable, in terms of suitability of the proposal, in the project Sector. At present, there are 874 Kendriya Vidyalayas spread across all States and UTs. Proposal are under consideration to open some more KVs in NE States during 1999-2000 to 2001-2002.

### *Navodaya Vidyalaya Samiti (NVS)*

This is another autonomous body which was set up to establish and manage fully residential co-educational schools covering class VIth to XIIth known as Jawahar Navodaya Vidyalayas (JNVs) with the aim of:

— To provide good quality modern education up to Senior Secondary stage to the talented children predominantly from rural areas, without regard to their family's socio-economic condition.

— To play the trend setter and pace setter role in their area.

— To serve, in each district, as a focal point for improvement in the quality of school education through sharing of experiences and facilities.

Admissions to the JNVs are made through competitive examination conducted by CBSE and children are admitted to Class VI. Education in Navodaya Vidyalayas is free. So far 404 Navodaya Vidyalayas are in operation covering 30 States/UTs in the country except the States of West Bengal & Tamil Nadu. The Scheme envisages establishment of NVs, on an average, one in each district in the country.

The Scheme started with 2 JNVs in 1985-86. As on date 404 districts have been covered in 30 States/Union Territories in the country except West Bengal and Tamil Nadu who have not opted for the scheme so far. The matter is being perused with the concerned State Governments for sanctioning Navodaya Vidyalayas in remaining uncovered districts. 1,16,108 students were on the rolls of Navodaya Vidyalayas during academic year 1997-98. Roughly 25,000 students are admitted every year from about 500,000 applicants. It is proposed to increase the capacity of existing 100 schools during the 9th Plan period.

For opening of a Navodaya Vidyalaya is based on the proposal from the concerned State/UT Governments offering 30 acres of suitable land free of cost, sufficient temporary building and other infrastructure free of rent or on permanent basis which could accommodate 240 students and staff for three to four years till Samiti constructs its own building at the permanent site.

### *Central Tibetan Schools Administration (CTSA)*

The Central Tibetan Schools Administration (CTSA) was set up in 1961 as an autonomous organisation by the Government of India. The main objectives of the CTSA are to run, manage and assist institutions for the education of children of Tibetan refugees in India. To keep the Tibetan Community abreast with all aspects of modern education and development while retaining essentials of their traditional system and culture, schools have been opened all over the country, where there is concentration of Tibetans, mostly in hilly areas. The Administration runs 79 schools.

### *Schemes and Programmes*

The development of Secondary Education sector is also supported by the following specific Centrally Sponsored Schemes:

— Vocationalisation of Secondary Education
— Integrated Education for Disabled Children
— Computer Literacy and Studies in Schools (CLASS)
— Education Technology
— Improvement of Science Education in Schools
— Promotion of Yoga in Schools
— Strengthening Culture and Values in Schools
— Strengthening Boarding and Hostel Facilities for Girls

*Vocationalisation of Secondary Education*

In accordance with the priority accorded to Vocational Education in the National Policy on Education, a Centrally Sponsored Scheme of Vocationalisation of Secondary Education was launched in February, 1988. The main objectives of the Scheme of Vocationalisation of Secondary education, as spelt out in the NPE are to provide diversification of educational opportunities so as to enhance individual employability, reduce the mismatch between demand and supply of skilled manpower and to provide an alternative for those pursuing higher education.

*Basic Components of the Scheme*

— Creation of separate administrative structure at the State, District, school level to manage vocational education programmes.

— Strengthening of SCERTs to provide technical support for research, development, training and evaluation.

— Conducting district vocational surveys in all the districts for assessment of labour market demand.

— Development of curriculum, instructional material, text books and guide material.

— Provision of two full time teachers per section, honorarium for part time experts, training of teachers.

— Provision for one workshed per section and basic equipment for the course.

*Integrated Education for Disabled Children (IEDC)*

Under the scheme, financial assistance is provided for education of disabled children which includes assistance towards books and stationery, uniforms, transport allowance, readers allowance for blind children, escort allowance for severely handicapped children, boarding and lodging charges for disabled children residing in hostels, salary of resource teachers and helpers, setting up and equipping resource rooms, survey and assessment of disabled children, purchase and production of instructional material, training and orientation of resource teachers, funds for making modifications in school buildings and salary of an administrative Cell at the State level to implement and monitor the programme.

According to the last survey conducted by the NSSO in 1991, the population of disabled children was estimated at 16.15 million which is currently estimated to have gone up to 20 million. Under the Persons with Disabilities Act it has become mandatory for the Central/State/local governments to provide basic education to children with disabilities up to 18 years of age. The Act also calls for a series of activities to promote the education of such persons and mainstream them in general school system. Based on the provisions of the Act and experiences in recent years it is proposed to revise the existing IEDC for which a group has been set up.

*Computer Literacy And Studies in Schools (CLASS)*

A revised CLASS Scheme has been introduced from the financial year 2001-02. Main Features of the scheme are :

— Each State/UT would be requested to formulate a Computer Education Plan (CEP). The CEP would indicate the steps already taken by the State Government/UTs and the assistance which they now require.

— The Department of Secondary & Higher Education would set up a Project Monitoring and Evaluation Group at the national level which would consider the CEPs. Funds would be allocated on the recommendations of the Project Monitoring and Evaluation Group.

— The State Governments would have to contribute a minimum of 25% of the funds required for the scheme.

*Education Technology*

This Scheme is being operated since 1972. The Scheme has been modified from 1987-88. Under the modified scheme, the entire cost of Radio-cum-Cassette Player, in Primary Schools and 75% cost of colour TV in upper Primary Schools is met by the Central Government. The States/UTs are required to provide audio software (cassettes) along with Radio-cum-Cassette Players.

To enable production of suitable programmes for these schools, six autonomous State Institutes of Education Technology, in U.P., Bihar, Orissa, Maharashtra, Gujarat and Andhra Pradesh, have been set up and are funded under the Scheme for the production of school programmes to be broadcast by the Akashvani and telecast by the Doordarshan. A new SIET ahs also been set up in Kerala by the Kerala Govt. and the programme production cost alone is being funded by the Central Govt. for the present.

Up to September 1999, 3,92,463 Radio-cum-Cassette Players and 75,903 Colour Televisions have been sanctioned to the States and UTs, for distribution to Primary and other category of Schools.

The Scheme has been evaluated by National Institute of Educational Planning and Administration (NIEPA). The report, inter-alia, recommends the continuance of the Scheme with certain improvements in its management. The Scheme has also been evaluated by the Social and Rural Institute (SRRI), New Delhi. The finding of the study clearly show a direct relationship between viewing of educational Telecasts and significantly better performance by children on factors such as language skills and Visual representation which satisfy their curiosity. The major findings of the study have been brought to the notice of the concerned States/UTs for taking necessary action.

## TECHNICAL AND VOCATIONAL EDUCATION

India has an extensive technical and vocational education system. This description of the national program may help distance educators in other countries.

### *Educational/Training Enterprise*

The Educational and Training Enterprize in India which operates at all conceivable levels from pre-school to post doctoral is of a monumental size. In the formal education system, the preschool years range from 1 to 3 followed by 10 years of high school and 23 years of higher secondary. The tertiary education is of mostly 3 to 4 years for under-graduate studies followed by Masters, M.Phil and Ph.D degrees. There are many Universities and institutions for the post-doctoral research and training. On the non-formal side the age group addressed 9 to 40 under two separate programmes for school age children and adults, respectively. The Open learning system has also started functioning in the country with the establishment of the National Open School and National Open University to provide the leadership and direction. At present there are 5 Open Universities and 4 Open Schools in India.

There are more than 7,40,000 formal schools. More than 3.6 million teachers are working on full time basis. There are more than 175 Universities offering under graduate and post graduate courses and about 6000 colleges affiliated to these universities. The educational structure in India is generally referred to as the Ten + Two + Three (10+2+3) pattern. The first ten years provide undifferentiated general education for all students. The +2 stage, also known as the higher secondary or senior secondary, provides for differentiation into academic and vocational streams and marks the end of school education.

In some states, the plus two stage is located in intermediate, junior or degree colleges but is not regarded as a part of the tertiary stage of education. Besides, the technician educational programme has been shown to exist after the ten year of general education. The location of one year or two year programmes of the Industrial Training Institutes have been shown at VIII+ and X+ levels followed by the apprenticeship training. The non formal systems operating at elementary stage, secondary stage (open school) and tertiary stage (open university) have been shown as shaded portions. Approximate retention in school as percent enrolment at various stages of education is also shown.

*Systems and Approaches of Vocational Education*

The Technical/Vocational Education and Training is multi-sectoral in nature. Each ministry/department in Central as well as State Governaments is responsible for manpower development in that sector. While some offer regular formal or non-formal courses, others draw from the general pool of educated and trained manpower. It is important to take up some of the major sectors and discuss their characteristics. For this purpose, it is desired to take up the industrial, health, and some of the agricultural, educational and commercial sector courses as examples.

In the sector of education there are three major types of vocational/ technical education and training programmes.

### *Technical Industrial Arts and Crafts Schools*

These technical schools which prepare students for the lower secondary stage Board examination are mainly located in the states of Maharashtra Gujarat, Andhra Pradesh, Karnataka and Kerala. There are 3720 such schools which enrolled 314104 students in 1987-88. In addition to the general school's curriculum for the tenth grade examination, the student is offered one vocational subject such as carpentry, blacksmithy, moulding, welding, fitting, turning, plumbing, building construction, rural techonology, textile techonology, wireman etc. These schools were started more as a feeder to polytechnics rather than for preparing young people for vocational fields. They continue today as an offshoot of the general schooling.

### *Higher Secondary Vocational Education*

The higher secondary vocationalisation programme aims to develop skilled manpower through diversified courses to meet the requirments of mainly the unorganised sector and to prepare people for the world of work in general through a large number of self employment oriented courses, not precluding wage employment orientation of many courses. Through diversification into production and service oriented courses, it is desired to reduce the aimless pursuit of higher education and thereby reduce pressure from the tertiary education.

In 1989–90 there were more than 150 courses in different states which are grouped under the major areas of agriculture, business and commerce, engineering and techonology health and para medical, home science and humanitiies. The design consists of theory and practice relating to the vocational field, related subjects, language and general foundation studies which includes enterpreneurship. In 1989–90 a total of 168.680 students were enrolled in the first year of the two ye ar programme. There are more than 5000 full time teachers teaching these courses.

*Technical Education*

This sub-system consists of a well knit chain of polytechnics which provide broad based education in engineering as well as some non-engineering areas. The minimum qualification for entry into a polytechnic is grade X certificate. The courses are generally of three year duration but a few range between two to four years. There are nearly 500 polytechnics with the annual admission capacity of 65000. The training is mostly institutional (with some industrial experience), the curricula predominantly theory oriented and location mostly urban. They aim to meet the manpower needs of the organised sector.

*Crafts Training Scheme*

The craftsman training is offered in nearly two thousand government run or privately managed Industrial Training Institutes. The intake capacity of these institutes amounted to about 327,000 in 1987–88. There are, in all, 64 trades of which 38 belong to the engineering group. The graduates of these courses find placement in organised public and private sector industrial and business establishments. Some of them go for self employment also. The ITIs offer both X+ and VIII+ level courses in nearly equal numbers. Most of the courses range in duration from one to two years. The National Council of Vocational Training is the supreme coordinating and policy making body which awards certificates to students on completion of courses. The curriculum is highly practice oriented and the elements of general education are kept at minimum. An ITI graduate is not eligible for university education.

*Appreniceship Training Scheme*

The scheme aims to regulate the programme of training of apprentices in the industry so as to conform to the prescribed syllabi of the Central Apprenticeship Council and to utilize fully the facilities available in the industry for practical training with a view to meet the requirment of skilled workers in industries. There are four categories of apprentice programme: Graduate Apprenticeship for engineering graduates, Technician Apprenticeship for diploma holders from polytechnics, Trade Apprenticeship for the graduates of ITIs and Technician (Vocational) Apprenticeship for the graduates of higher secondary vocational courses. There are 71 subjects and 12,000 technician apprentices training at a time.

The technician (vocational) apprenticeship is a recent inclusion with only twenty designed areas so far, with the expansion of trade list expected in near future. The trade apprenticeship programme has an intake capacity of over 190,000 of which about 132,000 are actually utilised. There are 140 apprenticeabl e trades which run for durations of one to four years. Appropriate rebate is allowed for the graduates of the craftsman training scheme. The Central Apprenticeship Council awards certificates to the graduates on successful completion of the training.

In addition to the two major training programmes presented above, the Ministry of Labour also runs advanced Vocational Training System and vocational training programmes particularly for women in separate institutes.

### *Health and Paramedical*

There are three councils at the national level to regulate the training programmes; in their respective areas such as the Indian Nursing Council, the Indian Pharmacy Council under the Ministry of Social Welfare. In other health and paramedical areas, the health departments of the state governments conduct their own training programmes to meet their health manpower requirments. These courses, under the control of a variety of authorities, are marked by an absence of standardised course content and proficiency level. it is difficult to make an estimate of output of the health manpower training and production system. Hospital based training, as an internal supply system, is also a prevelent mode. The curricula have little theoritical content in many situations and almost always these courses lead to a dead end in terms of opportunity for higher education.

*Agriculture*

The Indian Council of Agricultural Research is primarily concerned with graduate and post graduate agricultural educatuion and research. There are a few non formal training programmes for the rural youth through the Agricultural Science Centres and Agricultural Universities. There is hardly a system for production of middle level skilled manpower for the agricultural sector. In some states there are some government run agricultural schools but they often provide post induction training to village level workers and other personnel. A manpower production system aiming at vocational development for self employment hardly exists in India in the domain of agriculture.

*Business and Commerce*

The training system in the field of business and commerce is highly diverse. There are a large number of institutes and teaching shops throughout the country teaching many of the office trades and other vocations in salesmanship, marketing etc. There is no available estimate of the size of the supply system and the quality of its products.

**ROLE OF NCERT IN TVET**

The National Council of Education Research and Training is concerned so far only with the Hr.Secondary Vocationalization programme in formal schools. Its Department of Vocationalization of Education which is in the process of being converted into a Central Institute of Vocational Education is the nodal agency for all aspects relating to curriculum development, staff development, research, evaluation and monitoring and international contacts. The scope of the Department extends over the entire country but it has only an advisory and guiding role to perform. Having attained sufficient experience and expertise in Hr.

Secondary Vocationalization programmes the department is now actively associated with the development of various types of vocational courses for the under-graduate stage of education under the auspices of the University Grants Commission. In relation to the vocational training component under the Ministry of Labour the NCERT is represented on the National Council of Vocational Training which is t he apex decision making and coordinating body for its instituttions throughout the country. Similarly, in respect of Technical Education Programme, the NCERT is represented in the All India Council of Technical Education, a statutory body to look after technical and management education in the country.

## DISTANCE EDUCATION

The contact mode and the closed system delivery is, still by far, the most prevelent modality while significant beginning has been made through the national open learning institutions. The programmes generated by NCERT which are taught in more than 5000 hr.secondary schools as well as those in polytechnics and industrial training institutes, all use the contact delivery mode. However, the technical support institutions for all the above categories of institutions have accepted the significance of multi media approach in general and distance learning mode in particular for imparting technical/vocational education and training. With particular reference to the higher secondary courses, tile NCERT has developed some teaching-learning video films in electronics, automobile repairs and indigeneous handicrafts such as tie and dye, Ikat weaving etc. Sufficient stock of such materials are being built before schools are encouraged to use them for self paced and individualized learning.

The extent of post secondary TVET programme is not precisely quantified in India. A rough estimate would put the number as being close to a million in all programmes of one to three years duration. This number is more an indicator of the scale of operation rather than a statistical compilation. To be more specific, the first year of the higher secondary programme enrolled nearly 186000 students in 1989–90 which amounted to about 7% of the total enrolment in that grade in higher secondary institutions, taking the country as a whole. Broadly speaking, about 25 to 30% of the age cohort going to various types of education and training institutions may be estimated to be under TVET. This, however, does not include various formal or informal apprentice mode of learning or enterprize based training. The numbers would be fairly large but it would be proper to risk an estimate.

The formal programmes of TVET are by and large, directly or indirectly, state delivered. Even when private institutions are involved, they are mostly state financed. The entire enterprize, traditionally and by design, is highly subsidised, the students paying only a fraction of the public cost in the form of tution fees. The private cost is borne largely by the learners but on grounds of equity, certain sections get stipend and scholarships. The employers contribute hardly any thing by way of cost though they are the most direct beneficiaries. The social pressures and equity considerations gravitate against the argument of desubsidization as a vast majority of TVET learners come from relatively weaker sections of the society.

The NCERT studies have described the present state of management system development at the centre and in various states in terms of its structre and human component. The role of a proper management system manned by personnel with proper backgrounds and experiences is well accepted but its emergence has been rather slow and often erratic. Essentially, the management system consists of four distinct categories of functions for which structures are visualised to operate at four different levels. The functions are: a. policy and co-ordination,

b. administration (including supervision and financing), c. research and development, and d. examination and accreditation. The four levels at which these operate are: a. national, b. state, c. district, and d. school.

The higher secondary programmes by design are collaborative in nature. The schools offer theoretical instruction and basics in terms of vocational practice which is followed by on the job training or practical training at the actual work site. In the entire teaching-learning process the full time teachers are supported by a large number of part time instructors and guest lecturers drawn from the respective employment sectors. While the above is the suggested modality, many schools still depend on institutional instruction and training in place of collaboration mentioned above, but, the deployment of part time teachers is almost invariably ensured. At present when the programme implementation is in its infancy, the ground support is not upto the mark.

The students are evaluated at the end of two years by the Boards of Secondary/ Higher Secondary Education of different states while internal assessment is conducted. by the teaching faculty of the concerned school at periodic intervals. The internal evaluation is only for diagnostic purposes and the students' performance is judged by his scores in the final examination conducted by the Board. Vocational courses are offered only in those institutions which are accredited by the authorised board in the given state.

The in-service training of teachers is conducted under the guidance of NCERT by different states through courses varying in duration from 2 to 4 weeks. Preservice teacher preparation has so far not been initiated, but steps are underway for introducing teacher preparation courses in the regional colleges of education and other Universities.

## IMPROVEMENT OF SCIENCE EDUCATION IN SCHOOLS

To improve the quality of science education and promote

scientific temper, as envisaged in the National Policy on Education, 1986 this Scheme was initiated during 1987-88. Under the Scheme, financial assistance is provided to States/ UTs for science kits to upper primary schools; upgradation and strengthening of science laboratories in secondary/senior secondary schools supply of books on science related subject in secondary and senior secondary schools; and training of science and mathematics teachers.

With a view to identifying a nurturing talent in Mathematics, Physics and Chemistry at school level, the International Mathematical Olympiad (IMO), Internal Physics Olympiad (IPhO) and International Chemistry Olympiad (IChO) is held every year. India has been participating in these Olympiads since 1989, 1998 and 1999 respectively. Each participating country is required to send a team comprising not more than 6 secondary student contestants to IMO, 5 secondary student contestants at IPhO and 4 contestant students to IChO apart from a leader and deputy team leader.

### *Promotion of Yoga in Schools*

The NPE lays down that Yoga will receive special attention as a system which promotes the integrated development of the body and mind. The Scheme for promotion of Yoga in schools was launched in 1989-90. Under this scheme, financial assistance provided for training of teachers in Yoga and for building up of infrastructure necessary for the purpose. In addition, institutions of all India character are given assistance for maintenance as well as developmental expenditure for promotion of basic research and teacher training programmes in Yoga.

### *Culture and Value in Education*

The Scheme of Assistance to the Agencies for Strengthening Culture and Values in Education started since 1988-89. The Scheme has two broad components:

— Strengthening cultural and value education inputs in the school and non-formal education system.

— Strengthening the in-service training of art, craft, music and dance teachers.

— The assistance given under this scheme is 100% for new project/ programme taken up for implementation subject to a ceiling of Rs.5.00 lakhs per annum. Ordinarily, government agencies, educational institutions, Panchayati Raj Institutions, registered societies, public trusts and non-profit making companies are eligible for assistance under this scheme.

— Strengthening of Boarding and Hostel Facilities for Girl Students of Secondary and Higher Secondary Schools

### *Environmental Orientation to School Education*

The National Policy on Education (NPE), 1986, provides that the protection environment is a value. The Scheme was initiated in 1988-89. The Scheme envisages assistance to voluntary agencies. The voluntary agencies are assisted for conduct of experimental innovative programmes aimed at promoting integration of education programmes in schools with local environmental conditions.

## NATIONAL POPULATION EDUCATION PROJECT

National Population Education Project (School Education) was launched in April 1980 with a view to institutionalise population education in the school education system.

The objectives of the project are:

— Introduction of Adolescence Education (with major components like process of growing up, HIV/AIDS Education, Drug Abuse in Schools and Teachers Education); and

— Re-orientation, updating and improvement of the elements of Population Education in the light of Programme of Action adopted by the International Conference on Population and Development (ICPD), held in Cairo in 1984.

## *Technical Education*

The success of the software industry in India in terms of its global impact has clearly underscored the fact that Indian engineers can rival the best in the world. Software has provided a quick vehicle to demonstrate this point, although for those who have seen the achievements in nuclear, space and the missile development, this was obvious long ago. This image is strengthened by the observation that a number of Indian computer scientists have made it big in the U.S. as entrepreneurs, by going up the corporate ladder or being successful in academia after getting an excellent post-graduate education in the U.S. It is equally true that an entrepreneurial spirit in India has also spawned forth a number of successful software ventures. But these successes have also to be tempered with the fact that in terms of software products Indian firms have had negligible impact on the global market.

## *Engineering*

India has had a long tradition of research in the physical sciences starting from the pre-independence days. In the engineering or more broadly in the technical education field, it really started in a big way in the 50's thanks to the vision of Nehru. The Sarkar committee created the five Indian Institute of Technologies and each of them produced excellent engineers through state of the art curriculum. Indian Institute of Technology, Kanpur gave the lead in terms of a new approach to technical education through the introduction of a semester system, course wise promotion, integration of science with engineering, production of indigenous textbooks and finally starting the B.Tech, M.Tech and Ph.D degree programs in computer science.

Education being primarily a state subject, has seen phenomenal growth in Indian engineering colleges, and like in any other industrially advanced countries, we also have engineering institutions that can be calibrated in terms of quality. In the 50's, the vision of Nehru together with men like Bhabha, Sarabhai and Bhatnagar created the infrastructure of space, atomic energy, national as well as defense laboratories which have legitimately made India a self reliant country. Events like the Pokhran, Agni or the ISRO satellites are ample testimony to the high level of Indian expertise. It is also noteworthy that the success of these technologies relied very little on the graduates of the IITs.

For example, Bhabha Atomic Research Center (BARC) had its own in-house training program for the Bachelor degree holders in science. There is an important lesson to be learnt from this. The basic background of most of those seeking admission to degree-granting engineering schools is good. The successful and the well-prepared ones for the entrance examination get into the IITs. The rest get into other technical institutions. This is somewhat similar to the U.S., where there is fierce competition to get into the Ivy League or so-called elite schools. Recent research has shown that those graduating from these elite schools are better "connected" and have "peer" competition. In the long run they do slightly better than equally good students going through not so elite schools.

In India, those graduating from IITs have definitely a better chance of getting into post-graduate studies abroad in good schools. However, noting from the success of Indians in the Silicon Valley, there are a large number of non-IIT people who are equally successful. Assuming that an IIT student stays in India, it is difficult to guess whether in the long run they have an edge over other students. This is a point that authorities must consider before allocating resources to technical education.

### *Post-Graduate Education*

If the country has to catch up with the rest of the industrialized world in the next century, it can only be through quality postgraduate training on the same scale as the undergraduate training of the 50's and 60's. Only through such investments can real R&D flourish in the technical areas in India. Sciences have had a good track record by producing enough Ph.D's. But in Engineering there are not enough M.Tech's to go around and Ph.D's are a mere trickle. This may be one reason why the country cannot enter the software product area as opposed to services or hard core engineering design fields. On this base of manpower, the country cannot compete with the industrialized world.

What the country will witness is that the Multi-National Corporations (MNC's) will open up Research & Development (R & D) centers for the benefit of their parent companies, and the fruits of research will not be available to the country at large. This is the inevitable consequence of globalization, and there is no point in preventing it. Indian companies must compete for the best talent, and just as in the software services sector a level playing field may eventually result. But for that to happen the institutions must produce enough M.Techs and Ph.Ds of good quality to meet the demand.

Given the current scenario, only the IITs can increase the output of M.Techs and Ph.Ds. One possible solution, though drastic, is to convert IITs into post-graduate institutions only, just as the Indian Institute of Science (IISc) has done. IITs can take good talent from engineering schools and concentrate on R&D and postgraduate training. As indicated, this is a drastic solution and perhaps may not be welcomed by many. The other alternative is to have QIP type program for the industry. This is particularly needed for the engineering and software industry if they have to graduate to the level of producing products instead of services and collaboration. Academic institutions also need these products for maintaining their excellence. IITs & IISc must take a lead in Distance Education

(DE) at the post graduate level where many foreign universities are already making their presence felt.

## DEVELOPMENT OF TEACHER EDUCATION IN INDIA

The development of teacher education in India can be examined in two distinct periods, viz. before and after Independence. Its origin dates back to the early nineteenth century. The story of its development is impressive. Teacher education found its roots soon after its inception and quickly diversified itself. This could be due to several factors. The introduction of 'English education' in formal schools made it necessary for teachers to teach something which was quite new to them.

The content being non-religious and not based upon Indian culture, the known methodologies fell short of expectations; officers reporting from several places felt that learning by students was essentially by rote and that there were no appropriate books for them.1 The administration was keen that the money it spent on education led to proper results. There was eagerness on the part of private and missionary initiative to ensure success in their efforts. Lastly, the nature and relevance of teacher education programmes could not be ignored.

The development of teacher education has been continuous. It not only got established quickly but has also diversified into different programmes, each with a well-differentiated form and structure. A quick look at the way teacher education has evolved indicates that there have been three significant developments.

First, there was a physical growth in terms of number of institutions; this process has been fairly continuous from the pre-Independence period although tremendous expansion has taken place during the post-Independence period too.

Second, diversification of teacher education programmes took place across different stages of education such as pre-school, primary, secondary and higher secondary. This occurred during the pre-Independence period for the primary and secondary stages, while its spread to higher secondary and pre-primary are essentially recent developments.

The curricular and organisational structures for each of these have been generated in quite differentiated forms. Third, teacher education emerged in specific areas of specialisation like science education, mathematics education, special education, art education, physical education, language teaching and learning, and so on. As a result of these developments, teacher education today has become a significant component of our educational system with a large-scale network of various institutions and an area of academic specialisation.

It is pertinent to have an overview of how these developments have occurred during the past century and more. A brief resume of major events in the development of teacher education in India is presented below. The initial attempts formally made towards teacher education seem to have been by some private agencies in the three Presidencies under the East India Company, during the early decades of the century.

These were the Calcutta School Society formed in 1819, the Native Education Society of Bombay and the Madras School Society. These societies received grants specifically for training of teachers in their schools. The annual reports of the three Presidencies mention the attempts made by these societies to educate their teachers. In Madras, the Madras School Society's efforts were noted with appreciation and an amount was sanctioned in support of its activities even before 1824.2 This suggests that the earliest efforts in teacher education for working teachers were in the nature of private initiatives.

State initiative ensued towards the end of the eighteenth century and as an aftermath of the government assuming responsibility for education in India. Non-availability of an adequate number of schools, both vernacular and Anglo-vernacular, ineffective instruction provided in them and similar issues were continuously addressed by several officers. Lord Moira's Minute of 1815 on the judicial administration of the Presidency of Fort William is one of the earliest recorded views in support of the training needs of school teachers. It recorded,

> The village school-masters could not teach that in which they had themselves never been instructed; and universal debasement of mind, the constant concomitant of subjugation to despotic rule, left no chance that an innate sense of equity should in those confined circles suggest the recommendation of principles not thought worthy of cultivation by the government. The remedy for this is to furnish the village school-masters with little manuals of religious sentiments and ethical maxims, conveyed in such a shape as may be attractive to the scholars; taking care that while awe and adoration of the Supreme Being are earnestly instilled no jealousy be excited by pointing out any particular creed. The absence of such an objection, and small pecuniary rewards for zeal occasionally administered by the magistrates, would induce the school-masters to use those compilations readily.

It is significant to note that the recognition of training needs existed simultaneously with the development of a formal school system. Between 1815 and 1854, opinions in favour of teacher education accumulated and spread across different administrative levels. The increasing perception of the need for more schools was widespread. Alongside, there seems to have persisted a scepticism in respect of schools not regulated or supervised by the Europeans. This is reflected in a letter of the Secretary of Bombay Presidency to the Governor General of Bengal (1825),

> It seems one of the greatest objections of establishing numerous new schools at once is, that the persons who would be employed might be expected (from the experience we have already acquired) to oppose or to neglect the introduction of any improvements whether in the matter or the manner of instruction, without a much more vigilant European superintendence than could possibly be afforded.

While the European supervision was never doubted, training of teachers of schools gained attention as a possible mechanism for expanding the school system at a cheaper cost by using 'native' teachers and maintaining a certain quality. It is such a consideration which Thomas Munro, Governor of Madras, expressed in his proposal of 1826:

What is first wanted, therefore, is a school for educating teachers, as proposed by the Committee of Madras School Book Society, in the letter of the 25th October, 1824, which accompanied their second report. I think that they should be authorised to draw 700/- rupees monthly from the Treasury for the purpose which they have stated; namely, for the payment of the interest of money employed in building and the salaries of teachers, 500; and for the expenses of the press, 200. Along with providing financial support to private initiative, Munro also gave a detailed proposal for establishment of training schools in each collectorate as principal schools, with a continuous supply of trained teachers. Thereafter, one school could be provided for in each of the 300 *tahsils* under his Presidency. The Secretary of Bombay Presidency made a plea for a similar cause around the same time:

A great delay in the establishing of schools at the Presidency has arisen from the necessity of educating the school-master in the first instance, and a number of youths are with that view under instruction. If, therefore, it be resolved, that Government should assist in establishing schools where they are not, the first step for rendering them really useful would be to collect youths for the purpose of instructing them according to a proper system, and in proper books and branches of knowledge, and after they have attained sufficient maturity to qualify them for the duty at a school which can be ably superintended, to appoint them to the schools for which they have been selected.

As a result of several such developments, the three private societies were granted some sums of money. The reported impact of training of teachers was quite positive, though not fully effective. A recognition of the inevitable slowness in accruing more positive results in any new practice was also there. An example of such as perception is, in Munro's words,

Government initiative in teacher education came only as a consequence of Wood's Despatch of 1854. The general opinion thus generated among administrators received support after Wood's Despatch (1854) recognised 'the great deficiency in the facilities for teachers' training and 'desired to see the establishment, with as little delay as possible, of training.'9

As a sequel to this, normal schools for training primary school teachers were established in each Presidency, making formal the official acceptance of teacher training as an integral part of the Indian education system. The Presidency towns were the first to have normal training schools, with Madras in the lead (1856). These schools were found to be quite effective in the sense that their products were found to be superior to untrained teachers in schools. The actual number of teachers they trained was very small even in comparison to the low figures of enrolment in them. In 1859, Stanley's Despatch (1859) observed that 'the institution of training schools does not seem to have been carried out to the extent contemplated by the Court of Directors'.10

With continued and increased emphasis on normal school training for primary school teachers, there was an increased expansion of teacher education. After a decade, in 1881-82, the number of normal schools went up to 106. However, the total enrolment at these schools was low, viz. 3,886 teacher trainees, and the annual expenditure increased to Rs. 4 lakh. Records indicate that normal schools initially provided pedagogic training of some sort for teachers of primary schools.

The duration and nature of training seem to have varied across the Presidencies, though in all three stipends were given to teachers under training. Soon they were expanded to include prospective teachers who were 'bright, young men' willing to receive training with stipend. The Inspectorate selected persons for admission and not the headmasters of the schools. Significantly, separate training was given for prospective teachers for each class/grade. Separate schools for female teachers were also established at different places, though several headmistresses reported difficulty in attracting larger numbers for such training.

Gradually, school education expanded to include 'middle' classes and a little later, secondary classes. The establishment of universities after 1857 let to an increase in the number of colleges. This development had an impact on normal schools. While the main focus was on providing knowledge and pedagogy suited to particular grades, students were permitted, along with a special course on 'Method', to study subjects for matriculation which would facilitate their entering universities later.

Normal schools gradually began to attract more students for being selected for stipends and certification, which came to be seen as a surety for getting jobs. In fact, some annual reports from the Presidencies expressed concern about the 'wrong' youth getting selected which affected the quality of training. Several inspectors were irked by the increasing tendency on the part of students to perceive their selection to these schools as placing an obligation on the government to assure them subsequent placement on completion of their training.

In view of the expansion and diversification that had taken place in the educational system, the Indian Education Commission (1882) provided some definite directions for furthering teacher education in India. The commission not only approved of teacher training programmes for both elementary and secondary school teachers but also recommended a separate programme for secondary school, distinctly higher in level, form and method. Such a programme should include, in the view of the commission, 'an examination in the principles and practice of teaching... success in which should hereafter be a condition of permanent employment as a teacher in any secondary school, government or aided.'

The commission also recommended separate training programmes for graduates and undergraduates. As a sequel to the report of the Indian Education Commission (1882), training colleges were established for the first time and soon six training colleges came into existence, one each in Allahabad, Jabalpur (1890) Kurseong, Lahore, Madras, (1886) and Rajamundry (1894). Of these, the colleges at Madras and Rajamundry had their origins in normal schools which were upgraded to colleges when Licentiate in Teaching, equivalent to a degree, was introduced in them. Due to the lack of a building, the training college at Rajamundry was shifted to the local Arts College and functioned as part of that college. As a result, though it continued to provide a Licentiate in Teaching Programme during this period, the Madras college came to be recognised as the only exclusive training college for secondary school teachers for the entire Presidency till 1917. Besides these six training colleges, there were 50 training schools for secondary school teachers.

Thus, by the end of the nineteenth century, teacher education became established as a substantial structural set-up. Though it was predominantly a state-supported programme, there was an increase in private initiative too, mostly with state financial support. The institutional structure of teacher education diversified into normal schools, secondary training schools and training colleges, run by the state and private enterprise, and with well-differentiated training inputs as well as procedural and certification details.

The increasing needs of the field and the accruing experience of teacher education programmes as well as the growing knowledge base, brought to sharper focus the issues of appropriate streamlining of form, structure, content and methodology of teacher education. Such issues were the concern of the early twentieth century educational scene.

The onset of the twentieth century ushered in a period of real transition in the field of education as it did in political and social spheres in India. The seeds of transition were sown by the Viceroy, Lord Curzon (1902-05). He took several significant steps to improve the quality of education. His emphasis was on improvement of quality and not quantity at the university level, control and improvement at the secondary level and expansion and quality at primary level. He highlighted these concerns in his 'Resolution on Education Policy' (1904), which is more commonly known as the 'Government of India Resolution of 1904'.

The Resolution prescribed conditions to be satisfied by schools to be eligible for receiving grant-in-aid and recognition by the government. One of these conditions was that '... the teachers are suitable as regards character, number and qualifications...'. The Resolution emphasised the necessity of providing a large number of training institutions for primary teachers; the duration of training being a minimum of two years. Nurullah and Naik (1964) remark, '... by far his (Curzon's) greatest contribution to the subject was to emphasise the training of rural primary teachers in elementary agriculture which he desired to be taught in all rural primary schools which were mostly attended by the children of agriculturists.'

The other recommendations relevant to teacher education in the Government of India Resolution of 1904 were:

(i) the equipment of a training college should be as important as that of an arts college;

(ii) the training courses for graduates should be one-year university courses leading to a university degree, while training courses for undergraduates should be of two years;

(iii) the theory and practice of teaching should be included in training courses;

(iv) a practising school should be attached to each training college;

(v) every possible care should be taken to maintain a connection between a training college and schools.

Before the Resolution could be implemented, Curzon was recalled in 1905. The Resolution, however, provided direction to further action by subsequent Viceroys who decided to continue with these decisions. As a sequel to the Minto-Morley Reforms of 1909, the government passed another Resolution on Educational Policy in 1913 which, among other things, declared that '... eventually under the modern system of education no teacher should be allowed to teach without a certificate that he is qualified to do so.'

Within less than a decade after this, the Calcutta University Commission (1917-19) was set up under the chairmanship of Dr. Sadler. Though its terms of reference were limited to Calcutta University, it made some recommendations which had implications for other educational institutions as well. The commission laid stress on substantially increasing the output of trained teachers. It recommended that a Department of Education should be created in the Universities of Dacca (Dhaka, now the capital of Bangladesh) and Calcutta, and that education should be included as a subject of study in intermediate, B.A. and M.A. degree examinations. The commission was in session during World War I and the submission of its report coincided with the ending of the war, the Khilafat Movement and the Jallianwalabagh massacre. It was around this time that the Government of India Act 1917 was passed, providing for diarchy. Under this scheme elected provincial legislatures were given greater powers and made responsible for the transferred departments, which included education among them. This, no doubt, provided scope for more 'Indian' participation, but put an end to the interest shown earlier by the central government. This the Hartog Committee later termed as 'unfortunate'.

The Non-Cooperation Movement launched in 1920-21 and the Civil Disobedience Movement (1930-32), along with political developments in between did not allow diarchy to function for long. Not many new developments occured between 1920 and 1929, when the Hartog Committee was constituted. The various achievements in education of this period included a marginal increase in the number of educational institutions despite the large-scale boycott of English schools and colleges. The idea of a national education system received fresh impetus and institutions with explicit nationalist leanings mushroomed all over the country. More details of these are given in a later sub-section. One of the most significant new development in the year 1927 was the passing of the Compulsory Primary Education Act by most of the provincial governments.

The growing dissatisfaction with the educational system, its growing size and the revival of a parallel network of national education institutions alarmed the government about the falling quality of education making it 'largely ineffective and waseful'. In order to took into the matter more carefully and make relevant suggestions, the Auxiliary Committee of Indian Statutory Commission, more commonly known as the Hartog Committee, named after its Chairman, Sir Philip Hartog, was set up in 1929.

In the context of large-scale premature withdrawal of students from primary schools, the Hartog Committee (1929)15 made important recommendations about the training of primary school teachers:

(i) raising the standard of general education of primary school teachers;

(ii) lengthening the duration of training courses;

(iii) provision of adequate staff for training institutions;

(iv) improvement of service conditions of primary school teachers to attract and retain better quality of teachers.

In short, education, at all levels, will continue to grow, because it cultivates the human mind and makes people important and useful in the all-round development of a country.

# 2

# INDIGENOUS EDUCATION SCENARIO

From time immemorial, India has been a centre for learning. Thousands of years ago, great scholars used to teach through the scriptures. A variety of subjects such as philosophy, religion, medicine, literature, drama and arts, astrology, mathematics and sociology were taught and masterpieces on these subjects were written. Under the Buddhist influence, education was available to virtually everyone who wanted it and some world famous institutions arose out of the monasteries, such as Nalanda, Vikramshila and Takshashila. Nalanda, which flourished from the fifth to 13th century AD, was especially noteworthy.

During the 11th century, the Muslims established elementary and secondary schools, "*Madrasas*" or colleges, and even universities at cities like Delhi, Lucknow and Allahabad, mostly using Arabic as the medium of instruction. During the medieval period, there was excellent interaction between Indian and Islamic traditions in all fields of knowledge like theology, religion, philosophy, fine arts, painting, architecture, mathematics, medicine and astronomy.

With the arrival of the British, English education came into being with the help of the European missionaries. In 1817, Hindu College was established in Kolkata. The Elphinstone Institution was set up in 1834 in Mumbai. In 1857 three universities were set up at Kolkata, Chennai and Mumbai. Since then, Western education has made steady advances in the country. With 226 universities and thousands of colleges affiliated to them, 428 engineering colleges and technological institutes, more than a 100 medical colleges, scores of agricultural institutes and many other specialised centres of learning and research in every subject and discipline, India can claim its position as one of the leading countries providing quality higher education to its people as well as to students and scholars from countries all over the world.

Today Indian universities and institutes of higher education and research today have made a significant contribution to transmission of knowledge and enquiry into frontiers of science and technology. In the field of traditional subjects such as arts and humanities as well as in pure sciences, applied physics and chemistry, mathematics and in areas of technology, the universities and higher institutes have been playing a leading role in transforming the country into a modern industrialised, technologically advanced state.

Indian universities and institutes of higher learning have been playing their role to promote the needs and aspirations of higher education and research to Indian students and scholars. These centres have been extending their cooperation and friendship towards students of other developing countries also, where facilities for higher studies and research are not adequate. In addition, a number of overseas students are also drawn to Indian educational institutions providing high-quality education at very competitive prices.

## LINKING SCIENCE AND SOCIETY

### *The National Innovations Foundation (NIF)*

The NIF was registered as a society under the Society Act of 1860 with its head office in Ahmedabad – Gujarat. A few incubator projects are to be set up at various academic and other locations for converting innovations into viable business solutions. NIF will also mobilise leading experts in various fields both from within and from outside the country for value addition in local innovations. NIF is a giant step in the direction of making India innovative and it will ensure that the "I" in India stands for innovation.

The objectives of NIF are as follows:

— To help India become an inventive and creative society and global leader in sustainable technologies by scouting, spawning and sustaining grassroots innovations on a selective, time-bound and mission-oriented basis so as to meet the socio-economic needs of society.

— To set up incubator projects to convert innovations into products for eventual commercialisation while providing intellectual property support.

— To provide institutional support in scouting, spawning, sustaining, and scaling-up grassroots green innovations and helping their transition to self-supporting activities, seeking self-reliance through competitive advantage of innovation based enterprises and application of people-generated sustainable technologies at grassroots level.

— To evolve strategies and conduct, co-ordinate and support research, design and development efforts in the country on grassroots innovation in order to attain and maintain technological competence and enhance self-reliance.

— To build linkages between excellence in formal scientific systems and informal knowledge systems and create a knowledge network to link various stakeholders through application of information technologies.

### *The Society for Research and Initiatives for Sustainable Technologies and Institutions (SRISTI)*

SRISTI was registered in June 1993 under the Bombay Charitable Act of 1956, and the Society Act of 1860. It is located in Ahmedabad under the auspices of the India Institute of Management.

It is a developmental voluntary organisation with the following objectives:

— To expand space in society for grassroots initiatives and innovations with a special focus on women's indigenous knowledge.

— To document, analyse, and disseminate technological as well as institutional innovations developed by people themselves.

— To validate and add value to local innovations through experiments (on both farm and station) and laboratory research for generating nature-friendly sustainable technologies/products.

— To conserve local biodiversity through in situ as well as ex situ gene banks managed by local people.

— To protect intellectual property rights of grassroots innovators and to generate incentive models for recognising, respecting and rewarding grassroots creativity and associated ethical values and norms.

— To provide support to grassroots innovators to scale up their products and services through commercial and non-commercial channels.

— To embed the insights learnt from grassroots innovations in formal education systems in order to expand the conceptual and cognitive space available to these innovations.

### *Honey Bee Network*

The Honey Bee network is based at the Indian Institute of Management in Ahmedabad. Leadership for it is provided under the auspices of the Senior Professor, Anil Gupta, who is well-known and highly respected within India and world-wide. The philosophy of practice in linking science and society involves practical visible translation of transformative ideas to concrete practice, as illustrated below.

— Whatever is learnt from the people must be shared with them in their own language.

— All practices/innovations must be identified by the names and addresses of the individuals in order to acknowledge their contribution and pursue the protection of IPR of grassroots innovators.

— Whatever gains are made by those who document or add value to local knowledge, innovations or practices should be shared with the providers of knowledge and others who have contributed value addition in a fair and equitable manner.

The Honey Bee Network has outlined certain codes of conduct which are worth noting. In terms of academic work that is based on fieldwork with local communities, only papers and contributions which have been preceded by the following three things will be accepted:

— Every contribution must be acknowledged by the name and address of the contributor and communicator unless requested otherwise by the knowledge experts.

— The knowledge gained from the local communities must be shared with them in their language in an easily understandable manner along with reviews the author may have done of other studies.

— Researchers should ensure that any monetary gain from the research through value addition is shared fairly with the knowledge providers.

Honey Bee's strategies for documenting grassroots innovations consist of the following:

— A survey of innovations through students, i.e., undergraduate and postgraduate students in agriculture and rural development are oriented during their summer vacations to enable them to identify innovations.

— A survey of innovations through innovator, i.e., gets innovators to look for other innovators.

— Competition for innovation scouts, i.e., competitions have been organised among students of agricultural colleges and grassroots-level government level functionaries. No reference is made to the so-called rapid methods (RRAs) since the ability to scout for innovators depends far more on one's framework of understanding rural creativity than on any particular method. The entries sent in by participants are evaluated and the winners are awarded prizes. The innovators are honoured – which increases the esteem that such innovators now command in their villages and among peers.

— Biodiversity contest for documentation of innovation, i.e., organised among school children and adults.

— Lateral learning workshops, i.e., SRISTI provides scope for lateral learning among those who solve problems and not those who merely articulate the problem. In that sense, it experiments with the solution augmenting approach rather than just problem solving. By initiating a chain of experimenting farmers, and gradually getting them to host such meetings and share their innovations, it encourages farmers to take a major responsibility for networking and diffusion of ideas.

— Scanning old literature, i.e., language constraints have restrained the sharing of knowledge. There are many visionaries and experts at regional levels who do not get their due credit just because they were not good at English, and DID NOT PUBLISH IN ENGLISH. A lot of credit is therefore given for 'reinventing the wheel'.Scanning old literature helps to bring these unaccredited knowledge systems into the light. It is emphasised that the first step in participatory research should be to trace the living traditions that are rooted in local culture and history. Instead of grafting on alien terminology, concepts grounded in local philosophy, culture and traditions should be used as the initial building blocks.

— Dissertations by students, i.e., students are guided to prepare dissertations on IKS and women's IKS.

— Shodh Yatra, i.e., the journeys of exploration are undertaken with the objective of participatory learning and dissemination of experimental and inventive ethics among the community. SRISTI honoured men and women in almost every village during the journey.

— About 40 sacred groves have been identified around two major sanctuaries. These natural sacred elements ranges from stones, trees, plants, rivers and landscapes to waterbeds and are supplemented by man-made temples, flags, or other artefacts. The creation of the sacred groves that are watched by people is expected to keep local people as their own watchdogs in the conservation of the sanctuaries.

A database of grassroots innovations of outstanding examples of traditional knowledge has grown from 1500 in 1993 to 5 000 in 1997, to around 10 000 at present. Efforts are under way to:

— file patents in some cases,

— add value to develop commercialisable products, and

— disseminate other innovations by using information technology imaginatively.

A strategic objective is to expand the policy and institutional space for grassroots innovation.

### *The Gujarat Grassroots Innovation Augmentation Network (GIAN)*

The Gujarat Grassroots Innovation Augmentation Network (GIAN) filed a patent on behalf of Amrutbhai on the design of a tilting bullock cart. The right was assigned by the innovator to SRISTI (which also paid the cost) in order to help in the transfer of technology and the safeguarding of the interests of the innovator. The cart has since been licensed to three entrepreneurs for a period of five years for five districts in lieu of a one-off payment of Rs84000: about US$2 000).

This income of Rs84000 accrued to Amrutbhai was entirely due to the intellectual property provided through patent application process. Never before had a technology been transferred on the basis of district level boundaries and that for five years. Amrutbhai has exhibited his cart at several exhibitions, including the Indian Science Congress.

## PROTECTION AND THE LEGISLATIVE FRAMEWORKS IN INDIA

At present the Indian government has no formal laws to prevent anyone from appropriating knowledge from the indigenous community. It is recognised that protecting IKS innovations is quite a complex matter. The Intellectual Property Rights legislation that is in place in India has, to a large extent, been amended to provide some protection for IKS, having regard still to the parameters of the World Trade Organisation (WTO) - Trade Related Aspects of Intellectual Property Rights (TRIPS). These include the Patents Act of 1970, the Trade Marks Act, the Designs Act and the Copyright Act. It is also recognised that any legal framework should be flexible enough to allow exceptions such as the protection of cultural effects, cultural symbols, motifs and cultural marks.

The Patents Act of 1970, has the following important provisions:

> It does not grant patents to subject matter which was available to the public by means of use, written description or in any manner in any country, or which was used by local and indigenous communities prior to the date of filing the application for patents. The substantive examination of novelty in terms of their Patents Act ensures that requests for patents that are vested with knowledge of indigenous people or local communities are not granted.

## INDIGENOUS KNOWLEDGE SYSTEMS

As early as 1982, The Indian government initiated an IKS

National Programme with the aim of auditing, documenting and supporting research associated with Indigenous Knowledge Systems. This programme has grown substantially and offers an instructive model for other developing countries intending to support the development of IKS. The National programme comprises a variety of activities supported by government through the National Innovation Foundation (NIF) and the CSIR institutions.

The CSIR institutions range from centres dedicated to undertaking fundamental research on medicinal and aromatic plants and the National Institute of Immunology to those which spend major proportions of their time on applied research e.g. the Tropical Botanical Garden and Research Institute (TBGRI) in Kerala. These centres are also responsible for the training of postgraduate students (masters and Ph.D.s) in collaboration with universities. Indeed a number of scientists and administrators (trained at the Indian Institute of Management) graduate from these institutions.

The National Institute of Immunology plays a critical role in the IKS National Programme. The aim of the institute, within the context of the IKS National Programme, is to identify, document and patent immuno-modulatory molecules of plant material used by the community within the Ayurveda medical system and Folklore medicine. One of the outcomes for the research work is a database that will be deposited with major patenting offices in the world.

A major rationale behind this approach for protecting IKS knowledge is the fact that any knowledge that is in the public domain cannot be patented. However, in cases where new molecules are identified with potential for commercialisation, these molecules are patented and then passed on the innovation chain to the Central Drug Research Institute which further adds value and considers options for commercialisation. It was made very clear that the only way of protecting Folklore Knowledge is through the interface with the mainstream scientific system. By using scientific codification and validation the work will gain acceptability not only to the Indian research community but to the whole world.

The Lucknow Toxicology Institute's involvement in the whole IKS National Programme lies in testing for toxicity of traditional mixtures. The centre provides a service for chemical fingerprinting and for packaging and storage and functions as a quality control point. Most of the research work carried out relates to indigenous food. This has resulted in a scientifically well-developed database on indigenous food.

Another research centre participating in the IKS National Programme is the Indian National Botanical Institute. It is involved mainly in establishing an inventory and germ plasma collection of traditional medicinal plants. The institute is also involved in biodiversity research related to herbal plants, such as taxonomy, ethno-pharmacology and natural product chemistry. The Institute has been involved in bio-prospecting since 1984. The Institute regards prospecting for plant species that are endemic to India a first priority. Bio-prospecting is further undertaken together with the traditional Indian community (what Dr Pushpangadan called the children of the forests). One of their strategies is to collect and record traditional knowledge, which has not been documented before. The outcome of the bio-prospecting project is a national database. A national database will ensure the protection of traditional knowledge and may lead to the development of a national regulatory policy for access, harvesting and export.

The National Innovation Foundation established a "Honey Bee" movement. The aim of the movement is mainly to transform the conduct of intellectual researchers and other scholars to appreciate that what is learnt from the people must be shared with the people. The Foundation has established a National Registry of Small Innovations. The register is by no means the same as a Patent Database it offers documentation of the original source of innovation and can be used as documentary evidence in case of any challenge to patents anywhere in the world. In addition, Honey Bee has also established a Database of Innovation, which captures all the IKS innovations from the community in both English and own language through voice, text, and the use of interactive multimedia.

## *Medical and Health Systems*

The study revealed that India has the following three types of health systems:

### *The Allopathic medical system*

The Allopathic medical system (Western, curative medical system) is practised throughout India where the training of practitioners takes place in Western-styled medical schools. In some instances, there appears to be an attempt to integrate this system with the Ayurveda system by providing some training in homeopathy. However, this remains the most dominant mode of health delivery system and the government provides sufficient policy instruments, financial support and a supportive environment.

### *Ayurveda medical system*

The Ayurveda medical system (traditional Indian medical system) is practised in many parts of India. This medical system has its own separate and dedicated medical schools for training of its practitioners. The dominant form of treatment is homeopathy using extracts of natural plants and oils to treat diseases in an integrated way with nature. It was also interesting to note that this form of health system was considered one of the oldest in the world and may even have influenced the development of the Chinese health system. Fortunately, many of the homeopathic remedies used by the indigenous communities are already documented in the Indian Pharmacopoeia and hence cannot be easily pirated.

### *Folklore Medicine or Indian Traditional Medicine*

This is a third type of health system, which is largely undocumented and is used by "tribes" in remote areas of India. The IKS National Programme of India is targeting mainly this knowledge system which has been largely neglected, relegated to the periphery and therefore remains largely unprotected. Although there is support at government department level, through a directorate of Indigenous Medicine in the Department of Health, it appears that this operates on a shoe-string budget with very little capacity. In general, India lacks an enabling and protective policy environment for this particular knowledge system.

### *Research, Development and Technology Transfer*

The role of the Central Drug Research Institute, within the IKS National Programme, is to analyse the effectiveness of known traditional folklore preparations. The whole process involves analysis of single and multiple plant preparations, chemical fingerprinting through LC/MS, testing for activity or toxicity, testing for pharmacological activity in animal models, safety studies on animal models and finally, efficacy in human trials. This institute pays traditional communities to collect the material and pays for any other knowledge without any well-structured benefit-sharing scheme. It was stressed again that the only way to validate and authenticate Indigenous Knowledge is through scientific analysis and publication.

In the process of research some ethical issues arise with respect to drugs that are found to be toxic in animal models. The community usually rejects the outcome of scientific analysis on the basis that scientific studies are usually carried out in animals and not in humans. Should a plant species show promise during human trials, first priority to commercialise the product is given to Indian Bio-Pharmaceutical companies. This enables the tracking of the next generation of "super drugs" and the promotion of the local (or the national) pharmaceutical industry.

The involvement of the National Medicinal and Aromatic Plant Institute in the IKS National Programme has been that of agro-technological transfer. Research is undertaken to establish the best and optimum conditions for growing the traditional plants. In addition, the institute develops training courses, distributes the seeds and facilitates access to new markets.

The Medical Centre of Vaida Sala in Kotakkal is one of the medical centres that form part of the Indian Traditional medical system (Ayurvedic System). It is also participating in the IKS National Programme by making available samples of herbal medicines to the national programme.

### *Integration of IKS*

The components of the scientific community that are acting as the catalysts and agents of change in India combine within their ranks both critical and constructive perspectives that together are facilitating the gradual transformation of scientific ethos, ethics and practices, while developing a strong and committed system of protocols for protecting and developing IKS, biodiversity, and the intellectual property of local communities.

From the Centre for the Study of Developing Societies (CSDS, based in Delhi and headed by Professor Shiv Visvanathan), a strong development perspective on the relationship between mainstream science systems and the suppressed "others" is seen as one of the fundamental questions that needs to be addressed. Part of the legacy of colonialism, which lingers on in academic practice in general, is that non-western societies are taken as obsolescent, and in the rush towards modernity we, "the newly modernised," do not want to give the "obsolescent" victims a voice. In fact, as a group, victims are never part of scientific history or discourse. There is therefore a need to open up new moral and cognitive spaces within which constructive dialogue between people and between knowledge systems can occur.

The starting point for this is a realisation that new directions in the philosophy and sociology of science today are emerging, not from academia but from questions raised by grassroots movements. This brings to the fore the question of the link between universities and science and technology institutions on the one hand, and local communities on the other. In India, the grassroots movements represent dissenting organic academia and they raise issues that the universities are reluctant to confront. It is the grassroots movements and their determination of new directions in the philosophy and sociology of science that have constantly demonstrated that knowledge is an intrinsic part of democratic politics. It is through such voices that we have come to understand not only policy frameworks and the political economy of science, but also how the cosmology within which modern western science was embedded could be a source of violence. It is by undertaking this work of reconnecting systems that questions of cosmology and political economy can be linked to democratic theory.

During the visit, further insights were gained from the philosophy informing strategic actions by academics in other scientific institutions in India in their quest to assume greater responsibility for local/grassroots development. Good examples include the establishment of the National Innovations Foundation (headed by Dr Mashelkar, the Director-General of the CSIR), and the work of Dr Pushpangadan (Director of the National Botanical Research Institute (NBRI) at Lucknow), the Honey Bee Network, the Grassroots Innovation Augmentation Network (GIAN), the Society for Research and Initiatives for Sustainable Technologies and Institutions (SRISTI) all based at the Indian Institute of Management (IIM) in Ahmedabad, and headed by Senior Professor Anil Gupta.

These prominent scientists recognise that there is a gross asymmetry in the rights and responsibility of those who produce knowledge particularly in the informal sector, and those who go about valorising it in the formal sector. This brings to light the issue of the ethics of extraction and responsibility. It is strongly felt that there is no truth to the notion that Research and Development by small-scale firms or individual community-based scientists cannot generate globally valuable intellectual property.

At the same time, it is affirmed that they do not claim that local communities can better solve all problems. However, some problems which are solved by communities in a creative manner, indicate the riches that mainstream science and technology institutions have either failed to file, or even to notice. To that extent there exists tremendous scope for complementarity between the two knowledge systems (i.e. "formal" and "informal").

They also recognise that a major threat to the sustainability of natural resources is the erosion of people's knowledge, and the basic reason for this erosion is the low value attached to it. It is stated that the erosion of people's knowledge associated with natural resources is under greater threat than the erosion of the natural resources themselves. These scientists also ask why the most disadvantaged people have to carry the heaviest burden of maintaining genetic diversity for future generations.

Indigenous veterinary experts, herbalists and pastoralists know a lot about the habitats, the life cycles, and the many facets of plants and other resources. Yet, efforts to build upon knowledge systems of people who have maintained their natural resources so far are quite inadequate.

Language is felt to be another problem in revitalising local communities. For example it has been recognised that writing in English is valuable for connecting internationally, but that it alienates locally. The goal here is not only to feedback what (as scientists) we learn from local communities and individual innovators in their own language, but also to share with them what we learn from others (i.e., enhancing the public understanding of scientific developments).

A strong view is taken of unprofessional conduct on the part of scientists, especially the tradition of making local communities always anonymous in scientific practice even when these communities have played roles in divulging key information regarding certain plants or drugs. This must be stopped, and this change in the ethics of scientific practice should gradually impact on the basic tenor of academic discourse on local knowledge.

The issue of value addition is also taken very seriously in the practice of these institutions. Value addition to IK will help local communities co-exist with biodiversity resources by reducing primary extraction and generating long-term benefits. From this perspective, local communities are termed "knowledge-rich, but economically poor". The search is therefore for a middle way in the dialogue between and the linkage of IKS and formal knowledge systems. Any dynamic knowledge system therefore has to evolve through the continuance of traditional knowledge as well as contemporary innovations, and these should be pursued by individuals and communities. The spirit of sustainability, it is felt, can be achieved by blending the secular and the sacred streams of consciousness around the six E's: Ethics, Excellence, Equity, Efficiency, Environment and Education.

The aim is therefore to connect creative people engaged in generating local solutions, which are authentic and accountable, thus facilitating people to people learning. Some of these scientific institutions are therefore seriously concerned with the ethics of knowledge extraction, its documentation, dissemination, and incorporation into real life products/services or policy frameworks.

At the same time, scientists affirm that the discussion on biodiversity can only become authentic if we probe deep enough into knowledge traditions of each part of the world to discover the roots of sustainable ethics. But this discovery requires preparing our minds for visions, which collide with the dominant materialistic world-view. The existing epistemology relies excessively on the language and ethos of elites whose own record of sharing their rent with providers of knowledge is not very honourable. When they plead for reforms, they advocate action by everyone else in the world ranging from local governments to world bodies, but their own conduct and practice of life remains untouched by the logic of their appeal. It is with this in mind that it is urgent that such a code of conduct should be developed.

## *Integration to School Curriculum*

In India there is no formal mechanism for integrating IKS knowledge and innovations at either university or school level. However, the Honey Bee programme of the National Innovation Foundation has started to train both teachers and students to embed IKS innovations in their school activities. Honey Bee provides workshops to train primary level teachers and also encourages students to search for and document innovations from the community. A number of mechanisms have been adopted to promote the use and status of IKS innovations within the Indian community.

One that bears special mention at this point is the biodiversity contest for documentation of innovation. The aim is to scout for genius among little children and make them aware of their common ecological knowledge transferred from older generations to the younger ones. They are quizzed about the uses of the plants, and other nature-related aspects. These contests demonstrated that children from disadvantaged backgrounds showed an extraordinary ability to inventorise biodiversity and its local uses.

Ecological indicators such as prediction of rainfall and other climatic parameters, disease, pest attacks, fertility of soil, non-chemical agriculture, wild and as well as domesticated agro-biodiversity, declining water table, performance of animals and crops, non-sustainable practices, and the need for stemming the erosion of local ecological and technical knowledge were identified or discussed. Many of these indicators would have to be validated through systematic observation, or cross-cultural testing. These indicators embody the wisdom encoded in the form of "easy-to–interpret signals."

## DEVELOPMENT PROCESS AND INDIGENOUS PEOPLE

Most countries have enunciated policies and strategies to develop their indigenous population. But even without these policy statements, the normal economic, technological and social processes of development have to a large extent adversely affected the lives of millions of indigenous people. In central India, the forests, which once provided the playing fields for children, and the source of food and medicine, are no longer available to the indigenous peoples, as more and more forest areas go under government control as reserved forests.

The ruthless exploitation of the forest wealth, indiscriminate mining activities and the building of huge projects have displaced large numbers of indigenous peoples from their homeland, shoving them into congested rehabilitation centers where the children suffer from malnutrition, skin diseases and influenza as they come into contact with previously unencountered ailments. Diseases such as syphilis and tuberculosis, once not very prevalent among the indigenous peoples, have had a particularly harsh effect on the children.

Groups who were once self-sufficient, with enough food, milk and medicines from their own sources, have gradually been reduced to a dependent and confused people. The dwindling land resources, change in cropping pattern and the unavailability of forest resources for food, fuel, fodder and medicine have had their effects on the children particularly.

The impact of economic change for these tribes has been, according to Professor Haimendorf, an "enlarging of economic networks" and "interdependence" with the progressively expanding dominant population. The competition for scarce resources has resulted in many tribal peoples mortgaging their land to moneylenders, contractors and landlords, who surreptitiously manipulate the debt records holding children in bondage for their ancestors' debts. Such cases have greatly decreased since legislation banning bonded labor was passed, but it is difficult to detect and prove such cases due to the subtle informality of the arrangement.

Children in general are very vulnerable to development, but more so indigenous children, unused to outside contact. In particular, female children are still more vulnerable. Within indigenous populations, many studies have shown that there is a fair amount of equality among the sexes, particularly among children. But, when coming into contact with the dominant cultures, an indigenous female child has much more to overcome as she is faced with an unequal society where more than often a female child has a lower status than a male.

The consequences of such contact is that she is automatically slotted for less education, less pay for work, less health and nutritional care and often reduced to a sexual object. She has also to work harder in the family as family value systems disintegrate and more and more young men become the semi-educated unemployed and stop helping with household and agricultural work. The subtle molding of children of indigenous peoples to appreciate the clothes, consumerism, religion, art and living styles of the dominant cultures, abandoning the richness of their own values and wisdom, is a sad example of what the world is losing along with its flora, fauna and a clean environment.

### *Strategies for Development*

Not many studies have been done on the impact and effect of the development process on indigenous children. While all of the broad issues which affect indigenous people apply to women and children, specific issues like coping with the adverse effects of development on the domestic front and socio-psychological adjustments can be particularly hard to them. Most governments seem to hope for this situation so that the "problem" will be solved automatically. It is hoped that the unimaginative school systems with rote learning, noncreative approach, and promotion of the culture and the value systems of the powerful groups will bring the indigenous children into the "mainstream of national life."

The education system of the dominant groups has, in the name of eradicating illiteracy, produced a considerable number of semi-educated indigenous youth who remain unemployed with an acquired bias against traditional occupations and manual labor. With the increasing pressure on their lands and dwindling land holdings, the indigenous peoples have been forced to change their cropping patterns from food crops to cash crops which have impoverished them further and adversely affected nutritional intake. Often the youth migrate to semi-urban agglomerations where they may have to live in degradation and frustration.

Fortunately, there does, however, seem to be an alternative to this unhealthy strategy. It has been demonstrated in India that children of indigenous people can be given the opportunity to develop in their own genius and in their unique cultural milieu with dignity and pride and contribute significantly to the national life, without necessarily having to adopt the attitudes of the majority.

The way in which the tribal youth of Arunachal Pradesh of India have developed is a classic example. The enlightened policy by the government to selectively protect the tribal people from not only economic but also cultural exploitation has resulted in both the male and female youth of Arunachal Pradesh presently participating in all the spheres of the state and private activities with minimum of disadvantages and complexes. With the government acting only as a and complexes. With the government acting only as a catalyst - providing education, health, infrastructure and economic facilities to the population, with very little external interference in the culture and social organization of the people - the Apa Tani youth have retained their confidence and self-respect. Government schools have enabled the Apa Tani children to avail themselves of a sound education, irrespective of their parents' capacity to pay. The same, however, cannot be said about the tribal people of central India, who are much larger in number and more exposed to overall exploitation, due to their vulnerable geographical location.

In these areas the indigenous peoples are extremely dependent on the government machinery for protection of their rights and for development. This has led to much slower progress in the development of independent attitudes among the children. Similarly, the Nishis and the Miris have made considerable progress in the education of their youth. There are presently many university graduates among them and several boys and girls are enrolled outside Arunachal Pradesh for graduate studies. It is significant that as the members of the state legislature are largely from the "tribal" groups, aspirations of the people are usually reflected in state policies.

Unfortunately, the same cannot be said about the tribal people of central India, with some exceptions. The Gonds, Saoras, Bhils and Mundas are numerically much larger and have been more exposed to overall economic and cultural exploitation over centuries of contact with the dominant majorities.

The vulnerable geographic position, which allows easy access and exposure, has resulted in gradual displacement of the tribal peoples from their lands. In these areas the indigenous peoples are extremely dependent on the government for the protection of their rights and for their overall development. This has led to much slower progress in the development and independence of attitudes among the children. Government schools were established in Andhra Pradesh almost a decade earlier than in Arunachal Pradesh, yet relatively few Gonds or other tribal youth have become officers or professionals.

The educational system, which is focused on the dominant culture and excludes issues of relevance to indigenous peoples, tends to produce frustration and dissatisfaction among the youth. Many of them drop out of school to look for employment. The education of "tribal" children has caused concern to the government, which is presently discussing the components of the New Education Policy, which will have a specific and relevant focus on the educational curriculum of "tribal" children.

It is hoped that the new focus will include the historical and cultural aspects of the indigenous peoples, promotion of tribal dialects, vocational education, emphasis on female education, ashram schools for boys and girls and the introduction of basic information on technology to help in the understanding of the upgrading of their indigenous technology.

### *Government Policies*

Women and children have always been accorded a relatively low priority in the development objectives and strategies of most countries. It took the United Nations declaration of decades for women and children to activate most governments to focus some attention to the issues. And still comparatively less money is allocated toward the development of women and children in practically all sectors of government.

Accordingly, the effects are very marginal by the time they reach indigenous children. Due to the difficulties in communications, infrastructure facilities and political-bureaucratic factors there is always a considerable developmental gap between the more accessible and the remote regions. In most governmental programs, one finds a reluctance on the part of trained personnel to be posted in the areas where indigenous people live.

In fact, most developing countries still lack adequately trainee personnel to implement programs for women and children. Paired with no political or economic imperative to provide basic facilities for women and children, pressures to bring large industrial, hydroelectric, mining or deforestation projects in these areas work to the detriment of the original inhabitants.

Development seems to connote only that which is economically profitable. It is small wonder therefore that the development of women and children, particularly of the indigenous people, which is nonremunerative and not visible, is considered almost a soft option in the current concept of development. There must be a global perspective and goal in the development of indigenous children and peoples, to create an environment where indigenous children can grow up with dignity, fair play and justice while receiving the health and educational facilities which engender creativity and self-development. The more happy and well-adjusted children of today will be the more confident and productive citizens of tomorrow.

Indigenous people all over the world have for centuries through the present seen their lands taken away from them, their humanhood robbed and their culture destroyed and deprecated. Being people bred in solitude and natural surroundings, with spontaneous and intuitive responses they have developed their family systems based on their own genius, innate skills and requirements. The child is an integral part of the family and the family a part of the group tradition. So the child is in effect a cornerstone of the social fabric and economic system of the group.

The birth of a child in most indigenous communities, particularly among some tribes in India, is welcomed with an invocation to the world to bless the child. The elements such as the earth, the sky and the wind are requested to confer on the child the qualities associated with them. The birds, animals and even the humble earthworm are called upon to bless the child with their personal attributes. Such a child is brought up in the traditions of his forefathers and made to understand the value systems of the ancestors by the group itself. Normally, therefore, the child, the family and the group have a blended personality usually characterized by a common focus on the immediacy of the surrounding environment.

## CONTROLLING INDIGENOUS LIFE

All the possible institutions of civil society, right from the electronic media to primary schools, were applied by the champions of Hindutava to create a sensation of inferiority and thus to manipulate the masses. Among the indigenous people two processes were induced in parallel. One was the deliberate formation of institutions such as Vanvasi Kalyan Ashram and Dalit Sanghs to train-up youth cadres and thus to inculcate a feeling that indigenous tradition and culture is inferior to that of Hindu religion. Secondly, the insurgence of consumeristic culture in such areas. Both these process went in parallel and are inter-related and empowers the coexistence.

One of the outcomes of these trends is the crucial osmosis of Hindu strings and civilisation with all its flaws among the indigenous people. Nevertheless this fondness of controlling indigenous people has two basic reasons. One was to perpetuate the political power and right over their life though legitimising the social system and second to establish an unquestioned command over the resource zones of the country. Another vital part of the process is the development of internal colonisation. This is a vicious conspiracy by the Brahministic society to cohere the Dalits into their fold. Similarly Adivasis a wonderful model of egalitarianism have been transformed into an exploited class. Jharkhand and Bastar are the best examples to check the impact of such trends and processes. Earlier these aspects were efficiently engineered through the socio-religious structures, but today it is taking a political shape, which in fact is communalisation of polity or fascism is all about.

### *Communal-Fascist base among Dalits and Adivasis*

Communal-fascism is exploring its way to elaborate its base and activities and action. It appears that building of philanthropic and religious institutions like Vanvasi Kalyan Ashram, Dalit Sanghs, Deen Dayal Shodh Sansthan, Saraswati Sishu Mandir, Sanskriti Bihar, Vikas Bharit, Gayatri Pariwar, Brahmakumari Samaj, etc. are some of the strategies adopted to create inroads among the Dalits & Adivasis. Another strategy applied is the steady and systematic capturing of the community panchayats and organisations. The best example of this is Gujarat where the communal fascists have got their stranglehold. All these have added impelling force to the Hindutava card among Dalits and Adivasis. By and large this consists of concepts like de-Dalitisation and de-Adivasisation. Eventually this tendency empowers the fascist forces and broadens its space.

Expansion of fascism has so far and is disintegrating the Dalit-Adivasi ideology, theology, and identity and intimidated their very existence. Apparently this ruptures the community, deteriorates the noble notions of sharing, caring and co-operation, expansion of patriarchy and battered the inkling of community ownership over resources.

## *Fascism-Globalisation Nexus*

While going into further analysis, fascism acts close to the current process of globalisation. Both these are two inter-dependent and inter-linked facets of capitalism. While globalisation is supposed to capture the global economic and political power by cutting the national boundaries and establishing/capturing the market, fascist forces acts as their local agents in its approaches and attitudes with a bonus of suppressive socio-cultural and religious domination. The ideology of capitalism assumes absoluteness only through its offspring fascism. In India, Washington is taking a lenient view to prop up the communal fascist government of the BJP Hindu nationalists. The global governance can afford to accommodate and promote religious fundamentalist regimes as long as they are useful weapons in their hand because they have several things in common.

The political segments in India, by and large, strive and thrive to cater the global and national capitalistic market. As a part of this practice, there is an invisible 'safety net' around the capitalist camp. Having nothing to do with the people, the resources are rapidly being opened for the neo-colonisers to be explored and exploited. This great surrender before the global capital market implicates the momentum by which the fascist-capitalist nexus is plundering the resources. Targeting the resources is directly an assault on indigenous masses. Since their land, property, forest and other resources are the greenland for any sort of investment, strategies and planning are formulated in such a way to allure them so that they get entangled in the web and are unable to break it. This eventually culminates into large scale of displacement and migration, heavy loss of land and resources, robs them of their rich tradition and culture, and leads to the irreversible and perpetual loss of livelihood source. Therefore fascism is utmost visible in the market.

Never before in the history have we witnessed such a period of deliberate drift of further confusing and disempowerment of Dalits and Adivasis. It has constantly succeeded in gearing up its organisational tactics and mobilisation methods to subtly crush the energy of people, and divert it; thus draining off their capacity to fight for their rights and their ability to resist injustice. It is sucking them like a vampire day by day. Hence attack on Christians and other minorities is nothing but a direct assault on Dalits & Adivasis.

Under this circumstance, where humanitarian norms and values are degenerating and the indigenous people stand at the receiving end, is it possible for us to go back to these communities and unveil the wolf inside the goat's skin? Can we stand with the Dalits and Adivasis in developing a counter movement to combat the fascist-capitalist forces? Can we intentionally foster the indigenous people towards a socialist, secular, democratic and decentralised polity, which would lead us to the Kingdom values?

1) *The United Nations Permanent Forum on Indigenous Issues:* The Permanent Forum and Indigenous Children and Youth at its first session expressed its intention to make indigenous children and youth a focal point of its work in the years to come. The Permanent Forum submission addresses various recommendations to UNICEF, to the CRC and other monitoring bodies.

2) *International Labour Office (ILO):* Outlines the work of the ILO to address concerns of indigenous and tribal peoples around the world, primarily in relation to the Indigenous and Tribal Peoples Convention 1989. The ILO works on the basis of three priority methods: a) standard-setting and supervision, b) technical cooperation and assistance, c) research. This submission consists of 3 parts: 1) highlighting the ILO's rights-based approach, 2) technical cooperation efforts and 3) suggestions for the working group on non-discrimination and cultural specificity.

3) *International Institute for Child Rights and Development, University of Victoria, Canada:* Outlines recommendations on the theme of non-discrimination' access to basic services for indigenous children. Approaches which address the challenges of non-discrimination: should be a) rights-based (i.e. all rights are universal), b) indivisible (i.e. they may not be prioritized), c) interdependent. Health, education and protection should be integrated together.

4) *World Vision is an international Christian humanitarian organization, working with indigenous communities in a number of countries throughout the world*: The primary experiences drawn upon in this submission from the partnership they have with indigenous communities in Chile focus on culturally specificity and non-discrimination

5) *Isolated Communities and Ignored Claims:* Tribal Children's Right to Education in India. Tribal communities in India have been historically deprived of access to resources and opportunities, including the education. According to the author, unless the government undertakes urgent steps to

address this issue, its proclamations on child rights would remain empty rhetoric.

6) *Child Program:* The rights in the cultural diversity. This submission outlines the rights set out in the Indigenous Law approved by the Congress of the Union. These include the prohibition of discrimination for ethnic, cultural, religious reasons, or because of disability; the right to equal access to health and education services; and freedom of movement. It also address the question of education of indigenous children, who are marginalized, and considered as 'problems' rather than as people in the process of education and learning.

7) *Government of Norway:* This submission outlines the Governments efforts to promote and protect the human rights of children, because children need special protection and care and represent the future. Special efforts are therefore made to target certain groups of children and young people in Norway, including Sami children and young people, and great importance to the protection of children rights in its national and international efforts.

8) *The rights of indigenous children:* Theme: Cultural Specificity in the Canadian Educational Curriculum. This submission addresses the following issues: a) integrating indigenous staff within the school structure by encouraging indigenous people to become teachers, b) history books being reviewed by a diverse panel of community members.

9) *Religious Society of Friends (Quakers) in Australia Incorporated:* Indigenous Concerns Committee. This submission focuses on education, language and juvenile justice. It is based on information supplied by members of the Society of Friend, and by indigenous young people.

10) *The Bernard van Leer Foundation: Indigenous children and early childhood development programmes:* A matter of access and content. Presents lessons learned from four major early childhood development (ECD) programmes for indigenous children in Guatemala and Mexico. These case

studies are highlighted because the countries have large numbers of indigenous citizens, and because they illustrate approaches and strategies for ensuring appropriate education for young indigenous children.

11) *Government of Mexico:* Indigenous children begin their life in surroundings characterized by the extreme poverty and marginalization. This submission outlines Mexico's changes to public policy aimed at supporting the indigenous community and reducing disparities, including by increasing access to education and health services, and the creation of different government institutions such as the National Commission for the Development of Indigenous People. The National Commission recommends that the Committee encourage research on situation of indigenous children.

12) *UNICEF: Implementing the right to education for indigenous children:* Efforts in this regard have focused primarily on bilingual and intercultural education, and on the active participation of indigenous communities in the design and implementation of education projects and policies. Indigenous children must participate in all decisions regarding their children's right to education. An additional issue raised in the submission is appropriate training for indigenous teachers and other professional working with children.

13) *Centre for Organisation Research & Education (CORE):* Discrimination against indigenous children in India: Race, culture and class. Children's issues and indigenous children's issues need to be addressed by all sectors of society and civil society in particular. While anti-discrimination laws are a good starting point, implementation must take into acount their own realities: they are indigenous. Their survival, protection, development and participation depend on their identification as indigenous in the first place.

14) *Child Rights:* International Research Institute. There is a need for continuing dialogue with indigenous peoples about

the needs of their children. The Institute's annual international workshops on indigenous children and youth have become a major force for bringing international attention to the problems faced by indigenous children. The submission lists recommendations of the 4th international workshop. The Committee should regularly inquire about the status of indigenous children when reviewing State Party reports, and funds should be made available to allow indigenous to participate in relevant UN bodies.

15) *The child of Bangladesh:* Bangladesh is one of the poorest countries in the world and to establish child rights in this country, according to the authors, stakeholders need to unite and the government should engage in long term planning. 7 suggestions are listed to establish the rights of child, i.e. the government should develop programmes specifically for women.

16) *Human Rights Watch:* Discrimination Against Bedouin Children in Israel's Schools. Discrimination against Bedouin children colors every aspect of the Israeli education system. The classes they do have are often in poor condition, especially in the Negev. As a result of the classroom shortage, many classes in Arab schools are held in rented spaces, in some cases only a room in a private home, or in prefabricated buildings. The educational system has given a low priority to teacher training for the Arab school system and has taken no provisions to encourage Bedouin teachers.

17) *Violation of rights to children and young people pertaining to indigenous populations in Colombia:* Defense Association of the International Children. DNI Colombia. There are 92 different indigenous populations in Colombia, which use 64 distinct languages, and have their own symbolic, material and spiritual expressions cultural, forms and social mechanisms. This submission outlines the human rights situation of these populations and notes that of the 30,284 cases of human rights violations between August 2002 and

August 2003, 3,86% of these were related to indigenous populations in the Patumayo, Choco, Arauca, Risaralda y Cauca regions.

The Indian Government's commitment to the human rights standards enunciated in several key international instruments is exemplary. It has acceded to the International Covenant on Civil and Political Rights (ICCPR), the International Covenant on Economic, Social and Cultural Rights (ICESCR) and the International Convention on the Elimination of All Forms of Racial Discrimination (ICERD), indicating its willingness to be bound by the treaties in international law. However, the reality of India's human rights record reveals that this formal affirmation of human rights is deceptive.

The fundamental rights that the State has pledged to protect in the three aforementioned treaties continue to be routinely violated through the application of particular laws and the actions of State authorities. This disparity between the rhetoric and practice of the Indian Government is disturbing. It calls into question whether the Government's ratification of the ICCPR, the ICESCR and the ICERD is motivated by a genuine commitment to human rights, or the need to divert international scrutiny from the plight of its citizens.

### *The Caste System*

Caste-based discrimination remains endemic in Indian society. The groups occupying the lowest echelons of the caste system, particularly the Dalits or the Scheduled Castes, are regularly denied basic political, economic, social and cultural rights. The range of abuses to which they are subjected include torture, restrictions on their freedom of movement, and forced participation in such degrading tasks as manual scavenging. In spite of the fact that this constitutes a clear derogation from the provisions of the ICCPR, the ICESCR and the ICERD, the Indian Government has sought to frame caste-based discrimination as a social issue of purely domestic concern, rather than a human rights problem warranting international attention. This argument ignores indications that comparable kinds of discrimination exist in numerous countries in Asia and Africa. Even so, the Indian Government was successful in ensuring caste-based discrimination was omitted from the agenda of the World Conference against Racism, Racial Discrimination, Xenophobia and All Related Forms of Intolerance held in late 2001.

However, this reasoning has been unequivocally rejected by the Committee on the Elimination of Racial Discrimination, the monitoring body established under the Convention. The Committee has recognised caste-based discrimination as a form of discrimination based on descent and has passed a general recommendation reiterating this view, putting the question of the scope of the ICERD beyond doubt.

### *The Rights of Indigenous Peoples*

The rights of indigenous peoples are enshrined in various provisions of the ICERD, the ICCPR and the ICESCR. In particular, the right of all peoples to self-determination is recognised in Articles 1 of both the ICCPR and the ICESCR. Contrary to these provisions, the Indian Government has acted to suppress even peaceful movements for self-determination. Although the Indian Government ratified the ICCPR and ICESCR with reservations in respect of those Articles, this does not diminish the seriousness of the abuses systematically inflicted upon its indigenous populations. The tribal people of Northeast India, have suffered economic deprivation, social and cultural oppression and have been the victims of a discriminatory application of emergency laws such as the Armed Forces Act. Section 4(a) of the AFSPA provides that any commissioned officer or a person of equivalent rank in the Armed Forces is empowered to shoot to kill after giving such due warning as he may consider necessary.

### *The Rights of Religious Minorities*

Instances of the complicity of State agents in the persecution of religious minorities in India continue to undermine the Government's purported commitment to the protections contained in the ICERD. In the aftermath of the Gujarat riots in early 2002, overwhelming evidence emerged implicating members of the police force in the violence against Muslims. Furthermore, collusion between police and Government officials to protect the perpetrators of the violence from prosecution was reportedly widespread. Far from being an aberration in the behaviour of State officials, the tendency of law enforcement agencies to side with the Hindu majority in communal riots has been publicly acknowledged for some time. Indeed, the 1981 Report of the National Police Commission admitted to such a bias in the operations of its police officers.

The uncertain predicament of religious minorities in India is also apparent in the passage of anti-conversion laws in the early 1990s. Although ostensibly secular in purpose, the laws in fact operate to reinforce the dominance of the Hindu majority. The Special Rapporteur on Religious Intolerance shared this conclusion, reporting in 1992 on the forced conversions of Christians to Hinduism in the state of Madhya Pradesh, led by the Bharatiya Janata Party, which governed the state at the time. The same trend is apparent in more recent legislation enacted by the Jayalalitha Government in the state of Tamil Nadu and the controversial Government of the state of Gujarat.

In light of the range of human rights violations in India that contravene provisions of the ICERD, it is unsurprising that the Indian Government has been reluctant to submit its compliance reports to the CERD. It submitted its 16th and 17th reports after receiving four and three reminders from the Committee respectively.

In spite of its obligation under Article 6(6) of the ICCPR to work towards the abolition of the death penalty, the Indian Government has signalled its movement in the opposite direction by broadening the applicability of the death penalty as a punishment for 'terrorist acts' in its recent counter-terrorism legislation, the Prevention of Terrorism Act 2001. Furthermore, the Government is yet to amend the Indian Penal Code to ensure that persons are not executed for crimes committed when they were under the age of eighteen, in line with the requirements of Article 6(5) of the ICCPR. In conjunction with its reticence on the issue of signing the Second Optional Protocol to the ICCPR, this suggests a lack of good faith on the part of the Indian Government in its efforts to comply with the provisions of the ICCPR.

Although Article 4 of the ICCPR allows for the suspension of some of the rights contained in the Covenant in times of 'public emergency', it does not allow derogation from designated fundamental human rights under any circumstances. Several pieces of legislation enacted by the Indian Government clearly fall foul of this provision, including the AFSPA, the National Security Act and the Prevention of Terrorism Act. None of these Acts were enacted in an officially proclaimed emergency. Of greater concern, however, is the authorisation of measures such as arbitrary detention and other infringements upon fundamental human rights standards expressly prohibited by the ICCPR.

### *Official Immunity*

Both the ICCPR (in Article 2(3)) and the ICERD (in Article 6) enunciate the need for an effective remedy to be available to victims of human rights abuses. However, section 6 of AFSPA grants members of the armed forces immunity from prosecution. Given the regular allegations of human rights violations committed by India's armed forces in the past, this amounts to a denial of justice and of redress in the form of compensation.

The ICCPR provides for two complaints procedures – one available to individuals under the First Optional Protocol, and one available to States under Article 41 of the Covenant. However, the Indian Government has failed to consent to either of these mechanisms, depriving its citizens of an important alternative avenue of redress against the State. States that have acceded to the ICCPR are also expected to submit periodic reports to the Human Rights Committee detailing its compliance with the Covenants requirements. Each of the reports India has submitted thus far have been late, and the Committee is currently awaiting India's fourth report, which was due in 2001. The Indian Government's reports have often been criticised for focusing on describing the legal safeguards in place to protect human rights, rather than the practical effectiveness of their implementation.

# 3

# EDUCATION CHARTER, 1813

Up to 1813 the East India Company had followed the traditional pattern of governmental patronage to Indian learning. There was Warren Hastings college of Arabic and Persian studies in Calcutta and Jonathan Duncan's Sanskrit college in Benares. In 1813 the Charter Act sanctioned the annual sum of L 10,000 towards 'the revival and improvement of literature and the encouragement of the learned natives of India and for the introduction and promotion of a knowledge of the sciences among the inhabitants of the British territories of India'.

It was not until 1823 that a Committee of Public Instruction was formed to give effect to this provision. It immediately perceived the ambiguity between the promotion of oriental learning and the other western learning, and plunged into a lively controversy. This was the situation which Bentick found on his arrival and of which he took advantage.

In Calcutta he found a forward looking group of intellectuals led by Raja Ram Mohan Roy who had helped to found a college for western learning and advocated its introduction. In 1834 he received a powerful English reinforcement in the arrival of the Law member, Thomas Babington Macaulay. The result was the decision to launch English education and western knowledge into India. Macaulay declared in 1835 'that the great objects of the British government ought to be the promotion of European literature and science' and the available funds should 'be henceforth employed in imparting to the native population knowledge of English literature and science through the medium of the English language'.

From this time the government began to set up schools and colleges imparting western knowledge in the English language. To this was added another measure of greatest importance. English replaced Persian as the official state language and the medium of higher courts of law, local languages replacing Persian in the lower courts.

Western science was specifically introduced in the form of western medicine, of which the Calcutta Medical College was the first institution. Science also received attention in both schools and colleges. Western technology spread through engineering works like roads, canals, and later in 1853 by the introduction of Railways. The process was hastened by the increase in the number of Indian officers entering the administration as a result of Bentick's policy of Indianization.

Macaulay on his part started the codification of Indian public criminal law. The work was not completed until 1861 when the Indian Penal Code came into existence for the first time. Bentick heralded a age of social & administrative reforms in India although no other Governor General after him went to the extent he went yet the after effects of his reformist attitude went a long way in providing mobility to the stagnant Indian society.

Up to 1813 the company had followed the traditional pattern of governmental patronage to Indian learning. There was Warren Hastings college of Arabic and Persian studies in Calcutta and Jonathan Duncan's Sanskrit college in Benares. In 1813 the Charter Act sanctioned the annual sum of L 10,000 towards 'the revival and improvement of literature and the encouragement of the learned natives of India and for the introduction and promotion of a knowledge of the sciences among the inhabitants of the British territories of India'.

It was not until 1823 that a Committee of Public Instruction was formed to give effect to this provision. It immediately perceived the ambiguity between the promotion of oriental learning and the other western learning, and plunged into a lively controversy. This was the situation which Bentick found on his arrival and of which he took advantage.

In Calcutta he found a forward looking group of intellectuals led by Raja Ram Mohan Roy who had helped to found a college for western learning and advocated its introduction. In 1834 he received a powerful English reinforcement in the arrival of the Law member, Thomas Babington Macaulay. The result was the decision to launch English education and western knowledge into India. Macaulay declared in 1835 'that the great objects of the British government ought to be the promotion of European literature and science' and the available funds should 'be henceforth employed in imparting to the native population knowledge of English literature and science through the medium of the English language'.

From this time the government began to set up schools and colleges imparting western knowledge in the English language. To this was added another measure of greatest importance. English replaced Persian as the official state language and the medium of higher courts of law, local languages replacing Persian in the lower courts.

Western science was specifically introduced in the form of western medicine, of which the Calcutta Medical College was the first institution. Science also received attention in both schools and colleges. Western technology spread through engineering works like roads, canals, and later in 1853 by the introduction of Railways. The process was hastened by the increase in the number of Indian officers entering the administration as a result of Bentick's policy of Indianization.

Macaulay on his part started the codification of Indian public criminal law. The work was not completed until 1861 when the Indian Penal Code came into existence for the first time.

## EXPANSION AND TERRITORY

It was not until the middle of the 19th century that almost all of the territory that constitutes Pakistan and India came under the rule of the British East India Company. The patterns of territorial acquisition and rule as applied by the company in Sindh and Punjab and the manner of governance became the basis for direct British rule in the British Indian Empire and indirect rule in the princely states under the paramountcy of the Crown.

Although the British had earlier ruled in the factory areas, the beginning of British rule is often dated from the Battle of Plassey. Robert Clive's victory was consolidated in 1764 at the Battle of Buxar (in Bihar), where the emperor, Shah Alam II, was defeated. As a result, Shah Alam was coerced to appoint the company to be the diwan for the areas of Bengal, Bihar, and Orissa. The company thus became the supreme, but not the titular, power in much of the Ganges Valley, and company agents continued to trade on terms highly favorable to them. The area controlled by the company expanded during the first three decades of the 19th century by two methods. The first was the use of subsidiary agreements between the British and the local rulers, under which control of foreign affairs, defense, and communications was transferred from the ruler to the company and the rulers were allowed to rule as they wished (up to a limit) on other matters. This development created what came to be called the Native States, or Princely India, that is, the world of the maharaja and his Muslim counterpart the nawab. The second method was outright military conquest or direct annexation of territories; it was these areas that were properly called British India. Most of northern India was annexed by the British.

At the start of the 19th century, most of present-day Pakistan was under independent rulers. Sindh was ruled by the Muslim Talpur mirs in three small states that were annexed by the British in 1843. In Punjab, the decline of the Mughal Empire allowed the rise of the Sikhs, first as a military force and later as a political administration in Lahore.

The kingdom of Lahore was at its most powerful and expansive during the rule of Maharaja Ranjit Singh, when Sikh control was extended beyond Peshawar, and Kashmir was added to his dominions in 1819. After Ranjit Singh died in 1839, political conditions in Punjab deteriorated, and the British fought two wars with the Sikhs. The second of these wars, in 1849, saw the annexation of Punjab, including the present-day North-West Frontier Province, to the company's territories. Kashmir was transferred by sale in the Treaty of Amritsar in 1850 to the Dogra Dynasty, which ruled the area under British paramountcy until 1947.

As the British increased their territory in India, so did Russia expand in Central Asia. The East India Company signed treaties with a number of Afghan rulers and with Ranjit Singh. Russia backed Persian ambitions in western Afghanistan. In 1838 the Company's actions bought about the First Afghan War (1838- 42). Assisted by Sikh allies, the company took Kandahar and Kabul and made its own candidate amir. The amir proved unpopular with the Afghans, however, and the British garrison's position became untenable. The retreat of the British from Kabul in January 1842 was one of the worst disasters in British military history, as a column of more than 16,000 was annihilated by Afghan tribesmen as they struggled through the snowbound passes on their way back to India. The British later sent a punitive expedition to Kabul, which it burned in retribution, but made no attempt to reoccupy Afghanistan.

In Punjab, annexed in 1849, a group of extraordinarily able British officers, serving first the Company and then the British Crown, governed the area. They avoided the administrative mistakes made earlier in Bengal. A number of reforms were introduced, although local customs were generally respected. Irrigation projects later in the century helped Punjab become the granary of northern India. The respect gained by the new administration could be gauged by the fact that within ten years Punjabi troops were fighting for the British elsewhere in India to subdue the uprising of 1857-1858. Punjab was to become the major recruiting area for the British Indian Army, recruiting both Sikhs and Muslims.

## MOTIVES

A multiplicity of motives underlay the British penetration into India: commerce, security, and a purported moral uplift of the people. The "expansive force" of private and company trade eventually led to the conquest or annexation of territories in which spices, cotton, and opium were produced. British investors ventured into the unfamiliar interior landscape in search of opportunities that promised substantial profits. British economic penetration was aided by Indian collaborators, such as the bankers and merchants who controlled intricate credit networks.

British rule in India would have been a frustrated or half-realized dream had not Indian counterparts provided connections between rural and urban centers. External threats, both real and imagined, such as the Napoleonic Wars and Russian expansion toward Afghanistan, as well as the desire for internal stability, led to the annexation of more territory in India.

Political analysts in Britain wavered initially as they were uncertain of the costs or the advantages in undertaking wars in India, but by the 1810s, as the territorial aggrandizement eventually paid off, opinion in London welcomed the absorption of new areas. Occasionally the British Parliament witnessed heated debates against expansion, but arguments justifying military operations for security reasons always won over even the most vehement critics.

The British soon forgot their own rivalry with the Portuguese and the French and permitted them to stay in their coastal enclaves, which they kept even after independence in

1947. The British, however, continued to expand vigorously well into the 1850s. A number of aggressive governors-general undertook relentless campaigns against several Hindu and Muslim rulers. Among them were Richard Colley Wellesley, William Pitt Amherst, George Eden, Edward Law, and James Andrew Brown Ramsay. Despite desperate efforts at salvaging their tottering power and keeping the British at bay, many Hindu and Muslim rulers lost their territories: Mysore, the Maratha Confederacy, and Punjab.

The British success in large measure was the result not only of their superiority in tactics and weapons but also of their ingenious relations with Indian rulers through the "subsidiary alliance" system, introduced in the early 19th century. Many rulers bartered away their real responsibilities by agreeing to uphold British paramountcy in India, while they retained a fictional sovereignty under the rubric of Pax Britannica. Later, Dalhousie espoused the "doctrine of lapse" and annexed outright the estates of deceased princes of Satara, Udaipur, Jhansi, Tanjore, Nagpur, and Oudh.

European perceptions of India, and those of the British especially, shifted from unequivocal appreciation to sweeping condemnation of India's past achievements and customs. Imbued with an ethnocentric sense of superiority, British intellectuals, including Christian missionaries, spearheaded a movement that sought to bring Western intellectual and technological innovations to Indians. Interpretations of the causes of India's cultural and spiritual "backwardness" varied, as did the solutions.

Many argued that it was Europe's mission to civilize India and hold it as a trust until Indians proved themselves competent for self-rule. The immediate consequence of this sense of superiority was to open India to more aggressive missionary activity.

## POLICIES

The British Parliament enacted a series of laws, among which the Regulating Act of 1773 stood first, to curb the company traders' unrestrained commercial activities and to bring about some order in territories under company control. Limiting the company charter to periods of twenty years, subject to review upon renewal, the 1773 act gave the British government supervisory rights over the Bengal, Bombay, and Madras presidencies.

Bengal was given preeminence over the rest because of its enormous commercial vitality and because it was the seat of British power in India, whose governor was elevated to the new position of governor-general. Warren Hastings was the first incumbent. The India Act of 1784 sometimes described as the "half-loaf system," as it sought to mediate between Parliament and the company directors, enhanced Parliament's control by establishing the Board of Control, whose members were selected from the cabinet. The Charter Act of 1813 recognized British moral responsibility by introducing just and humane laws in India, foreshadowing future social legislation, and outlawing a number of traditional practices such as *sati* and *thagi*.

As governor-general from 1786 to 1793, Charles Cornwallis, professionalized, bureaucratized, and Europeanized the company's administration. He also outlawed private trade by company employees, separated the commercial and administrative functions, and remunerated company servants with generous graduated salaries. Because revenue collection became the company's most essential administrative function, Cornwallis made a compact with Bengali zamindars, who were perceived as the Indian counterparts to the British landed gentry. The Permanent Settlement system, also known as the zamindari system, fixed taxes in perpetuity in return for ownership of large estates; but the state was excluded from agricultural expansion, which came under the purview of the zamindars. In Madras and Bombay, however, the *ryotwari* settlement system was set in motion, in which peasant cultivators had to pay annual taxes directly to the government.

Neither the zamindari nor the ryotwari systems proved effective in the long run because India was integrated into an international economic and pricing system over which it had no control, while increasing numbers of people subsisted on agriculture for lack of other employment. Millions of people involved in the heavily taxed Indian textile industry also lost their markets, as they were unable to compete successfully with cheaper textiles produced in Lancashire's mills from Indian raw materials.

Beginning with the Mayor's Court, established in 1727 for civil litigation in Bombay, Calcutta, and Madras, justice in the interior came under the company's jurisdiction. In 1772 an elaborate judicial system, known as *adalat*, established civil and criminal jurisdictions along with a complex set of codes or rules of procedure and evidence. Both Hindu pandits and Muslim qazis were recruited to aid the presiding judges in interpreting their customary laws, but in other instances, British common and statutory laws became applicable. In extraordinary situations where none of these systems was applicable, the judges were enjoined to adjudicate on the basis of "justice, equity, and good conscience."

The legal profession provided numerous opportunities for educated and talented Indians who were unable to secure positions in the company, and, as a result, Indian lawyers later dominated nationalist politics and reform movements. Education for the most part was left to the charge of Indians or to private agents who imparted instruction in the vernaculars. But in 1813, the British became convinced of their "duty" to awaken the Indians from intellectual slumber by exposing them to British literary traditions, earmarking a paltry sum for the cause. Controversy between two groups of Europeans - the "Orientalists" and "Anglicists" - over how the money was to be spent prevented them from formulating any consistent policy until 1835 when William Cavendish Bentinck, the governor-general from 1828 to 1835, finally broke the impasse by resolving to introduce the English language as the medium of instruction. English replaced Persian in public administration and education.

The company's education policies in the 1830s tended to reinforce existing lines of socioeconomic division in society rather than bringing general liberation from ignorance and superstition. Whereas the Hindu English-educated minority spearheaded many social and religious reforms either in direct response to government policies or in reaction to them, Muslims as a group initially failed to do so, a position they endeavored to reverse.

Western-educated Hindu elites sought to rid Hinduism of its much criticized social evils: idolatry, the caste system, child marriage, and sati. Religious and social activist Ram Mohan Roy, who founded the Brahmo Samaj in 1828, displayed a readiness to synthesize themes taken from Christianity, Deism, and Indian monism, while other individuals in Bombay and Madras initiated literary and debating societies that gave them a forum for open discourse. The exemplary educational attainments and skillful use of the press by these early reformers enhanced the possibility of effecting broad reforms without compromising societal values or religious practices. The 1850s witnessed the introduction of the three "engines of social improvement" that heightened the British illusion of permanence in India. They were the railroads, the telegraph, and the uniform postal service, inaugurated during the tenure of Dalhousie as governor-general. The first railroad lines were built in 1850 from Howrah inland to the coalfields at Raniganj, Bihar, a distance of 240 kilometers. In 1851 the first electric telegraph line was laid in Bengal and soon linked Agra, Bombay, Calcutta, Lahore, Varanasi, and other cities.

The three different presidency or regional postal systems merged in 1854 to facilitate uniform methods of communication at an all-India level. With uniform postal rates for letters and newspapers - one-half anna and one anna, respectively - communication between the rural and the metropolitan areas became easier and faster. The increased ease of communication and the opening of highways and waterways accelerated the movement of troops, the transportation of raw materials and goods to and from the interior, and the exchange of commercial information.

The railroads did not break down the social or cultural distances between various groups but tended to create new categories in travel. Separate compartments in the trains were reserved exclusively for the ruling class, separating the educated and wealthy from ordinary people.

## WESTERN EDUCATION IN NINETEENTH-CENTURY INDIA

The history of English language and literature in colonial India in order to highlight why they should retain high cultural status in the post independence years. Inevitably this was an ongoing process when results of which reflect the fusion of a wide range of social, political, and cultural influences. However, it can be seen that certain policies and publications had a particular potency and effect. Through outlining the most influential of these it will be possible to register how their reverberations continue to impinge upon the social and cultural milieu of post independence India today. In the field of post-colonial studies the question of whether to write in the language of the former oppressor becomes a hotly debated subject giving rise to much difference of opinion.

## SHAPING OF A LANGUAGE CULTURE

The Charter Act of 1813 decreed that English would be taught in the Indian education system although not as a replacement for indigenous languages. Instead, it was anticipated that English would co-exist with Oriental studies as a means by which moral law could be reinforced.

The 1817 publication of John Mill's *History Of British India* proved to be a defining text in the theories of how education policies should be formed. Mill was situated firmly in the

Enlightenment tradition and disdainful of notions that Indian culture and tradition was of relevant value for an advancing nation. He dismissed cultural history on the basis that it was not primarily motivated by reason and therefore was illogical, irrational and defunct.

Relying on missionary accounts of Hindu society Mill condemned Indian behaviour as immoral in comparison to European codes of conduct. India and Indians were deemed a childish, superstitious and backward nation with a huge potential for development. In the world view of Mill and others the crude emerging civilisation of India could be directed and moulded by the morally superior colonial power. Mill advocated the introduction of European knowledge to counter balance Indian traits judged to be irrational. Instilling ideals of reason would accordingly 'reform' Indians by the example of Western systems of thought and outlook.

The ideas contained within the *History Of British India* discredited Indian culture, language and literature even as its assumptions of moral superiority authorise and justified the presence of the British in India. In 1835 Lord William Bentninck revitalised the earlier Charter Act with his New Education Policy which determined that English should be the official language of the courts, diplomacy and administration. Prior to this Persian had been the accepted language of diplomacy. Bentninck's motive was ostensibly to "regenerate" society, but the ramifications were boundless. From this moment on only those with Western style education and a knowledge of English were eligible for government employment or for a career in public life. Thomas MacAuley's infamous 'Minute On Indian Education' encapsulates both the overt and covert agendas for such a policy.

In 1854 Sir Charles Wood published his Education Dispatch which was aimed at widening the availability of Western oriented knowledge. Universities were established under the London examining model in Calcutta, Bombay, and Madras.

However, in order to popularise this style of education and education in general, third level entry standards were lowered.

Lord Ripon's Hunter Commission of 1882 somewhat belatedly attempted to rectify the omissions of earlier policies through advocating that there should be increased provision of education at primary level and for women. The theory was that there would be a subsequent rise in the calibre of applicants for third level entry. The inevitable result was that an Indian-based education was viewed as being second rate in comparison to. an English-based education. With the focus being on quantity rather than quality an Indian intellectual elite did not develop quite as intended. In the post mutiny era there was a fresh impetus toward Western style education as a means of control. This went hand-in-hand with widespread condemnation of traditional Indian beliefs which conflicted with the rationalist point of view. Lord Ripon's Hunter Commission in 1882 advocated more primary and female education in order to raise third level entry standards.

## THE CULTURAL AND SOCIAL CONSEQUENCES

For the aspirational Indian knowledge of English became a major tool for economic and social advancement. It was no longer essential to belong to a literary caste: rather, acquisition of English enabled the individual to transcend the formerly impenetrable barriers of caste and class. Although the first was admitted into the Indian civil service in 1864 it had been a technical possibility since 1833.

The widespread dissemination of Western knowledge and literature created a climate of opinion wherein British ascendancy and power seemed to be a natural prerogative arising from a perceived and implied intellectual and moral refinement. Indians became increasingly motivated by the desire to emulate and acquire the body of knowledge which appeared to be at the roots of the coloniser's power.

This attitude was promoted by the British tendency to imbue their national literature with a moral imperative. By stressing an imaginary moral superiority the colonial administration managed to obscure the underlying motivation and reality of a first world power exploiting a technically inferior country for its own economic advantage. As MacAuley's 'Minute' shows , English literature was employed to prevent the risk of native insubordination under the "guise of a liberal education".

The cultural consequences of the 1854 Education Dispatch were that the ease with which one could acquire an Indian contributed to its subsequent devaluation. A consensus of opinion arose which held that a truly educated Indian had received a university tuition in England. Third level education retained a Geographical elitism. With the focus being on quantity rather than quality an Indian intellectual elite did not develop quite as had been intended. However, official policies meant that , for the first time, Indians of differing caste and religious persuasions had access to a common language and pool of ideas.

Similarities in education for Hindu, Muslim and Jain resulted in a fusion of social and cultural ideals. The formation of The Indian National Congress in 1885 reflected this cultural synthesis as it mainly consisted of Western educated lawyers, teachers and professionals who made a forward looking component of Indian society. It was this group which created the impulse and movement for the formation of an independent India. In brief, while English language and literature had originally worked as strategies of containment they also played a significant role in the de colonising process. The reverberations of a colonial past continue to be felt as English became widespread and retained much of the aura of power and prestige.

The history of education in India under the British rule has yet to be properly written. It should be remembered that in the pre-British period, India was not an illiterate country. This land was far more advanced in education than many a

Christian country of the West. Almost every village had its school for the diffusion of not only 3 but 4 R's – the last R being religion or the Ramayana. That work has contributed not a little to the preservation of Hindu culture.

Stress has not been laid on another fact, which is, that educational institutions were not established in this country as soon as the East India Company obtained political supremacy here. It took the Christian merchant "adventurers" just a century to come to the decision that it was for their benefit to impart education to the swarthy "heathens" of India. The battle of Plassey was fought in 1757; and the Wood's Despatch, commonly called the Educational Charter of India, is dated 1854. This should show that the system of education was not introduced in hot haste but after the mature deliberation of nearly a century. It should also not be lost sight that the Indians themselves were the pioneers of introducing Western education in this country. The Hindu College of Calcutta was established long before Macaulay penned his celebrated minute or wood sent out his Educational Despatch to India.

When the East India Company attained political supremacy in India, they did not bestow any thought on the education of the inhabitants of their dominions. Gold was their watchword. Everyone of their servants who came out to India tried to enrich himself as quickly as possible at the expense of the children of the soil. It was on this account that Edmund Burke described them as "birds of prey and passage" in India.

According to Herbert Spencer, "The Anglo-Indians of the last century – "birds of prey and passage, " as they were styled by Burke – showed themselves only a shade less cruel than their prototype of Peru and Mexico." These residents of Britain after making their fortunes retired in England, where they were known as "Indian Nabobs." The Christian "Indian Nabobs" looked on the heathens of India in the same light as their co-religionists of America did on their Negro slaves.

But as years rolled on, it became patent to some thoughtful Anglo-Indians, that their dominion in India could not last long unless education – especially Western – was diffused among the inhabitants of that land. But this proposition struck terror and dismay into the hearts of the generality of the people of England. It should be remembered that India was a country inhabited by savages and barbarians.

In the pre-British period, India possessed educational institutions of a nature which did not exist in the countries of the West. That even in the beginning of the Nineteenth century, India, in the matter of education, was in advance of the European countries is proved by the fact of her teaching those countries a new system of tuition, to which attention was drawn by the Court of Directors in their letter to the Governor-General-in-Council in Bengal, dated 3rd June, 1814, extracts from which have been already given above. Very few in India know that the system of "mutual tuition" – which has been practiced by Indian school-masters since time immemorial – has been borrowed by the Christian countries of the West from India.

The man who first introduced it into Great Britain was a native of Scotland by the name of Dr. Andrew Bell. The village communities of India had not then been destroyed, and it being the duty of every village communities to foster education, a school formed a prominent institution in every village of any note.

The decimation of the Indian education system thus created a vacuum that then had to be filled. Into that vacuum, eager and waiting, went the missionaries, who swiftly set up their own church-sponsored schools and taught Indian children their own literature and history according to the gospel of Max Muller. It is by now a well-established fact that education was a means to Christianize and "domesticate" the native population and render it loyal to the British empire.

With the destruction of the village communities and the impoverishment of the people which are inseparably connected with the British mode of administration of India, educational institutions which used to flourish in every village of note became things of the past. Walter Hamilton, writing in 1828 from official records said: "It has long been remarked that science and literature are in a progressive state of decay among the natives of India, the number of learned men being not only diminished, but the circle of learning,....the principal cause of this retrograde condition of literature may be traced to the want of that encouragement which was formerly afforded to it by princes, chieftains and opulent individuals, under the native governments, now past and gone. The British administrators of India of those days were actuated by political motives in keeping Indians ignorant.

## CONVERSION AND EDUCATION OF HINDUS: THE SITUATION IN 1813

In the Charter Act of 1813, to promote the happiness of the heathens of India, it was proposed that: "such measures ought to be adopted as may tend to the introduction among them of useful knowledge, and of religious and moral improvement; and in furtherance of the above objects, sufficient facilities ought to be afforded by law to persons desirous of going to and remaining in India, for the purpose of accomplishing those benevolent designs."

Before proceeding further, it is necessary to point out the diplomatic language of the above clause of the Charter Act. It is language befitting a Machiavelli or a Talleyrand – which does not so much express as conceal the thought and objects which the framers of the Act had in view. Who are the persons referred to as "desirous of going to and remaining in India, for the purpose of accomplishing those benevolent designs?" They were Christian missionaries. At the time of the East India Company charter of 1813, education in England was still under the control of the Church. Hence, the framers of the charter could not think of imparting education to Indians without ecclesiastical agency. This explains the diplomatic language of the Charter.

It would have been outraging the feelings of Indians to have informed them of the ecclesiastical Department that they were going to be saddled with, for the benefit of the Christian natives of England. Hence the diplomatic language of the Charter Act.

Warren Hastings was asked by the Lords' Committee: "would the introduction of a Church establishment into the British territories in the East Indies, probably be attended with any consequences which would be injurious to the stability of the Government of India?"

Hastings and Malcolm and others, opposed the introduction of Christian missionaries in India and imparting of knowledge to its inhabitants from considerations of political expediency. But it was on grounds of political expediency, too, that these two measures were advocated. It was Charles Grant, described as the Christian Director of the East India Company, who was the first to press upon the British public the expediency of sending Christian missionaries to India for the conversion of its heathen inhabitants, and the imparting them education. In order to succeed in his endeavor, he did what the Christian missionaries are in the habit of doing to this day, that is, vilifying, and painting the natives of India in the blackest color possible. The Christian nations and countries of the West sent missionaries of their faith to non-Christian nations, not so much for the spiritual welfare of the latter, as for the worldly good which these missionaries bring to the Christian nations.

Charles Grant wanted to keep the natives of India perpetually under the leading strings of his own countrymen. He wrote that, "We can foresee no period in which we may not govern our Asiatic subjects, more happily for them than they can be governed by themselves or any other power; and doing this we should not expose them to needless danger from without and from within, by giving the military power into their hands."

According to him, neither conversion to Christianity nor imparting of instruction to the natives was calculated to inspire them with any desire for liberty. Neither Charles Grant nor the natives of England were prompted by any motive of philanthropy or altruism to grant these measures to India. It was sordid considerations of worldly gain which led the people of England to adopt the above measures under the cloak of philanthropy. As it seems to be the opinion of some of the gentlemen who compose the Committee of Public Instruction, that the course which they have hitherto pursued was strictly prescribed by the British Parliament in 1813, and as, if that opinion be correct, a legislative act will be necessary to warrant a change, we have thought it right to refrain from taking any part in the preparation of the adverse statements which are now before us, and to reserve what we had to say on the subject till it should come before me as a member of the Council of India.

It does not appear to me that the Act of Parliament can, by any art of construction, be made to bear the meaning which has been assigned to it. It contains nothing about the particular languages or sciences which are to be studied. A sum is set apart "for the revival and promotion of literature and the encouragement of the learned natives of India, and for the introduction and promotion of a knowledge of the sciences among the inhabitants of the British territories." It is argued, or rather taken for granted, that by literature, the Parliament can have meant only Arabic and Sanscrit literature, that they never would have given the honorable appellation of "a learned native" to a native who was familiar with the poetry of Milton, the Metaphysics of Locke, and the Physics of Newton; but that they meant to designate by that name only such persons as might have studied in the sacred books of the Hindoos all the uses of cusa-grass, and all the mysteries of absorption into the Deity.

This does not appear to be a very satisfactory interpretation. To take a parallel case; suppose that the Pacha of Egypt, a country once superior in knowledge to the nations of Europe but now sunk far below them, were to appropriate a sum or the purpose of "reviving and promoting literature, and encouraging learned natives of Egypt," would anybody infer that he meant the youth of his pachalic to give years to the study of hieroglyphics, to search into all the doctrines disguised under the fable of Osiris, and to ascertain with all possible accuracy the ritual with which cats and onions were anciently adored? Would he be justly charged with inconsistency, if, instead of employing his young subjects in deciphering obelisks, he were to order them to be instructed in the English and French languages, and in all the sciences to which those languages are the chief keys?

The words on which the supporters of the old system rely do not bear them out, and other words follow which seem to be quite decisive on the other side. This lac of rupees is set apart, not only for "reviving literature in India," the phrase on which their whole interpretation is founded, but also for "the introduction and promotion of a knowledge of the sciences among the inhabitants of the British territories,"—words which are alone sufficient to authorise all the changes for which contend.

If the Council agree in my construction, no legislative Act will be necessary. If they differ from me, I will prepare a short Act rescinding that clause of the Charter of 1813, from which the difficulty arises. The argument which we have been considering, affects only the form of proceeding. But the admirers of the Oriental system of education have used another argument, which, if we admit it to be valid, is decisive against all change. They conceive that the public faith is pledged to the present system, and that to alter the appropriation of any of the funds which have hitherto been spent in encouragmg the study of Arabic and Sanscrit, would be down-right spoliation. It is not easy to understand by what process of reasoning they can have arrived at this conclusion.

The grants which are made from the public purse for the encouragement of literature differed in no respect from the grants which are made from the same purse for other objects of real or supposed utility. The rights of property are undoubtedly sacred. But nothing endangers those rights so much as the practice, now unhappily too common, of attributing them to things to which they do not belong. Those who would impart to abuses the sanctity of property are in truth imparting to the institution of property the unpopularity and the fragility of abuses. If the Government has given to any person a formal assurance; nay, if the Government has exdted in any person's mind a reasonable expectation that he shall receive a certain income as a teacher or a learner of Sanscrit or Arabic, we would respect that person's pecuniary interests—we would rather err on the side of liberality to individuals than suffer the public faith to be called in question.

But to talk of a Government pledging itself to teach certain languages and certain sciences, though those languages may become useless, though those sciences may be exploded, seems to me quite unmeaning. There is not a single word in any public instructions, from which it can be inferred that the Indian Government ever intended to give any pledge on this subject, or ever considered the destination of these funds as unalterably fixed. But had it been otherwise, we should have denied the competence of our predecessors to bind us by any pledge on such a subject.

Suppose that a Government had in the last century enacted in the most sole, in manner that all its subjects should, to the end of time, be inoculated for the smallpox: would that Government be bound to persist in the practice after Jenner's discovery? These promises, of which nobody claims. the performance, and from which nobody can grant a release; these vested rights, which vest in nobody; this property without proprietors; this robbery, which makes nobody poorer, may be comprehended by persons of higher faculties than mine.— We consider this plea merely as a set form of words, regularly used both in England and in India, in defence of every abuse for which no other plea can be set up.

We now come to the gist of the matter. We have a fund to be employed as Government shall direct for the intellectual improvement of the people of this country. The simple question is, what is the most useful way of employing it? All parties seem to be agreed on one point, that the dialects commonly spoken among the natives of this part of India, contain neither literary nor scientific information, and are, moreover, so poor and rude that, until they are enriched from some other quarter, it will not be easy to translate any valuable work into them. It seems to be admitted on all sides, that the intellectual improvement of those classes of the people who have the means of pursuing higher studies can at present be effected only by means of some language not vernacular amongst them.

What then shall that language be? One-half of the Committee maintain that it should be the English. The other half strongly recommend the Arabic and Sanscrit. The whole question seems to me to be, which language is the best worth knowing? How, then, stands the case? We have to educate a people who cannot at present be educated by means of their mother-tongue. We must teach them some foreign language. The claims of our own language it is hardly necessary to recapitulate. It stands pre-eminent even among the languages of the west. It abounds with works of imagination not inferior to the noblest which Greece has bequeathed to us; with models of every species of eloquence; with historical compositions, which, considered merely as nar- ratives, have seldom been surpassed, and which, considered as vehicles of ethical and political instruction, have never been equalled; with just and lively representations of human life and human nature; with the most profound speculations on metaphysics, morals, government, jurisprudence, and trade; with full and correct information respecting every experimental science which tends to preserve the health, to increase the comfort, or to expand the intellect of man.

Whoever knows that language has ready access to all the vast intellectual wealth, which all the wisest nations of the earth have created and hoarded in the course of ninety generations. It may safely be said, that the literature now extant in that language is of far greater value than all the literature which three hundred years ago was extant in all the languages of the world together. Nor is this all. In India, English is the language spoken by the ruling class. It is spoken by the higher class of natives at the seats of Government. It is likely to become the language of commerce throughout the seas of the East. It is the language of two great European communities which are rising, the one in the south of Africa, the other in Australasia; communities which are every year becoming more important, and more closely connected with our Indian empire. Whether we look at the intrinsic value of our literature, or at the particular situation of this country, we shall see the strongest reason to think that, of all foreign tongues, the English tongue is that which would be the most useful to our native subjects.

The question now before us is simply whether, when it is in our power to teach this language, we shall teach languages in which, by universal confession, there are no books on any subject which deserve to be compared to our own; whether, when we can teach European science, we shall teach systems which, by universal confession, whenever they differ from those of Europe, differ for the worse; and whether, when we can patronise sound Philosophy and true History, we shall countenance, at the public expense, medi- cal doctrines, which would disgrace an English farrier,—Astronomy, which would move laughter in girls at an English boarding school,—History, abounding with kings thirty feet high, and reigns thirty thousand years long,—and Geography, made up of seas of treacle and seas of butter.

History furnishes several analogous cases, and they all teach the same lesson. There are in modern times, to go no further, two memorable instances of a great impulse given to the mind of a whole society,—of prejudices overthrown,—of knowledge diffused,—taste purified,—of arts and sciences planted in countries which had recently been ignorant and barbarous.

The first instance to which refer, is the great revival of letters among the Western nations at the close of the fifteenth and the begining of the sixteenth century. At that time almost every thing that was worth reading was contained in the writings of the ancient Greeks and Romans. Had our ancestors acted as the Committee of Public Instruction has hitherto acted; had they neglected the language of Cicero and Tacitus; had they confined their attention to the old dialects of our own island; had they print- ed nothing and taught nothing at the universities but Chronicles in Anglo-Saxon, and Romances in Norman-French, would England have been what she now is? What the Greek and Latin were to the contemporaries of More and Ascham, our tongue is to the people of India. The literature of England is now more valuable than that of classical antiquity.

Another instance may be said to be still before our eyes. Within the last hundred and twenty years, a nation which has previously been in a state as barbarous as that in which our ancestors were before the crusades, has gradually emerged from the ignorance in which it was sunk, and has taken its place among civilized communities. There is now in that country a large educated class, abounding with persons fit to serve the state in the highest ftmctions, and in no wise inferior to the most accomplished men who adorn the best circles of Paris and London. There is reason to hope that this vast empire, which in the time of our grandfathers was probably behind the Punjab, may, in the time of our grandchildren, be pressing close on France and Britain in the career of improvement.

And how was this change effected? Not by flattering national prejudices: not by feeding the mind of the young Muscovite with the old women's stories which his rude fathers had believed: not by filling his head with lying legends about St. Nicholas: not by encouraging him to study the great question, whether the world was or was not created on the 13th of September: not by calling him "a learned native," when he has mastered all these points of knowledge: but by teaching him those foreign languages in which the greatest mass of information had been laid up, and thus putting all that information within his reach. The languages of Western Europe civilized Russia. We cannot doubt that they will do for the Hindoo what they have done for the Tartar. And what are the arguments against that course which seems to be alike recommended by theory and by experience? It is said that we ought to secure the cooperation of the native public, and that we can do this only by teaching Sanscrit and Arabic. We can by no means admit that when a nation of high intellectual attainments undertakes to Superintend the education of a nation comparatively ignorant, the learners are absolutely to prescribe the course which is to be taken by the teachers. It is not necessary, however, to say any thing on this subject. For it is proved by unanswerable evidence that we are not at present securing the Cooperation of the natives. It would be bad enough to consult their intellectual taste at the expense of their intellectual health. But we are consulting neither,—we are withholding from them the learning for which they are craving, we are forcing on them the mock-learning which they nauseate.

This is proved by the fact that we are forced to pay our Arabic and Sanscrit students, while those who learn Engiish are wiling to pay us. All the declamations in the worid about the love and reverence of the natives for their sacred dialects will never, in the mind of any impartial person, outweigh the undisputed fact, that we cannot find, in all our vast empire, a single student who will let us teach him those dialects unless we will pay him.

Other evidence is not wanting, if other evidence were required. A petition was presented last year to the Committee by several ex-students of the Sanscrit College. The petitioners stated that they had studied in the college ten or twelve years; that they had made themselves acquainted with Hindoo literature and science; that they had received certificates of proficiency: and what is the fruit of all this! "Notwithstanding such testimonials," they say, "we have but little prospect of bettering our condition without the kind assistance of your

Honorable Committee, the indifference with which we are generally looked upon by our countrymen leaving no hope of encouragement and assistance from them."

They therefore beg that they may be recommended to the Governor General for places under the Government, not places of high dignity or emolument, but such as may just enable them to exist. "We want means," they say, "for a decent living, and for our progressive improvement, which, however, we cannot obtain without the assistance of Government, by whom we have been educated and maintained from childhood." They conclude by representing, very pathetically, that they are sure that it was never the intention of Government, after behaving so liberally to them during their education, to abandon them to destitution and neglect.

All these petitions, even the most unreasonable of them, proceeded on the supposition that some loss had been sustained- that some wrong had been inflicted. These are surely the first petitioners who ever demanded compensation for having been educated gratis, for having been supported by the public during twelve years, and then sent forth into the world well furnished with literature and science. They represent their education as an injury which gives them a claim on the Government for redress, as an injury for which the stipends paid to them during the infliction were a very inadequate compensation. And we doubt not that they are in the right. They have wasted the best years of life in learning what procures for them neither bread nor respect.

Surely we might, with advantage, have saved the cost of making these persons useless and miserable; surely, men may be brought up to be burdens to the public and objects of contempt to their neighbours at a somewhat smaller charge to the state. But such is our policy. We do not even stand neuter in the contest between truth and falsehood. We are not content to leave the natives to the influence of their own hereditary prejudices. To the natural difficulties which obstruct the progress of sound science in the East, we add fresh difficulties of our own making. Bounties and premiums, such as ought not to be given even for the propagation of truth, we lavish on false taste and false philosophy.

By acting thus we create the very evil which we fear. We are making that opposition which we do not find. What we spend on the Arabic and Sanscrit colleges is not merely a dead loss to the cause of truth; it is bounty-money paid to raise up champions of error. It goes to form a nest, not merely of helpless place-hunters, but of bigots prompted alike by passion and by interest to raise a cry against every usetul scheme of education. If there should be any opposition among the natives to the change which we recommend, that opposition will be the effect of our own system. It will be headed by persons supported by our stipends and trained in our colleges.

The longer we persevere in our present course, the more formidable will that opposition be. It will be every year reinforced by recruits whom we are paying. From the native society left to itself, we have no difficulties to apprehend; all the murmuring will come from that oriental interest which we have, by artificial means, called into being, and nursed into strength. There is yet another fact, which is alone sufficient to prove that the feeling of the native public, when left to itself, is not such as the supporters of the old system represent it to be.

During the last three years, about sixty thousand rupees have been expended in this manner. The sale of Arabic and Sanscrit books, during those three years, has not yielded quite one thousand rupees. In the mean time the School- book Society is selling seven or eight thousand English volumes every year, and not only pays the expenses of printing, but realises a profit of 20 per cent. on its outlay.

The fact that the Hindoo law is to be learned chiefly from Sans- crit books, and the Mahomedan law from Arabic books, has been much insisted on, but seems not to bear at all on the question. We are commanded by Parliament to ascertam and digest the laws of India. The assistance of a law Commission has been given to us for that purpose. As soon as the code is promulgated, the Shasster and the Hedaya will be useless to a Moonsiff or Sudder Ameen.

But there is yet another argument which seems even more untenable. It is said that the Sanscrit and Arabic are the languages in which the sacred books of a hundred millions of people are written, and that they are, on that account, entitled to peculiar encouragement. Assuredly it is the duty of the British Government in India to be not only tolerant, but neutral on all religious questions.

But to encourage the study of a literature admitted to be of small intrinsic value, only because that literature inculcates the most serious errors on the most important subjects, is a course hardly reconcileable with reason, with morality, or even with that very neutrality which ought, as we all agree, to be sacredly pre- served. It is confessed that a language is barren of useful know- ledge. We are to teach it because it is fruittul of monstrous superstitions. We are to teach false History, false Astronomy, false Medicine, because we find them in company with a false religion.

It is taken for granted by the advocates of Oriental learning, that no native of this country can possibly attain more than a mere smattering of English. They do not attempt to prove this; but they perpetually insinuate it. They designate the education which their opponents recommend as a mere spelling book education. They assume it as undenlable, that the question is between a profound knowledge of Hindoo and Arabian literature and science on the one side, and a superficial knowledge of the rudiments of English on the other. This is not merely an assumption, but an assumption contrary to all reason and experience. We know that foreigners of all nations do learn our language sufficiently to have access to all the most abstruse knowledge which it contains, sufficiently to relish even the more delicate graces of our most idiomatic writers. There are in this very town natives who are quite competent to discuss political or scientific questions with fluency and precision in the English language.

Secondary education coincides with education of grades 6 through 12 or the second stage of education that commences after primary education and continues up to beginning of higher education. Ancient period In the early Vedic period education was a family responsibility, being given by the father to the son. In the later Vedic age, the age of upanisads, education was institutionalised and it look a definite shape. In this period Brahmanic education entered Bengal.

With the formal ceremony of Upanayan the guru or the teacher accepted his pupil. The normal age of upanayan was 8 for a brahman, 11 for a ksatriya and 12 for a vaishya. The guru's home was the school where the pupils lived for the whole period of education as a member of the family. Thus a residential feature was seen in the education imparted in ancient India. No tuition fees were charged but pupils used to render personal manual services. In the early Vedic schools, education was confined to young Brahmans. In the later Vedic period before 500 BC, the education of the Ksatriyas and Vaisyas came under Brahman control.

For others education was craft oriented. Traders ie, the Vaisyas studied grammar and trade crafts. Their education was organised according to apprentice system. The sudras were involved in agricultural and related economic activities and numerous arts and crafts. Their education was also production and craft centred. In later Vedic period the rigidity of caste system made access to education restricted. Towards the end of ancient period two types of schools were developed: The tol or pathsala and network of indigenous elementary schools.

The tols were seats of higher learning including secondary education. They imparted instruction through sanskrit and provided traditional classical learning. In early Vedic period, boys and girls at the age of eight after upanayan enjoyed equal educational facilities. Girls started their studentship at guru's home. Young maidens completing their education were married to learned persons. In Vedic society a wife was a regular partner in the sacrificial offering of the husband. So she had to acquire Vedic knowledge which was essential for performing religious rites and ceremonies. But as a result of social changes in later period, women lost their liberal social status as well as opportunity for education. In later period, Brahmanic education flourished along with Buddhist education. It also continued throughout Muslim and British periods. In Bangladesh, tols are the secondary level institutions of Brahmanic education. Buddhist education centred around monasteries or viharas. The primary idea of buddhism was to provide for proper instruction of the novice in the doctrines of the Buddhist faith and to secure supervision over his conduct while he was becoming habituated to the monastic life.

The first step of admission or initiation in Buddhism is called *prabbajja* and after admission, the candidate becomes a novice and is placed under a discipline of a preceptor. After completion of the novitiating period he becomes a *bhikshu* (monk), a full-fledged member of the order. From this provision for the instruction of novices arose the Buddhist education system. In Buddhist system, the pupil does all the menial work and renders the services the preceptor requires. In turn, the teacher gives the pupil all possible intellectual and spiritual help and guidance by teaching and instruction. A competent bhikshu generally accepts 2 novices. The group of young bhikshus lived in the vihara. Such residential viharas were developed in various parts of India including the present territory of Bangladesh.

Viharas were seats of higher learning and were supported by a system of elementary education. No secondary level institution was developed as such at that time. But elementary level courses prepared the students for advanced specialised studies at the viharas. So it is presumable that elementary education covered both primary and secondary level of education.

Huen Tsang who stayed in India from 629 to 645 AD found that primary course started at the age of 8 and continued up to the age of 15 and subjects like grammar, arts and crafts, medicine, reasoning and inner science were taught. I Tsing who stayed in India from 673 to 687 AD observed that at elementary level pupils studied five major *vidyas* such as grammar and lexicography, arts, medicine, logic and science of universal soul or philosophy. After completion of this stage, the period of specialised higher studies began. Buddhist monastery primarily prepared the students to teach sacred literature.

Buddha with great reluctance consented to admit women as disciples on their renouncing the household stage. Rules were developed for regulating the life of the nuns under complete subjugation of monks. Gradually, an order of nuns was created for education and training of the nuns. But there is lack of evidence of details of actual training they had in nunneries. One of the contributions of Buddhist education was that through offering the secular curricula along with religious ones in viharas and admission of laymen and non-Buddhists to attend those institutions, Buddhism stimulated the demand for education among common people.

Muslim period Since the establishment of Muslim rule in India (around 1204-1206), Bengal was ruled as a province of Delhi empire and sometimes it was an independent state. The subahdars, the independent rulers and nawabs established maktabs and madrasahs as educational institutions. Maktabs provided primary education and madrasahs were seats of secondary education and higher learning. The madrasahs of Bengal were in a flourishing condition during Muslim rule. These were run with state funds. The nobility and the private individuals were also found to set up and run madrasahs at their own initiative. Many illustrious scholars, administrators and officials were graduates of madrasahs in Muslim Bengal. In the school of Shah Mubarak his sons Faizi and Abul Fazl, historian Badauni and other scholars studied. In the madrasah run by Sharafuddin Abu Taoama in sonargaon students studied both secular and religious subjects. During the rule of emperor Shahjahan the madrasahs of Jahangirnagar specialised in teaching science, theology, philosophy and mathematics.

Madrasah education was free. The teacher enjoyed high status in the society. The courses of madrasah generally included religious subjects like the quran, the hadith, theology and other Islamic studies. Secular subjects such as history, logic, geography, algebra, astronomy, medical science, chemistry and other technical, vocational, professional subjects were more cultivated in some centres.

The medium of instruction was Persian but Arabic was compulsory for Muslims students. Teaching of history was one special feature of madrasah education during Muslim period. As a result, these learning centres could produce some illustrious historians in the subcontinent. Generally Muslim students studied in madrasah. Akbar adopted a policy so that Hindu youths can study at madrasah.

Women during Muslim rule did not have opportunity for education due to purda system. But there are evidences that in harems of kings, nawabs and nobles some ladies, daughters, sisters of kings and nobility received education and some of them attained great distinction. But great mass of Muslim women received no education at all except some domestic training in performance of household duties.

The tradition of madrasah education continued during the British period but its nature and character of flourishing period changed to a great extent. In early 19th century as reported by Adam (1835-1838) there were various types of madrasahs and wide range of courses such as Grammatical works, Rhetoric, Logic, Law, Doctrines of Islam, Ptolemy and Astronomy; courses of Natural Philosophy, Science, History and Literature were also taught. Role learning was given a large place and the main aim of a teacher was to pass on the pupil the learned tradition, which he himself had received.

During the decadence of Muslim power due to lack of state patronage, financial support from the landed aristocracy and nobility and change of official language from Persian to English madrasah education lost its past.glory. Rather it assumed conservative character and used classical language as medium of instruction. Madrasah education with some modifications is continuing in Bangladesh.

British period European trading companies began their commercial activities in India from 1600 AD. Gradually, the Portuguese, the French, the Dutch and the English settled in some important parts and commercial centres. Among them the English east india company was ultimately able to establish their rule in India. Till the early 19th century, they did not evolve any definite educational policy.

It was only in the Charter Act of 1813 that education of the Indian people was included within the duties of the East India Company and an annual sum of 10,000 pounds was provided for their educational activities. However, the company mainly spent the money for oriental learning. The progressive reformers of Bengal such as rammohun roy protested against this and demanded western education for the people of this country. But the company did not pay any attention to this. However, as per the Charter, missionaries were allowed to work in the country. This had great impact upon the development of modern type of English schools at primary and secondary levels.

One of the important events of this period was the endorsement of Macaulay's Minute in Lord bentinck's Despatch of 7 March 1835, which provided that western learning should be spread through the medium of English language. Use of English as medium of instruction in public education was announced as a formal policy. As a result, a good network of English high schools and colleges were established in Bengal, mostly due to government initiative and support. The new high schools demonstrated fairly high standard of instruction in language and literature, but their standard was low in practical subjects. The syllabus was mainly bookish.

Secondary education received a new orientation in wood's education despatch of 1854. It provided that the provincial government would give grant-in-aid to high schools on fulfillment of some conditions. Specifically, schools should provide secular education. This policy ultimately enabled the government to withdraw from the field of educational activities and shoulder the responsibility upon the Indians. However, grant-in-aid system, scholarship scheme for students of all levels and creation of department of Public Instruction resulted in appreciable expansion of secondary education in Bengal.

The Indian Education Commission of 1882 addressed the issue of secondary education at a great length. The government accepted its recommendations to transfer all government secondary schools to private bodies and to establish a model government high school in each district headquarters. By the beginning of the 20th century the province of Bengal experienced a spectacular growth of secondary education. There were 3,097 English high schools in India in 1901-1902 and nearly a half of them were in Bengal. At the district level, Bengal had more schools than any other presidency. There was an English secondary school for every 104.3 square miles. It also had the largest number of unaided schools. With low fees and easy admission these schools came up to cater to the demand for western education.

Secondary education experienced a setback as a result of lord curzon's regressive education policy adopted on the basis of Simla conference (1901) for strict control over high schools by the universities and the Education Department. However during Curzon's period, the partition of bengal in 1905 offered a better opportunity for the development of education in East Bengal. Henry Sharp, the first Director of Public Instruction of East Bengal, initiated educational improvement programme. He arranged a special aid programme for Muslim students such as scholarships at every level of education and provision of free places in government aided schools for eight percent of Muslim students.

For greater participation a Muslim hostel was established in every government school. As a result, there was a substantial increase in the number of Muslim students in primary and secondary schools. The increase was about 35% from 425,800 in 1906-1907 to 575,700 in 1911-1912. The policy of promoting education in eastern Bengal was continued under unified government of Bengal throughout the rest of British period.

Under diarchical rule in 1921-1937, there was an increase in the number of secondary schools in rural areas, large expansion in secondary education of girls, adoption of mother tongue as a medium of instruction, some improvement in training and service conditions of teachers. During the World War II the development of secondary education was slackened. In the post war period, some efforts were made to introduce vocational courses in high schools and establish technical, commercial and agricultural high schools.

On the eve of the Partition of Bengal in 1947, two types of schools, middle school and high schools provided secondary education. Middle schools offered education of grades one through six and high schools grades seven through ten. There were nearly 20,000 middle schools and 2,000 high schools. More than a half of them were supported from tuition fees and donations contributed by the people. Less than 40% of the high schools received grant-in-aid from the state. Forty schools were directly supported by the state. For teachers' training of middle school there were five normal schools. Two training colleges, one in Calcutta and the other in Dhaka were set up to train high school teachers.

It was J E D Bethune who first established a regular secular girls' high school in 1849 in Calcutta with six pupils. Bethune's experiment was so successful that it became a model of girls' school in other provinces of India. But progress of girls' secondary education was very humble. By the end of the century (1896-1897), there were only two girls' English high schools, one was Bethune School in Calcutta and the other Eden School in Dhaka.

The impetus of girls' education came from the Indian Education Commission of 1882. According to the several recommendations of the commission the government of Bengal started to give higher grants to girls' schools. Special subjects suited to the girls were included in the curricula. Enrolment of girls in mixed schools was started. The District and Municipal Boards also started to contribute a fare share of funds for girls' education. Education of Muslim girls entered into the scene particularly with the efforts of Nawab faizunnesa choudhurani and roquiah sakhawat hossain. Gradually, the opening of female training schools, starting of fee concession, prize and scholarship schemes greatly helped promote girls' education in Bengal.

### *Pakistan period*

The first task of the government of East Bengal within the framework of independent Pakistan was to readjust vacuum created in the educational scene of the province due to large scale exodus of Hindu teachers, administrators and staff to India. On Partition of India, Calcutta University ceased to have any jurisdiction over the schools and colleges located in East Bengal. To fill up the gap, the government of East Bengal promulgated the East Bengal Educational Ordinance 1947 following which the former Dhaka Board of Intermediate and Secondary Education was replaced by a new East Bengal Secondary Education Board (EBSEB) and immediately, all high schools came under the control of this board.

During the period between from 1947 to 1960, no major policy on reforms and reorganisation of secondary education was undertaken by the central government of Pakistan. However, some measures adopted by the government had significant influence on the development of education in the province. The Pakistan Educational Conference of 1947 held at Karachi recognised Urdu as the lingua franca of Pakistan and proposed compulsory teaching of Urdu from grade 6 in areas where Urdu was not the medium of instruction at the primary stage. This resolution had repercussions in East Bengal and public movement against this resolution started. Ultimately, as a result of the language movement in East Pakistan, Bangla was recognised as one of the two state languages of Pakistan and the condition of compulsory teaching of Urdu in the secondary schools in East Bengal was relaxed.

Secondary education was recognised as a separate academic and administrative unit and its duration extended from 5 to 7 years consisting of three sub-stages: middle (grade 6-8), secondary (grade 9-10), and higher secondary (grade 11-12). A uniform curriculum was followed in the junior schools or middle stage. Diversification was introduced in the secondary stage. Along with compulsory subjects, pupils may choose courses from any one of the diversified streams - humanities, science, commerce, industrial arts, home economics and agriculture.

The higher secondary stage was separated from the control of the university. Curricula of this stage included mother tongue and English as compulsory subjects for all students. Students could choose required number of courses from any one of the following streams: humanities, science, commerce, fine arts, Islamic studies and agriculture. The administration of secondary education was carried out by the provincial education directorate headed by the director of public instruction (DPI).

The academic control over secondary schools was previously carried out by a single Board of Education. In pursuance of the new policy, four boards were set up at Dhaka, Comilla, Jessore and Rajshahi to conduct SSC and HSC examinations within their respective jurisdiction. The curricula and syllabi of the secondary and higher secondary stages were prepared and prescribed by the boards. The curricula of the middle stage were prescribed by the Education Department.

The minimum qualification for the teachers of middle schools was HSC, for the secondary schools a bachelor degree with professional training, and for the teachers of higher secondary education masters degree.

In the past, financing of secondary education was basically a responsibility of private enterprises. The government maintained only a small number of schools. The Pakistan Education Commission, as well as the Second Five-Year Plan (1960-65) emphasised reliance on private effort rather than on government resources. During Pakistan period, the cost of running a private school in East Pakistan increased enormously. The schools paid minimum salary to teachers. Qualified teachers were not attracted by such poor salary. This resulted in the deterioration of standard of secondary education.

During Pakistan period, the number of girls' secondary schools expanded considerably. In 1947, there were about 200 girls' high schools and by 1970, the number rose to about 700. In addition, girls were found to attend mixed secondary schools, particularly in the rural areas. By 1972-73, girls' enrolment in secondary schools stood at 0.27 million or 16% of total secondary school enrolment.

### *Bangladesh period*

Immediately after independence, the new government of Bangladesh took initiative to formulate a new education policy and formed an Education Commission on 26 July 1972, with Dr muhammad qudrat-i-khuda as chairman. The commission produced its report covering all aspects of national education. As for secondary education it made far-reaching recommendations. But before the adoption of the report the political scene of the country changed with the assassination of the president of the country in August 1975. Later in 1975, the National Curriculum and Syllabus Committee was formed in 1975 and the curricula and syllabi prepared by the committee for the secondary level were implemented during 1980-85. This constituted a major curricula thrust for secondary education till it was replaced in 1996 by the new curricula.

The present secondary education curricula and syllabi were prepared by the initiative of the National Curricula Co-ordination Committee (NCC) of 1993 and it was implemented from the academic session of 1996.

At present, the secondary education consists of three sub-stages: lower secondary, secondary and higher secondary, and may be termed as a 3+2+2 plan. Lower secondary education (grade 6 to 8) is offered in junior high schools. Many high schools and a few intermediate colleges also offer lower secondary education. Most junior high schools have primary classes attached to them. The secondary stage (grade 9-10) is offered in institutions of various types: schools having one to ten grades or twelve grades, three to ten grades; and six to ten grades. Higher secondary education (grade 11-12) is offered in some high schools, intermediate colleges and degree colleges.

The objectives of secondary education of Bangladesh are formulated on the basis of the guidelines prepared by the Bangladesh Education Commission of 1974, the National Curriculum and Syllabus Committee of 1975 and the National Curricula and Co-ordination Committee of 1993. The aim is to enable the learners to acquire new knowledge, skills, use modern science and technology, develop positive outlook and scientific attitude, to acquire skills for self-employment and to inspire them with patriotism, and religious, moral, cultural and social values. The present curricula renewal and modernisation process started in 1993.

One of the features of present secondary education is that general secondary education, vocational education and madrasah education (*Dakhil* and *Alim* stage) are brought under one system for maintaining uniformity, standard and mobility. In the general sub-system of education the curricula of lower secondary education comprises Bangla, English, mathematics, religious education, social science, home economics, arts and crafts, physical education and health as compulsory subjects. The pupils may take elective subjects such as Arabic, advanced Bangla and advanced English.

At present (2001), there are six compulsory subjects in the secondary stage: Bangla, English, mathematics, religious education, social science, home economics, agriculture, social science or general science. In addition, pupils can take courses from any one of the diversified streams such as science, humanities, business education, home economics and Islamic studies. The students can study one more elective subject. The total marks in the SSC examination were 1100. In the higher secondary stage students study one of the specified areas, such as science, humanities, business education, home economics and Islamic studies. Bangla and English are compulsory for all students. Students may also study one elective subject.

The Ministry of Education is the national policy making organ for educational development in Bangladesh. Secondary education is the direct responsibility of the Directorate of Secondary and Higher Education headed a director general. The Directorate has four divisional and eight zonal offices. Under the jurisdiction of eight zonal offices, there are 64 district education offices. The district education officers are responsible for management and inspection of junior high schools and high schools within their districts.

Government high schools and colleges are managed according to the rules and regulations issued by the government. All junior high schools and non-government secondary schools have their managing committee for management and supervision of the schools. The schools follow the rules and regulation of the respective Board of Intermediate and Secondary Education for constitution of the managing committees.

The non-government intermediate colleges are managed by their governing bodies constituted as per the rules set by the boards. The examination system in the secondary schools and the administration and management of the SSC and HSC examinations remained almost same in Bangladesh period as it was before 1972. Scholarships are awarded to the meritorious students on the basis of marks obtained in the secondary and higher secondary examinations.

Bachelor's degree is a minimum qualification for a high school teacher. It is a requirement that the teacher should have a professional training, which is offered in 11 teachers' training colleges and also by the Bangladesh Open University. In 1995, about 34.5% of the teachers had professional degrees. For teaching students of intermediate classes, the requirement is a master's degree.

From the very inception, Bangladesh government has been encouraging women's education. Facilities and opportunities for girls' participation were created at all levels. At secondary level enrolment of girl students expanded greatly since 1994 due to adoption of various financial assistance projects and free tuition for girls studying in grades 6 to 10. More and more female teachers are being appointed to increase girls' enrolment in secondary schools.

There were over 12,000 secondary level institutions in Bangladesh in 1995. All junior schools are privately managed. There are 170 government secondary schools for boys and 147 for girls. Of the nine government intermediate colleges, three are for girls. There are 11 cadet colleges. Some secondary level institutions are run by the autonomous bodies such as universities, banks, mills, and public sector corporations.

At present, 85% of primary school graduates enrol in secondary schools. The figure was less than 50% a decade ago. This is due to adoption of universal primary education programme by the government in 1991. About 5.12 million students (54% boys and 46% girls) were enrolled in secondary schools in 1995. This is 62% higher compared to that in 1991. Average number of students in a secondary school was 426. Teacher-student ratio and school-teacher ratio were 1:37 and 1:13 respectively.

Secondary education could not contribute much in terms of supply of semi skilled manpower due to lack of programmatic education policy and financial allocation during Pakistan period. The government of Bangladesh in its first, second and third five year plans stressed the need for linking secondary education with employment situation of the country. But the major achievement was ensured in the field of secondary education during the fourth plan (1990-1995). Main areas were infrastructure development of institutions, strengthening of administration and management, renewal and modernisation of curricula of secondary level institutions and teachers training colleges through the Secondary Education Development Project (SEDP). Enhancement of female education participation was another great achievement in this plan period.

To supply more trained teachers, double shifts were introduced in the training colleges. B Education and M Education curricula were modernised. A scheme was taken up for training 7,000 female teachers for rural secondary schools. For continuous observation and monitoring of implementation of the new curricula and ensuring quality of education an Educational Management and Information System was set up. Bangladesh Open University offers SSC course for students who cannot continue in formal schools as regular students.

The Fifth Five Year Plan provided for creation of additional classrooms in 7,000 schools, introducing double shifts in selected rural and urban secondary schools, development of science laboratories with modern equipment and continuation of present financial assistance programme for female students studying in grades 11 and 12. One innovative policy adopted in the plan is the involvement of community and private efforts in educational activities

Christian Missionaries an organised group of people engaged in the evangelical work of spreading the gospel, were active in Bengal in the colonial period, though their contact started since the 16th century AD. Legend traces that St. Thomas was the first Christian missionary to come to India in

50 AD and convert a group of people of the Malabar coast by 58 AD. Since then various missionaries-Syrian, Roman Catholic and particularly the Jesuits-visited India at different times. But Christianity in India remained almost confined to the coastal areas in South India.

Bengal's contact with the Christian mission started with the coming of Jesuit missionaries-Father Antony Vaz and Father Peter Dias in 1576 and the group of Augustinian Friars in 1580. Bandel, a Dutch town, became the centre of their activities. The Christian mission started as an organised movement in Bengal with the arrival of British Protestant missionaries in the last decade of the 18th century. The great Evangelical Revival in contemporary England to preach the gospel to all nations resulted in the formation of quite a few missionary societies. The Baptist Missionary Society (BMS), the London Missionary Society (LMS) and the Church Missionary Society (CMS) formed in 1792, 1795 and 1799 respectively were the major ones.

The first two were non-conformist bodies and the third was Anglican. The Church of Scotland started its mission in Bengal decades later in 1830 under alexander duff (1806-1878). But all these churches made an evangelical alliance in the field of Bengal mission. The formation of the interdenominational Calcutta Missionary Conference (CMC) in 1831 was the best illustration of such evangelical spirit. The Christian missionaries in Bengal followed the humanitarian ideas of the early evangelicals in England and emphasised the 'social aspects' of the missionary programme. The Scottish Missionaries and the Irish Presbyterians, too, followed this programme. Their united efforts made the 19th century the greatest century of Christian missionary activities. This was also a great age of European colonial expansion. The Western commerce and culture began to dominate the colonized countries. This commercial expansion created favourable conditions for foreign missions. The Protestant powers like Germany, Netherlands, Sweden and Denmark entered the mission field.

It was only the English Protestant missionaries who showed ardent or permanent missionary zeal. With the growth of British power, Bengal became the main centre of their activities. The English east india company, however, initially opposed their organised work. The first organised missionary work in Bengal started under william carey, a Baptist, after his arrival in Bengal in 1800. Carey started the first Baptist Mission in that year at serampore, then under Danish control. His two associates were Joshua Marshman (1768-1837) and William Ward (1769-1823) and they formed the famous Serampore Trio. The LMS too started their mission work under Nathaniel Forsyth in 1798 in the Dutch town of chinsura. The CMS entered India after the company's charter of 1813 removed the restriction on missionary enterprise in India. Greenwood and Schroeter were the first church missionaries to arrive in Calcutta in 1816.

In the cultural encounter between Christianity and religions of the subcontinent the missionaries failed to influence the followers of Islam. As believers in one God Muslims could not accept the doctrine of 'Trinitarian' Christianity. Some adverse comments about the prophet Muhammad (Sm) in a pamphlet issued from Serampore Baptist Missionary press in 1809 created a widespread commotion among the Muslims. The Seramore Trio judged the publication as an imprudent act and never again published anything which could offend the Muslims. Henceforth the Baptists became more cautious about preaching among the Muslims. The Muslim society in general remained beyond the missionary efforts and there were very few mission stations in the Muslim dominated rural eastern Bengal.

Carey in Bengal realised, as early as in 1796, the need for women missionaries to address such issues. In 1820 William Ward, referring to degraded condition of Indian women, appealed to English women for joining mission to improve it.

During the decade between 1823 and 1833 the missionaries established more of such girls' schools in their different mission stations in Bengal. The missionaries' wives generally took charge of these schools in their respective mission stations. The curriculum here was similar to that in the boys' schools. Disillusioned over negligible success of the girls' day schools the missionaries began to concentrate more on the boarding schools. Every natural calamity brought more inmates to these schools. Shelter and food was provided to these destitute. With time these schools played a key role in conversion to Christianity.

After 1855, the government-aided girls' schools managed by Bengalis turned out to be rivals of the mission schools. The Indian Education Commission of 1882 reported that most of the students attending 7,000 missionary girls' schools all over India were Christians. The boarding schools ultimately became the 'nurseries' of education of Christian women folk.

Along with it missionaries concentrated on the 'Zenana System' (a system of domestic instruction mostly by wives of missionaries). The Education Despatch of 1854 mentioned the system introduced in the early 19th century. Indicating its success the Education Commission (1882) recommended special grants for running the system. Some leading Brahma and Hindu families, encouraged this system since they wanted their women to be educated. In 1871 there were more 'Zenana' pupils in Bengal than in other presidencies put together.

With the arrival in Calcutta of Mary Carpenter and Annette Akroyd, Unitarian women educationists, in 1866 and 1872 respectively, a phase of co-operation between the Brahma/Hindu reformists and the Unitarian Christians regarding women's education began. Both of them helped in the foundation of the Brahma Normal School and the Hindu *Mahila Vidyalaya*. But the Christian missionaries mostly controlled the institutions for training women teachers. In 1932, five of the seven Teachers Training Colleges in India were Christian institutions and over 100 out of 157 students were Christians. By all means the Christian missionaries remained pioneers in the field of formal and professional education of women in colonial Bengal.

The Christian mission in 19th century Bengal also became involved in a crucial issue - the tribal question. The Santals, the largest tribe of Eastern India, attracted their attention for evangelisation. Considering the tribal tradition as a significant factor in the pluralist Bengal society, they penetrated the obscure Santal world and tried to identify themselves with their life and thinking. Apart from a few colonial bureaucrats, the missionaries had been the pioneers in 'Tribal Studies' - now an important stream of social science. They made invaluable contribution to it. The works of PO Bodding - *A Santal Dictionary* and numerous outings of LO Skrefsrud in Santali and English still occupy a pre-eminent position in this study.

Misionaries were in favour of imparting education among the Santals through their mother tongue and were keen to improve their socio-economic condition as a prerequisite for evangelisation. The Santal mission of the Northern Churches later became the largest among the tribal missions and attracted considerable attention in India and abroad. The CMS and the BMS, were the two most active missionary societies in this field. The CMS started its work in 1854 and the BMS in 1867. Before that A Leslie and T Christian were sent out to preach among the Santals in 1824-41 and 1826 respectively, but Christian died within a year and Leslie, a victim of 'jungle fever' also left his station. E Droese, the German missionary of the CMS, started mission work in 1854.

Shortly afterward the santal rebellion (1855) marked a turning point in the Santal mission of the CMS. Believing that 'utter want of education', and 'gross absurdity of Santal's religious belief' caused the insurrection, the Bengal Government requested the CMS to prepare a plan for educating the Santals and agreed to provide financial assistance for this purpose. The scheme submitted by the Calcutta Committee stressed the need of vocational training along with formal primary education. The India government accepted the scheme (1856) but the outbreak of the sepoy revolt (1857) prevented its execution. Undaunted by this initial setback the CMS opened the Santal branch of

Bhagalpur mission in 1859. The Santal mission was formed as an independent unit under EL Puxley.

New mission stations were established in some parts of the newly created Santal Parganas (1856) which included some parts of Bengal proper. Puxley stressed the need for 'Santalizing' the teaching organisations with cooperation of Santal *manjhis* (headmen). He established a Teachers' Training School (1863) with Santali as the medium of instruction. He gave Santali a written form in Roman character. By 1866 he completed the Santal vocabulary, Santal dictionary, Bible History, part of St. Mathew's Gospel and Anglican Prayer Book. Puxley's performance was quite impressive. Starting with 10 'useless' schools in 1862 he left 36 schools with 348 students at the time of his departure in 1868. The Training School proved to be a great success and a centre of 'movement towards Christianity'.

Puxley's success attracted a group of Church Missionaries (such as J Brown, ET Cole, A Stark, H Davies and HW Shackell) to the Santal mission between 1868 and 1871. More textbooks were published in Santali by the Calcutta Bible Society. Missionary efforts created a growing urge for education among the Santals since missionaries made them believe that education was the only safeguard against the oppression of zamindars and mahajans. The rise and growth of the Kherwar movement, 1871- 81 (the word, Kherwar was derived from the word 'khair' which meant man - a movement for spiritual and social regeneration of the Santal community) had also a role behind this zeal for education. A group of Santals, longing for English education, was ready to pay for it. Forty Santal students were admitted to English schools in Santal Parganas in 1880. George Campbell's keen interest in Santal mission and a special grant towards Santal education encouraged the missionaries. Up to the end of the 19th century the task of educating the Santals was exclusively left to the missionary societies.

The main aim of the Christian Missionaries-changing the cultural and social fabric of the Bengal society by Christianising it-was never fulfilled. The mission itself indeed remained outside the main stream of the Bengal society. Its future largely lay in the conversion of the 'outcastes and tribals, exiled communities as they themselves were'. The largest number of the converts of the Church and Baptist Missions came from the *kartabhajas* (worshippers of Lord), a Hindu egalitarian religious sect developing among the 'lowest' orders of the Hindus like *Chandals* and *Namashudras*.

In 1838 - 39 about 3,000 *Kartabhajas* embraced Christianity after a flood of Jalangi river in the Krishnanagar district. Flood relief from the missionaries probably encouraged this 'great movement'. A large number of *Kartabhajas* from Barisal and Jessore (BMS Stations) also became Christians in 1840s. This was the first and most notable instance of 'mass movement' towards Christianity in 19th century Bengal.

In the 20th century, Christian churches adopted some new measures amounting to a 'revolution in missions'. Social welfare, vocational training, educational and medical institutions replaced the old methods of preaching and Christian teaching. With the growth of a more rational outlook to non-Christian religions and cultures, they also began to consider these new measures as different ways to the fulfilment of God's mission on earth; 'Not to destroy, but to fulfil' - this commandment became the watchword of many of them. Giving up Euro-centric views they were fast moving towards forming an international, inter-racial and inter-denominational church.

Ever since W Carey proposed a World Missionary Conference in 1810, a section of Bengal missionaries were thinking of forming such an organisation. The Calcutta Missionary Conference was the first step towards it. Such thinking led to the preparation for a universal movement that started with the World Missionary Conference at Edinburgh in 1910.

# 4

# MACAULAY'S MINUTES

The British Parliament in 1813 made it mandatory to the East India Company to set aside Rs 1 lakh annually "for the revival and promotion of literature and the encouragement of the learned natives of India, and for the introduction and promotion of a knowledge of the sciences among the inhabitants of the British territories".

The Company officials were divided into two camps over the kind of education to be encouraged as well as the medium of instruction. The Orientalist camp insisted that the existing Indian indigenous system of education was great, with Sanskrit and Persian being the medium of instruction. The Anglicist camp, led by Lord Macaulay, valiantly argued for the European system of education for India with English as the medium of instruction. Governor General Bentinck approved Macaulay's position on March 7, 1835, with a slight modification.

The latter in the 1820s conducted a vigor-ous campaign against what they viewed as barbarism and supersti-tion, attacking in particular the suttee, a Hindu religious practiceof burning alive a man's widow on his funeral pyre. The decisionof the East India Company in 1833 to admit Indians into its civilservice precipitated a new round in this old debate. Although bothsides agreed that the education of Indians should be promoted,they differed on its proposed form. The Orientalists favored Arabicand Sanskrit learning. The Anglicists urged the introduction ofwestern scholarship taught in English. The most prominent westernizer was Thomas Babington Ma-caulay (1800-1859), a member of the Supreme Council of India.Already a distinguished essayist, and later renowned for hisHistoryof Englandfrom the Accessionof James the Second, Macaulay never doubted the superiority of English civilization. The history of England since 1688 was, he wrote, "eminently thehistory of physical, of moral, and of intellectual improvement." It was Britain's duty therefore to uplift the Indians by blessing themwith western learning, an argument made most dogmatically in his Minute on Indian Education (1835).

Macaulay's Minute on Indian Education is a public document. Macaulay's Minute on Education was dated February 2, 1835. The Governor General of India, William Bentinck approved the Minute on March 7, 1835 and it became the cornerstone of British India educational policy.

We may question the logic and the arguments of Macaulay, particularly his diatribe against Indian culture, religion, theology, arts, and sciences. He wrote these words nearly 175 years ago, and as a representative of a ruling power. Some of his words certainly hurt us even today when we read him, and if he were to write to this generation, he have no doubt that he would have been perhaps more circumspect, and would have been "restrained by the necessity of paying a decent reverence to the practices of an established religion".

However, we all know that the number of Indians who wish to learn and use English has been growing steadily for the last two centuries. We all know that English has come to stay in India. The ruling Indian castes or classes have embraced English with suitable modifications as to the contents of lessons and the lexicon that are used in textbooks and taught in classes. English has become the language of higher castes and the affluent in the Indian subcontinent. The lower castes and poorer classes try to emulate the model set by their peers. The net result is that English will continue, and no central or state government will dare to abolish it from the curriculum in India. Globalization makes English a value added language, the access to which becomes a passport for jobs around the world.

Many during Macaulay's tenure in India actually fought for the use of Indian languages as media of instruction. Even as English contains excellent Christian literature, it also is home for secular literature. Secular Humanism found its way in many lands through the learning of English language and literature. Macaulay's project for the use of English in Indian schools did actually accomplish this goal. Its "ennobling" characteristic as a tool and purveyor of culture, the scientific knowledge it opens up for those who learn it, the ease with which one could transact business using it, all have more or less overshadowed the deep Christian foundation upon which the language, literature and culture is built.

Aided by the influence of secularism, many Christian teachers of English have more or less abandoned the Christian program while teaching English. Ethics and morals portrayed in literature were interpreted not as emerging from the Christian base but from universal humanism. English is still pregnant with Christian metaphors, idioms and set phrases, which cannot be wholly understood and used without a grasp of the underlying Christian message.

Perhaps because of the reason last mentioned, most nations have embarked upon a process of textbook contextualization when it comes to teaching English. The original pieces of writing by the native speakers of English are sought to be replaced by the writings of the nationals who are masters of English prose and poetry. In their creative writing, metaphors, idioms, and set phrases from the national languages, which imply local culture and religion, are more freely used. Translations from the local tales are more frequently substituted for tales from Europe. In addition, government-inspired documents on ideology become part of the textbook. Nations want to appropriate English as a language minus the culture and religion it represents and communicates. And this trend has been successfully established in the last fifty years in India. Macaulay's diatribe is simply a nuisance at the moment for the ruling castes and classes, but his momentous decision to introduce English in the Indian School System is followed with a force never before seen in the Indian subcontinent for any language.

It is also recognized that English could not and would not be taught by the native speakers of English in India. This is economically impractical, and politically inconvenient, and sometimes would be viewed as a disastrous step. The former colonies of Britain such as India, Pakistan, Bangladesh, Sri Lanka, and several African nations have provided for the teaching of English mainly through their nationals. Some countries like Japan and China open their doors to more number of native speakers of English to teach English. This step has far-reaching consequences for the quality of English language instruction and use in India, but the people of the Indian subcontinent have admirably "resolved" the problem with their own nuances. Better schools and colleges continue to seek a competence for their students similar to that of native English speakers. It is possible that this trend would gain momentum as Indians begin to generate more wealth.

When English is introduced in the school curriculum as a language to be learned in addition to a national language or languages, it is inevitable that governments and institutions would look for training their own nationals to meet the demand.

Missionaries in the past responded to this by training nationals in the art of teaching English as a foreign or second language, while noting all the time the inadequate skills attained in pronunciation and naturalness of usage. Macaulay's letters and minutes make subtle references to the nuances of Indian English, without looking down upon such innovations. The missionaries and others involved in teaching English have recognized that a perfect duplication of the native speakers' language is neither possible nor desirable.

Learning English is closely associated with the study of English literary pieces in the Indian subcontinent. Even as many adult students in short term English courses may not care for the literary benefits of learning English, many more do not feel satisfied with just learning the language and using it only for practical ends. They do, indeed, seek to understand, enjoy and appreciate what English literature offers them. School curriculum always blends learning English language with learning and enjoying English literature.

The following sections present Lord Macaulay's Minute on Indian Education, written on February 2, 1835, and approved by the Governor General William Bentinck on March 7 in the same year. The subsection headings are not part of the original document. Introduce these subheadings to help our readers to pursue Macaulay's line of thought on the subject.

## "MACAULAY'S MINUTE ON EDUCATION, 2ND FEBRUARY, 1835"

### *Legislative Act Necessary to Change Current Practice? Macaulay's Minute*

As it seems to be the opinion of some of the gentlemen who compose the Committee of Public Instruction, that the course which they have hitherto pursued was strictly prescribed by the British Parliament in 1813, and as, if that opinion be correct, a legislative act will be necessary to warrant a change, I have thought it right to refrain from taking any part in the preparation of the adverse statements which now before us, and to reserve what I had to say on the subject till it should come before me as a member of the Council of India.

### *Definiiton of Literature*

It does not appear to me that the Act of Parliament can, by any art of construction, be made to bear the meaning which has been assigned to it. It contains nothing about the particular languages or sciences which are to be studied. A sum is set apart 'for the revival and promotion of literature and the encouragement of thelearned natives of India, and for the introduction and promotion of a knolwdge of the sciences among the inhabitants of the British territories.'

It is argued, or rather taken for granted, that by literature, the Parliament can have meant only Arabic and Sanscrit literature, that they never would have given the honorable appellation of 'a learned native' to a native who was familiar with the poetry of Milton, the Metaphysics of Locke, and the Physics of Newton; but that they meant to designate by that name only such persons as might have studied in the sacred books of the Hindoos all the uses of cusa-grass, and all the mysteries of absorption into the Deity. This does not appear to be a very satisfactory interpretation. To take a parallel case: suppose that the Pacha of Egypt, a country once superior in knowledge of the nations of Europe, but now sunk far below them, were to appropriate a sum for the purpose of 'reviving and promoting literature, and encouraging learned natives of Egypt,' would anybody infer that he meant the youth of his pachalic to give years to the study of hieroglyphics, to search into all the doctrines disguised under the fable of Osiris, and to ascertain with all possible accuracy the ritual with which cats and onions were anciently adored? Would he be justly charged with inconsistency, if, instead of employing his young subjects in deciphering obelisks, he were to order them to be instructed in the English and French languages, and in all the sciences to which those languages are the chief keys?

The words on which the supporters of the old system rely do not bear them out, and other words follow which seem to be quite decisive on the other side. This lac of rupees is set apart, not only for 'reviving literature in India,' the phrase on which their whole interpretation is founded, but also for 'the introduction and promotion of a knowledge of the sciences among the inhabitants of the British territories,' -words which are alone sufficient to authorize all the changes for which we contend. If the Council agree in my construction, no legislative act will be necessary. If they differ from me, we will prepare a short Act rescinding that clause of the Charter of 1813, from which the difficulty arises.

### *No Pledge given on support to India Language Education*

The argument which we have been considering, affects only the form of proceeding. But the admirers of the Oriental system of education have used another argument, which, if we admit it to be valid, is decisive against all change. They conceive that the public faith is pledged to the present system, and that to alter the appropriation of any of the funds which have hitherto been spent in encouraging the study of Arabic and Sanscrit, would be down-right spoliation. It is not easy to understand by what process of reasoning they can have arrived at this conclusion.

The grants which are made from the public purse for the encouragement of literature differed in no respect from the grants which are made from the same purse for other objects of real or supposed utility. We found a sanatarium on a spot which we suppose to be healthy. Do we thereby pledge ourselves to keep a sanatarium there, if the result should not answer our expectation? We commence the erection of a pier. Is it a violation of the public faith to stop the works, if we afterwards see reason to believe that the building will be useless?

The rights of property are undoubtedly sacred. But nothing endangers those rights so much as the practice, now unhappily too common, of attributing them to things which they do not belong. Those who impart to abuses the sanctity of property are in truth imparting to the institution of property the unpopularity and the fragility of abuses. If the Government has given to any person a formal assurance; nay, if the Government has excited in any person's mind a reasonable expectation that he shall receive a certain income as a teacher or a learner of

Sanscrit or Arabic, we would respect that person's pecuniary interests-we would rather err on the side of liberality to individuals than suffer the public faith to be called in question.

But to talk of a Government pledging itself to teach certain languages and certain sciences, though those languages may become useless, though those sciences may be exploded, seems to be quite unmeaning. There is not a single word in any public instructions, from which it can be inferred that the Indian Government ever intended to give any pledge on this subject, or ever considered the destination of these funds as unalterably fixed.

But had it been otherwise, we should denied the competence of our predecessors to bind us by any pledge on such a subject. Suppose that a Government had in the last century enacted in the most solemn manner that all its subjects should, to the end of time, be inoculated for the small-pox: would that Government be bound to persist in the practice after Jenner's discovery? These promises of which nobody claims the performance, and from which nobody can grant a release; these vested rights, which vest in nobody; this property without proprietors; this robbery, which makes nobody poorer, may be comprehended by persons of higher faculties than mine. We consider this plea merely as a set form of words, regularly used both in England and in India, in defence of every abuse for which no other plea can be set up.

We hold this lac of rupees to be quite at the disposal of the Governor-General in Council, for the purpose of promoting learning in India, in any way which may be thought most advisable. We hold his Lordship to be quite as free to direct that it shall no longer be employed in encouraging Arabic and Sasnscrit, as he is to direct that the reward for killing tigers in Mysore shall be diminished, or that no more public money shall be expended on the chanting at the cathedral.

We now come to the gist of the matter. We have a fund to be employed as government shall direct for the intellectual improvement of the people of this country. The simple question is, what is the most useful way of employing it?

All parties seem to be agreed on one point, that the dialects commonly spoken among the natives of this part of India, contain neither literary nor scientific information, and are, moreover, so poor and rude that, until they are enriched from some other quarter, it will not be easy to translate any valuable work into them. It seems to be admitted on all sides, that the intellectual improvement of those classes of the people who have the means of pursuing higher studies can at present be effected only by means of some language not vernacular amongst them.

### *What then shall That Language Be?*

What then shall that language be? One-half of the Committee maintain that it shouldbe the English. The other half strongly recommend the Arabic and Sanscrit. The whole question seems to me to be, which language is the best worth knowing?

We have no knowledge of either Sanscrit or Arabic. -But I have done what we could to form a correct estimate of their value. We have read translations of the most celebrated Arabic and Sanscrit works. We have conversed both here and at home with men distinguished by their proficiency in the Eastern tongues. The intrinsic superiority of the .Western literature is, indeed, fully admitted by those members of the Committee who support the Oriental plan of education. It will be hardly disputed, suppose, that the department of literature in which the eastern writers with any Orientalist who ventured to maintain that the Arabic and Sanscrit poetry could be compared to that of the great European nations. But when we pass from works of imagination to works in which facts are recorded, and general principles investigated, the superiority of the Europeans becomes absolutely immeasurable. It is, I believe, no exaggeration to say, that all the historical information which has been collected from all the books written may be found in the most paltry abridgments used at preparatory schools in England. In every branch of physical or moral philosophy, the relative position of the two nations is nearly the same.

### *Indians Cannot be educated by means of their Monther-Tongue: English is the language*

How, then, stands the case? We have to educate a people who cannot at present be educated by means of their mother-tongue. We must teach them some foreign language. The claims of our own language it is hardly necessary to recapitulate. It stands pre-eminent even among the languages of the west. It abounds with works of imagination not inferior to the noblest which Greece has bequeathed to us; with models of every species of eloquence; with historical compositions, which, considered merely as narratives, have seldom been surpassed, and which, considered as vehicles of ethical and political instruction, have never been equaled; with just and lively representations of human life and human nature; with the most profound speculations on metaphysics, morals, government, jurisprudence, and trade; with full and correct information respecting every experimental science which tends topreserve the health, to increase the comfort, or to expand the intellect of man.

Whoever knows that language has ready access to all the vast intellectual wealth, which all th wisest nations of the earth have created and hoarded int 4he course of ninety generations. It may be safely said, that the literature now extant in that language is of far greater value than all the literature which three hundred years ago was extant in all the languages of the world together. Nor is this all. In India, English is the language spoken by the ruling class.

It is spoken by the higher class of natives at the seats of Government. It is like to become the language of commerce throughout the seas of the East. It is the language of two great European communities which are raising, the one in south of

Africa, the other in Australasia; communities which are every year becoming more important, and more closely connected with our Indian empire. Whether we look at the intrinsic value of our literature, or at the particular situation of this country, we shall see the strongest reason to think that, of all foreign tongues, the English tongue is that which would be the most useful to our native subjects.

### *Do we abdicate our Responsibility?*

The question now before us is simply whether, when it is in our power to teach this language, we shall teach languages, by which, by universal confession, there are not books on any subject which deserve to be compared to our own; whether, when we can teach European science, we shall teach systems which, by universal confession, whenever they differ from those of Europe, differ for the worse; and whether, when we can patronise sound Philosophy and true History, we shall countenance, at the public expense, medical doctrines, which would disgrace an English farrier, —Astronomy, which would move laughter in girls at an English boarding school,—History, abounding with kings thirty feet high, and reigns thirty thousand years long,—and Geography, made up of seas of treacle and seas of butter.

We are not without experience to guide us. History furnishes several analogous cases, and they all teach the same lesson. There are in modern times, to go no further, two memorable instances of a great prejudices overthrown, —of knowledge diffused,—of taste purified,—of arts and sciences planted in countries which had =recently been ignorant and barbarous.

The first instance to which I refer, is the great revival of letters among the Western nations at the close of the fifteenth and the beginning of the sixteenth century. At that time almost every thing that was worth reading was contained in the writings of the ancient Greeks and Romans. Had our ancestors acted as the Committee of Public Instruction has hitherto acted; had they neglected the language of Cicero and Tacitus; had they confined their attention to the old dialects of our own island; had they printed nothing and taught nothing at the universities but Chronicles in Anglo-Saxon, and Romances in Norman-French, would England have been what she now is?

What the Greek and Latin were to the contemporaries of More and Ascham, our tongue is to the people of India. The literature of England is now more valuable than that of classical antiquity. I doubt whether the Sanscrit literature be as valuable than that of classical antiquity. I doubt whether the Sanscrit literature be as valuable as that of our Saxon and Norman progenitors. In some departments, —in History.

Another instance may be said to be still before our eyes. Within the last hundred and twenty years, a nation which had previously been in a state as a barbarous as that in which our ancestors were before the crusades, has gradually emerged from the ignorance in which it was sunk, and has taken its place among civilized communities. There is now in that country a large educated class, abounding with persons fit to serve the state in the highest functions, and in no wise inferior to the most accomplished men who adorn the best circles of Paris and London. There is reason to hope that this vast empire, which in the time of our grandfathers was probably behind the Punjab, may, in the time of our grandchildren, be pressing close to on France and Britain in the career of improvement.

And how was this change effected? Not by flattering national prejudices: not by feeding the mind of the young Muscovite with the old women's stories which his rude fathers had believed: not by filling his head with lying legends about St. Nicholas: not by encouraging him to study the great question, whether the world was or was not created on the 13th of September: not by calling 'a learned native,' when he has mastered all these points of knowledge: but by teaching him those foreign languages in which the greatest mass of information had been laid up, and thus putting all that information within his reach. The languages of Western Europe civilized Russia. I cannot doubt that they will do for the Hindoo what they have done for the Tartar.

### *The Learns cannot Prescribe what the Teachers should Teach*

And what are the arguments against that course which seems to be alike recommended by theory and by experience? It is said that we ought to secure the co-operation of the native public, and that we can do this only by teaching Sanscrit and Arabic.

We can by no means admit that when a nation of high intellectual attainments undertakes to superintend the education of a nation comparatively ignorant, the learners are absolutely to prescribe the course which is to be taken by the teachers. It is not necessary, however, to say anything on this subject. For it is proved by unanswerable evidence that we are not at present securing the co-operation of the natives. It would be bad enough to consult their intellectual taste at the expense of their intellectual health. But we are consulting neither, — we are withholding from them the learning for which they are craving, we are forcing on them the mock-learning which they nauseate.

This is proved by the fact that we are forced to pay our Arabic and Sanscrit students, while those who earn English are willing to pay us. All the declamations in the world about the love and reverence of the natives for their sacred dialects will never, in the mind of any impartial person, outweigh the undisputed fact, that we cannot find, in all our vast empire, a single student who will let us teach him those dialects unless we will pay him.

We have now before me the accounts of the Madrassa for one month, — the month of December 1833. The Arabic students appear to have been seventy-seven in number. All receive stipends from the public. The whole amount paid to them is about 500 rupees a month. On the other side of the account stands the following item: Deduct amount realized from the out-students of English for the months of May, June and July last, 103 rupees.

### *Do we pay people to Learn what they want to Learn?*

We have been told that it is merely from want of local experience that I am surprised at these phenomena, and that it is not the fashion for students in India to study at their own charges. This only confirms me in my opinion. Nothing is more certain than that it never can in any part of the world be necessary to pay men for doing what they think pleasant and profitable. India is no exception to this rule. The people of India do not require to be paid for eating rice when they are hungry, or for wearing woolen cloth in the cold season. To come nearer to the case before us, the children who learn their letters and a little elementary Arithmetic from the village school-master are not paid by him. He is paid for teaching them. Why then is it necessary to pay people to learn Sanscrit and Arabic? Evidently because it is universally felt that the Sanscrit and Arabic are languages, the knowledge of which does not compensate for the trouble of acquiring them. On all such subjects the state of the market is the decisive test.

Other evidence is not wanting, if other evidence were required. A petition was presented last year to the Committee by several ex-students of the Sanscrit College. The petitioners stated that they had studied in the college ten or twelve years; that they had made themselves acquainted with Hindoo literature and science; that they had received certificates of proficiency: and what is the fruit of all this! 'Notwithstanding such testimonials,' they say, 'we have but little of bettering our condition without the kind of assistance of your Honorable Committee, the indifference with which we are generally looked upon by our countrymen leaving no hope of encouragement and assistance from them.'

They therefore beg that they may be recommended to the Governor General for places under the Government, not places of high dignity or emolument, but such as may just enable them to exist. 'We want means,' they say, 'for a decent living, and for our progressive improvement, which, however, we cannot obtain without the assistance of Government, by whom we have been educated and maintained from childhood.' They conclude by representing, very pathetically, that they are sure that it was never the intention of government, after behaving so liberally to them during thei education, to abandon them to destitution and neglect.

### *The Context between Truth and Flasehood*

We have been used to see petitions to Government for compensation. All these petitions, even the most unreasonable of them, proceeded on the supposition that some loss had been sustained-that some wrong had been inflicted. These are surely the first petitioners whoever demanded compensation for having been educated gratis, — for having been supported by the public during twelve years, and then sent forth into the world well furnished with literature and science.

They represent their education as an injury which gives them a claim on the Government for redress, as an injury for which the stipends paid to them during the infliction were a very inadequate compensation. And I doubt not that they are in the right. They have wasted the best years of life in learning what procures for them neither bread nor respect. Surely we might, with advantage, have saved the cost of making these persons useless and miserable; surely, men may be brought up to be burdens to the public and objects of contempt to their neighbours at a smaller charge to the state. But such is our policy.

We do not even stand neuter in the contest between truth and falsehood. We are not content to leave the natives to the influence of their own hereditary prejudices. To the natural difficulties which obstruct the progress of sound science in the East, we add fresh difficulties of our own making. Bounties and premiums, such as ought not to be given even for the propagation of truth, we lavish on false taste and false philosophy.

### *Expenditure on Sanscrit and Arabic Learning is dead Loss*

By acting thus we create the very evil which we fear. We are making that opposition which we do not find. What we spend on the Arabic and Sanscrit colleges is not merely a dead loss to the cause of truth; it is bounty-money paid to raise up champions of error. It goes to form a nest, not merely of helpless place-hunters, but of bigots prompted alike by passion and by interest to raise a cry against every useful scheme of education. If there should be by opposition among the natives to the change which we recommend, that opposition will be the effect of our own system. It will be headed by persons supported by our stipends and trained in our colleges.

The longer we persevere in our present course, the more formidable will that opposition be. It will be every year reinforced by recruits whom we are paying. From the native society left to itself, we have no difficulties to apprehend; all the murmuring will come from that oriental interest which we have, by artificial means, called into being, and nursed into strength.

### *The Real Desire of Indian*

There is yet another fact, which is alone sufficient to prove that the feeling of the native public, when left to itself, is not such as the supporters of the old system represent it to be. The Committee have thought fit to lay out above a lac of rupees in printing Arabic and Sanscrit books. Those books find not purchasers. It is very rarely that a single copy is disposed of. Twenty-three thousand volumes, most of them folios and quartos, fill the libraries, or rather the lumber-rooms, of this body. The Committee contrive to get rid of some portion of their vast stock of oriental literature by giving books away. But they cannot give so fast as they print. About twenty thousand rupees a year are spent in adding fresh masses of waste paper to a hoard which, I should, is already sufficiently ample. During the last three years, about sixty thousand rupees have been expended in this manner. The sale of Arabic and Sanscrit books, during those three years, has not yielded quite one thousand rupees. In the mean time the School-book Society is selling seven or eight thousand English volumes every year, and not only pays the expenses of printing, but realizes a profit of 20 per cent. on its outlay.

### *The Indian Penal Code will replace Sanscrit and Arabic Texts*

The fact that the Hindoo law is to be learned chiefly from Sanscrit books, and the Mahometan law from Arabic books, has been much insisted on, but seems not to bear at all on the question. We are commanded by Parliament to ascertain and digest the laws of India. The assistance of a law Commission has been given to us for that purpose. As soon as the code is promulgated, the Shastras and the Hedaya will be useless to a Moonsief or Sudder Ameen. I hope and trust that before the boys who are now entering at the Madrassa and the Sanscrit college have completed their studies, this great work will be finished. It would be manifestly absurd to educate the rising generation with a view to a state of things which we mean to alter before they reach manhood.

### *India Government will be Tolerant and Neutral to all religious*

But there is yet another argument which seems even more untenable. It is said that the Sanscrit and Arabic are the languages in which the sacred books of a hundred millions of people are written, and that they are, on that account, entitled to peculiar encouragement. Assuredly it is the duty of the British Government in India to be not only tolerant, but neutral on all religious questions. But to encourage the study of a literature admitted to be of small intrinsic value, only because that literature inculcates the most serious errors on the most important subjects, is a course hardly reconcileable with reason, with morality, or even with that very neutrality which ought, as we all agree, to be sacredly preserved. It is confessed that a language is barren of useful knowledge.

We are to teach it because it is false History, false Astronomy, false Medicine, because we find them in company with a false religion. We abstain, and we trust shall always abstain, from giving any public encouragement to those who are engaged in the work of converting natives to Christianity. And while we act thus, can we reasonably and decently bribe men out of the revenues of the state to waste their youth in learning how they are to purify themselves after touching an ass, or what text of the Vedas they are to repeat to expiate the crime of killing a goat?

### *Indians can atttain excellence in English*

It is taken for granted by the advocates of Oriental learning, that no native of this country can possibly attain more than a mere smattering of English. They do not attempt to prove this; but they perpetually insinuate it. They designate the education which their opponents recommend as a mere spelling book education. They assume it as undeniable, that the question is between a profound knowledge of Hindoo and Arabian literature and science on the one side, and a superficial knowledge of the rudiments of English on the other. This is not merely an assumption, but an assumption contrary to all reason and experience. We know that foreigners of all nations do learn our language sufficiently to have access to all the most abstruse knowledge which it contains, sufficiently to relish even the more delicate graces of our most idiomatic writers.

There are in this very town natives who are quite competent to discuss political or scientific questions with fluency and precision in the English language. I have heard the very question on which I am now writing discussed by native gentlemen with a liberality and an intelligence which would do credit to any member of the Committee of Public instruction. Indeed it is unusual to find, even in the literary circles of the continent, any foreigner who can express himself in English with so much facility and correctness as we find in many Hindoos. Nobody, we suppose, will contend that English is so difficult to a Hindoo as Greek to an Englishman.

Yet an intelligent English youth, in a much smaller number of years than our unfortunate pupils pass at the Sanscrit college, becomes able to read, to enjoy, and even to imitate, not unhappily, the compositions of the best Greek Authors. Less than half the time which enables an English youth to read Herodotus and Sophocles, ought to enable a Hindoo to read Hume and Milton.

We think it clear that we are not fettered by the Act of parliament of 1813; that we are not fettered by any pledge expressed or implied; that we are free to employ our funds as we choose; that we ought to employ them in teaching what is best worth knowing; that English is better worth knowing than Sanscrit or Arabic; that the natives are desirous to be taught English, and are not desirous to be taught Sanscrit or Arabic; that neither as the languages of law, nor as the languages fo religion, have the Sanscrit and Arabic any peculiar claim to our engagement; that it is possible to make natives of this country thoroughly good English scholars, and that to this end our efforts ought to be directed. In one point I fully agree with the gentlemen to whose general views I am opposed. I feel with them, that it is impossible for us, with our limited means, to attempt to educate the body of the people. We must at present do our best to form a class who may be interpreters between us and the millions whom we govern; a class of persons, Indian in blood and colour, but English in taste, in opinions, in morals, and in intellect. To that class we may leave it to refine the vernacular dialects of the country, to enrich those dialects with terms of science borrowed from the Western nomenclature, and to render them by degrees fit vehicles for conveying knowledge to the great mass of the population. She would strictly respect all existing interests. She would deal even generously with all individuals who have had fair reason to expect a pecuniary provision. But I would strike at the root of the bad system which has hitherto been fostered by us.

We would at once stop the printing of Arabic and Sanscrit books, would abolish the Madrassa and the Sanscrit college at Calcutta. Benares is the great seat of Brahmanical learning; Delhi, of Arabic learning. If we retain the Sanscrit college at Benares and the Mahometan college at Delhi, we do enough, and much more than enough in my opinion, for the Eastern languages. If the Benares and Delhi colleges should be retained, would at least recommend tht no stipends shall be given to any students who may hereafter repair thither, but that the people shall be left to make their own choice between the rival systems of education without being bribed by us to learn what they have no desire to know. The funds which would thus be placed at our disposal would enable us to give larger encouragement to the Hindoo college at Calcutta, and to establish in the principal cities throughout the Presidencies of Fort William and Agra schools in which the English language might be well and thoroughly taught.

If the decision of his Lordship in Council should be such as we anticipate, we shall enter on the performance of my duties with the greatest zeal and alacrity. If, on the other hand, it be the opinion of the government that the present system ought to remain unchanged, we beg that we may be permitted to retire from the chair of the Committee. we feel that we could not be of the smallest use there-ww feel, also, that we should be lending my countenance to what we firmly believe to be a mere delusion. We believe that the present system tends, not to accelerate the progress of truth, but to delay the natural death of expiring errors.

We conceive that we have at present no right to the respectable name of a Board of Public Instruction. We are a Board for wasting public money, for printing books which are of less value than the paper on which they are printed was while it was blank; for giving artificial encouragement to absurd history, absurd metaphysics, absurd physics, absurd theology; for raising up a breed of scholars who find their scholarship an encumbrance and a blemish, who live on the public while they are receiving their education, and whose education is so utterly useless to them that when they have received it they must either starve of live on the public all the rest of their lives. Entertaining these opinions, Naturally desirous to decline all share in the responsibility of a body, which, unless it alters its whole mode of proceeding, we must consider not merely as useless, but as positively noxious.

Macaulay was not a racist. Indians were not inferior as people; they simply had an inferiorculture. As Greece had civilized Rome and Rome had civilized Britain, now Britain, a link in the chain of progress, must transferthat benefit to India.Macaulay and others recognized that education might contri-bute to the end of British political rule in India. Nevertheless, Britain would create a more enduring empire: The sceptre may pass from us. Victory may be inconstant to our arms. But there are triumphs which are followed by no reverse. There is an empire exempt from all natur-al cause of decay. Those triumphs are the pacific triumphs of reason over barbarism;that empire is the imperishable empire of our arts and our morals, our literature and our laws. Regardless of the merits of the case, the government of India'sadoption of Macaulay's recommendations was of great impor-tance. Although alienating many Indians and perhaps contributingto the Indian Mutiny of 1857, the westernization and moderniza-tion of India was begun.

# 5

# Wood's Despatch

The history of education in India under the British rule has yet to be properly written. It should be remembered that in the pre-British period, India was not an illiterate country. This land was far more advanced in education than many a Christian country of the West. Almost every village had its school for the diffusion of not only 3 but 4 R's – the last R being religion or the Ramayana. That work has contributed not a little to the preservation of Hindu culture.

Stress has not been laid on another fact, which is, that educational institutions were not established in this country as soon as the East India Company obtained political supremacy here. It took the Christian merchant "adventurers" just a century to come to the decision that it was for their benefit to impart education to the swarthy "heathens" of India. The battle of Plassey was fought in 1757; and the Wood's Despatch, commonly called the Educational Charter of India, is dated 1854. This should show that the system of education was not introduced in hot haste but after the mature deliberation of nearly a century.

It should also not be lost sight that the Indians themselves were the pioneers of introducing Western education in this country. The Hindu College of Calcutta was established long before Macaulay penned his celebrated minute or wood sent out his Educational Despatch to India.

When the East India Company attained political supremacy in India, they did not bestow any thought on the education of the inhabitants of their dominions. Gold was their watchword. Everyone of their servants who came out to India tried to enrich himself as quickly as possible at the expense of the children of the soil. It was on this account that Edmund Burke described them as "birds of prey and passage" in India.

According to Herbert Spencer, "The Anglo-Indians of the last century – "birds of prey and passage, " as they were styled by Burke – showed themselves only a shade less cruel than their prototype of Peru and Mexico."

These residents of Britain after making their fortunes retired in England, where they were known as "Indian Nabobs."

The Christian "Indian Nabobs" looked on the heathens of India in the same light as their co-religionists of America did on their Negro slaves. Writes a historian: "On the contrary, the education of Negroes was expressly forbidden. Here, for instance, are some passages from the Code of Virginia in 1849; "Every assemblage of Negroes for the purpose of instruction in reading or writing shall be an unlawful assembly.

But as years rolled on, it became patent to some thoughtful Anglo-Indians, that their dominion in India could not last long unless education – especially Western – was diffused among the inhabitants of that land. But this proposition struck terror and dismay into the hearts of the generality of the people of England.

It should be remembered that India was a country inhabited by savages and barbarians. In the pre-British period, India possessed educational institutions of a nature which did not exist in the countries of the West. That even in the beginning of the Nineteenth century, India, in the matter of education, was in advance of the European countries is proved by the fact of her teaching those countries a new system of tuition, to which attention was drawn by the Court of Directors in their letter to the Governor-General-in-Council in Bengal, dated 3rd June, 1814, extracts from which have been already given above. Very few in India know that the system of "mutual tuition" – which has been practiced by Indian school-masters since time immemorial – has been borrowed by the Christian countries of the West from India. The man who first introduced it into Great Britain was a native of Scotland by the name of Dr. Andrew Bell (1753-1832). The village communities of India had not then been destroyed, and it being the duty of every village communities to foster education, a school formed a prominent institution in every village of any note.

The decimation of the Indian education system thus created a vacuum that then had to be filled. Into that vacuum, eager and waiting, went the missionaries, who swiftly set up their own church-sponsored schools and taught Indian children their own literature and history according to the gospel of Max Muller. It is by now a well-established fact that education was a means to Christianize and "domesticate" the native population and render it loyal to the British empire.

With the destruction of the village communities and the impoverishment of the people which are inseparably connected with the British mode of administration of India, educational institutions which used to flourish in every village of note became things of the past.

Walter Hamilton, writing in 1828 from official records said: "It has long been remarked that science and literature are in a progressive state of decay among the natives of India, the number of learned men being not only diminished, but the circle of learning,....the principal cause of this retrograde condition of literature may be traced to the want of that encouragement which was formerly afforded to it by princes, chieftains and opulent individuals, under the native governments, now past and gone.

The British administrators of India of those days were actuated by political motives in keeping Indians ignorant. Thus one gallant Major General Sir Lionel Smith, K.C.B., at the enquiry of 1831, said: "The effect of education will be to do away with all the prejudices of sects and religions by which we have hitherto kept the country – the Mussalmans against Hindus, and so on; the effect of education will be to expand their minds, and show them their vast power."

## CONVERSION AND EDUCATION OF HINDUS: THE SITUATION IN 1813

In the Charter Act of 1813, to promote the happiness of the heathens of India, it was proposed that: "such measures ought to be adopted as may tend to the introduction among them of useful knowledge, and of religious and moral improvement; and in furtherance of the above objects, sufficient facilities ought to be afforded by law to persons desirous of going to and remaining in India, for the purpose of accomplishing those benevolent designs."

Before proceeding further, it is necessary to point out the diplomatic language of the above clause of the Charter Act. It is language befitting a Machiavelli or a Talleyrand – which does not so much express as conceal the thought and objects which the framers of the Act had in view. Who are the persons referred to as "desirous of going to and remaining in India, for the purpose of accomplishing those benevolent designs?" They were Christian missionaries. At the time of the East India Company charter of 1813, education in England was still under the control of the Church. Hence, the framers of the charter could not think of imparting education to Indians without ecclesiastical agency. This explains the diplomatic language of the Charter. It would have been outraging the feelings of Indians to have informed them of the ecclesiastical Department that they were going to be saddled with, for the benefit of the Christian natives of England. Hence the diplomatic language of the Charter Act.

Warren Hastings was asked by the Lords' Commitiee: "would the introduction of a Church establishment into the British territories in the East Indies, probably be attended with any consequences which would be injurious to the stability of the Government of India?" Sir Malcolm told the Lords Committee: "With the most perfect conviction upon my mind, that, speaking humanly, the Christian religion has been the greatest blessing that could be bestowed on mankind....In the present extended state of our Empire, our security for preserving a power of so extraordinary a nature as that we have established, rests upon the general division of the great communities under the Government, and their subdivision into various castes and tribes; while they continue divided in this manner, no insurrection is likely to shake the stability of our power. "

Hastings and Malcolm and others, opposed the introduction of Christian missionaries in India and imparting of knowledge to its inhabitants from considerations of political expediency. But it was on grounds of political expediency, too, that these two measures were advocated.

It was Charles Grant, described as the Christian Director of the East India Company, who was the first to press upon the British public the expediency of sending Christian missionaries to India for the conversion of its heathen inhabitants, and the imparting them education. We read in his biography that Grant always kept his eye fixed on the chief object of his heart – the evangelization of India. In order to succeed in his endeavor, he did what the Christian missionaries are in the habit of doing to this day, that is, vilifying, and painting the natives of India in the blackest color possible.

That is quite true. The Christian nations and countries of the West sent missionaries of their faith to non-Christian nations, not so much for the spiritual welfare of the latter, as for the worldly good which these missionaries bring to the Christian nations. That Indian patriot, Lala Lajpat Rai, who was deported out of India without any trial and without knowing the nature of the charges against him, wrote in a letter from America, which he visited in 1905: "The other day there was held a conference of missionaries in which President Copen is said to have advocated the extension of the mission work for the benefit of the American trade. He said, in part, we need to develop foreign missions to save our nation commercially....It is only as we develop missions that we shall have a market in the Orient which will demand our manufactured articles in sufficient quantities to match our increased facilities. The Christian man is our customer. The heathen, has, as a rule, few wants. It is only when man is changed that there comes this desire for the manifold articles that belonged to the Christian man and the Christian home. The missionary is everywhere and always the pioneer of trade.."

Commenting on the above extract, Lala Lajpat Rai very rightly observed: "The Indian admirers and friends of Christian missions ought to note this commercial ideal of the American missionary. The missionary is not 'the pioneer of trade' only but also the pioneer of the political supremacy of the Boston people of the East. I think the frank statement of leading Christians ought to open the eyes of all who see no danger in the work of the Christian Missions in the East."

If truth be told, it must be admitted that Christian nations are not anxious to save the souls of the heathens but wish to enrich themselves, and, therefore, send missionaries to non-Christian lands. Charles Grant wanted to keep the natives of India perpetually under the leading strings of his own countrymen. He wrote that, "We can foresee no period in which we may not govern our Asiatic subjects, more happily for them than they can be governed by themselves or any other power; and doing this we should not expose them to needless danger from without and from within, by giving the military power into their hands."

According to him, neither conversion to Christianity nor imparting of instruction to the natives was calculated to inspire them with any desire for liberty. Neither Charles Grant nor the natives of England were prompted by any motive of philanthropy or altruism to grant these measures to India. It was sordid considerations of worldly gain which led the people of England to adopt the above measures under the cloak of philanthropy.

As it seems to be the opinion of some of the gentlemen who compose the Committee of Public Instruction, that the course which they have hitherto pursued was strictly prescribed by the British Parliament in 1813, and as, if that opinion be correct, a legislative act will be necessary to warrant a change, we have thought it right to refrain from taking any part in the preparation of the adverse statements which are now before us, and to reserve what we had to say on the subject till it should come before me as a member of the Council of India.

It does not appear to me that the Act of Parliament can, by any art of construction, be made to bear the meaning which has been assigned to it. It contains nothing about the particular languages or sciences which are to be studied. A sum is set apart "for the revival and promotion of literature and the encouragement of the learned natives of India, and for the introduction and promotion of a knowledge of the sciences among the inhabitants of the British territories." It is argued, or rather taken for granted, that by literature, the Parliament can have meant only Arabic and Sanscrit literature, that they never would have given the honorable appellation of "a learned native" to a native who was familiar with the poetry of Milton, the Metaphysics of Locke, and the Physics of Newton; but that they meant to designate by that name only such persons as might have studied in the sacred books of the Hindoos all the uses of cusa-grass, and all the mysteries of absorption into the Deity.

This does not appear to be a very satisfactory interpretation. To take a parallel case; suppose that the Pacha of Egypt, a country once superior in knowledge to the nations of Europe but now sunk far below them, were to appropriate a sum or the purpose of "reviving and promoting literature, and encouraging learned natives of Egypt," would anybody infer that he meant the youth of his pachalic to give years to the study of hieroglyphics, to search into all the doctrines disguised under the fable of Osiris, and to ascertain with all possible accuracy the ritual with which cats and onions were anciently adored? Would he be justly charged with inconsistency, if, instead of employing his young subjects in deciphering obelisks, he were to order them to be instructed in the English and French languages, and in all the sciences to which those languages are the chief keys?

The words on which the supporters of the old system rely do not bear them out, and other words follow which seem to be quite decisive on the other side. This lac of rupees is set apart, not only for "reviving literature in India," the phrase on which their whole interpretation is founded, but also for "the introduction and promotion of a knowledge of the sciences among the inhabitants of the British territories,"—words which are alone sufficient to authorise all the changes for which I contend.

If the Council agree in my construction, no legislative Act will be necessary. If they differ from me, we will prepare a short Act rescinding that clause of the Charter of 1813, from which the difficulty arises.

But the admirers of the Oriental system of education have used another argument, which, if we admit it to be valid, is decisive against all change. They conceive that the public faith is pledged to the present system, and that to alter the appropriation of any of the funds which have hitherto been spent in encouragmg the study of Arabic and Sanscrit, would be down-right spoliation. It is not easy to understand by what process of reasoning they can have arrived at this conclusion.

The grants which are made from the public purse for the encouragement of literature differed in no respect from the grants which are made from the same purse for other objects of real or supposed utility. We found a sanatarium on a spot which we suppose to be healthy. Do we thereby pledge ourselves to keep a sanatarium there, if the result should not answer our expectation? We commence the erection of a pier. Is it a violation of the public faith to stop the works, if we afterwards see reason to believe that the building will be useless?

The rights of property are undoubtedly sacred. But nothing endangers those rights so much as the practice, now unhappily too common, of attributing them to things to which they do not belong. Those who would impart to abuses the sanctity of property are in truth imparting to the institution of property the unpopularity and the fragility of abuses. If the Government has given to any person a formal assurance; nay, if the Government has exdted in any person's mind a reasonable expectation that he shall receive a certain income as a teacher or a learner of Sanscrit or Arabic, we would respect that person's pecuniary interests—we would rather err on the side of liberality to individuals than suffer the public faith to be called in question.

But to talk of a Government pledging itself to teach certain languages and certain sciences, though those languages may become useless, though those sciences may be exploded, seems to me quite unmeaning. There is not a single word in any public instructions, from which it can be inferred that the Indian Government ever intended to give any pledge on this subject, or ever considered the destination of these funds as unalterably fixed. But had it been otherwise, we should have denied the competence of our predecessors to bind us by any pledge on such a subject. Suppose that a Government had in the last century enacted in the most sole,nn manner that all its subjects should, to the end of time, be inoculated for the smallpox: would that Government be bound to persist in the practice after Jenner's discovery? These promises, of which nobody claims the performance, and from which nobody can grant a release; these vested rights, which vest in nobody; this property without proprietors; this robbery, which makes nobody poorer, may be comprehended by persons of higher faculties than mine. We consider this plea merely as a set form of words, regularly used both in England and in India, in defence of every abuse for which no other plea can be set up. We hold this lac of rupees to be quite at the disposal of the Governor General in Council, for the purpose of promoting learning in India, in any way which may be thought most advisable. We hold his Lordship to be quite as free to direct that it shall no longer be employed in encouraging Arabic and Sanscrit, as he is to direct that the reward for killing tigers in Mysore shall be diminished, that no more public money shall be expended on the chanting at the cathedral.

## A CASE FOR DISTANCE EDUCATION

Universities in British India have a 145 - years old history. On the recommendations of the Wood's Despatch (1854), three Universities were established, one each in Calcutta, Madras and Bombay. These were supposed to be on the lines of London University, which then was a purely examining body, non-resident and non-teaching in its basic character. The Punjab and the Allahabad universities were incorporated on the lines of the old universities in 1882 and 1887 respectively. By 1901-02, there was a very rapid expansion of college education. As against 68 colleges in 1881-82, there were 179 affiliated colleges in 1901-02, 138 in the so-called British India, 32 in Indian princely states and 9 in Ceylon.

In 1902, during Lord Curzon's Viceroyalty, the India University Commission was appointed. The recommendations of this Commission gave birth to the Indian Universities Act of 1904. Within ten years of this Act, however, the position changed vastly and new Universities had to be started. In 1916, Banaras and Mysore came into being. Into 1917, Patna became the seat of a new university. The same year saw the emergence of the S.N.D.T. Women's University at Bombay, followed closely, the next year, by a university at Hyderabad.

In 1916, the Calcutta University started post-graduate departments where direct university involvement in teaching, transcending its affiliating or examining character, was witnessed for the first time. The Calcutta University Commission recommendation brought about a sea change in the scene of higher education in India. A number of new universities sprang up. These included Dhacca and Rangoon in 1920, Aligarh and Lucknow in 1921, Delhi in 1922, Travancore in 1937, Utkal in 1943, Sagar in 1946 and Sind as also Rajputana in 1947. This is the short history of higher education in India during the British period.

Since enrolment in various courses in inalienably related to the manpower needs in terms of the faculty strength, the projected increase in the vital sector of higher education can be easily predicted. Given 80 students per faculty member, an additional number of 68,000 new faculty members and 1,480 additional arts, science and commerce colleges will be needed every five years. Understandably, therefore, the Education Commission observed in June 1966 : "If the present rate of expansion (10% a year) is assumed to continue for the next 20 years, the total enrolment in higher education would be between 7 and 8 million by 1985-86 or more than twice the estimated requirements for manpower for national development. An economy like ours can neither have the funds to expand higher education at this scale nor the capacity to find suitable employment for the millions of graduates who come out of the educational system at this level of enrolment."

The essence of the matter is that the existing educational apparatus has reached a point of saturation beyond which it can be stretched only with danger both to the system and to the economy of the country. While on the one hand the solution may lie in faster economic growth, on the other it lies in diversification of the modes of education which at present remain deeply embedded in the traditional soil. One way out is the expansion and steady growth of non-traditional modes. "So long as the basic imbalances persist, there is no escape from containing the enrolment within available resources while stretching the resources to the utmost through part-time and correspondence or distance education". The Education

Commission in this connection observed : "An economy like ours can neither have the funds to expand higher education on this scale nor the capacity to find suitable employment for the millions of graduates who would come annually out of the educational system at this level on enrolment."

The Commission was of the view that admission to the institutions of higher education should be made selective. This view, no doubt tenable from one angle, was found unacceptable by political pundits who held the reigns of power. They opined that the development of a democracy primarily depends on the quality and quanta of education which a State can give to its citizens. Indeed, the observation had been made in almost all the five year plans.

Education is the most important single factor in achieving rapid economic development and technological progress and in creating a social order founded on the values of freedom, social justice and equal opportunity.... It has been one of the major aims of the Five Year Plans to expand and intensify the education effort so that from now on, in all branches of national life, education becomes the focal point of planned development.

This view, contrary to the Kothari Commission Report, was held by many educationists also. But the stresses and strains of a stagnant economy, which had to be further subjected to wasteful expenditure of a nature and magnitude unheard of, were factors responsible not only for the reasons behind the Kothari Commission's view, but also for others who thought in the same manner. It was also recommended that the admissions to colleges should be open only to those who 'deserved being in a college'. However, the statistics again made a nonsense of what was being thought of at the levels of planning and implementation.

It is a statistical fact that only one in every forty men of the age-group 20-25 now goes to the college. Even if the stipulated increase in the number of college-going students become a hard fact by 2000, the ratio of college-going and non-college-going students will not change. Thus every time 39 students will prefer not to go to a college, only one will do so. Will it be worthwhile or even desirable to shut the gates of colleges to some of the 25 young men or women out of a thousand of the relevant age-group in the Indian population who want to seek admission ? In an egalitarian society it becomes more of an imperative than a choice to throw open avenues of betterment to all those who desire.

Whether or not they deserve is a question which should engage attention either in a totalitarian state or in an absolute, monarchical order of things. Naturally, therefore, the Report of the Education Commission (1964-65) had given detailed comments on the equalization of educational opportunities. It has said that inequalities of educational opportunities arise in various ways which include the non-location of institutes of higher learning in rural, hilly or backward areas. While the recommendation of the Commission was "this handicap should be overcome by the widest dispersal of educational institutions, consistent with economy and efficiency," it also noted with dismay that "another cause of inequality of educational opportunity is the poverty of large sections of the population and the relative affluence of a small minority" with the result that "even in the neighbourhood of an educational institution, children from poor families do not have the same chance as those who come from, richer ones".

Among other recommendations such as the progressive abolition of fee, provision for free books and scholarship, the Commission stressed the need for the Indian universities to take upon their shoulders the task of community service, through adult education programmes, extension lectures, correspondence courses and establishment of evening institutions. About programmes of adult education, it said :

Another special responsibility of the Indian universities is to develop programmes of adult education in a big way, and to that end, evolve widespread network of part-time and correspondence courses. The universities have to provide these courses in all their faculties, not only as extramural preparation for their examinations, but also as programmes of in-service education if professional workers in all walks of life. General adult education programmes are also needed to create a unity of outlook and faith between the masses and the intelligentsia.

The concept of a university may be defined as "an organised and degree giving institution, intended for the study and advancement of higher branches of learning, self-governing in its nature, and, to a greater or lesser extent, national in scope". The university may further be defined as "a corporation or society which devotes itself to a search after knowledge for the sake of its intrinsic value". Neither of the two definitions enable it appropriate to include the 'methodology' or 'medium' of teaching to be of such intrinsic value to be incorporated in the definition of university.

However, today's university has a greater role to play than - say - the ancient universities of Takshashila and Nalanda or *stadium generale* of Bologna, Salamanca, Paris, Oxford or Prague. Let us understand the point this way. It is a national institution, hence it cannot keep itself aloof from the main currents of national life. If cannot become recluse in its 'ivory tower' of culture. It will have to bring its policies and programmes into line with social and national problems, and keep itself in contact with the needs of all sections of our population, well-educated and illiterate, workmen and labourers, artisans and farmers. In short, it should provide suitable extension programmes too. Thus, a university in Free India will have four main functions : (i) instruction, (2) research, (3) affiliation, and (4) extension.

Under 'extension', comes adult education programmes and community service. The initiation of correspondence courses is a part of the extension of the university to the doorstep of the receiver. It is the university that goes out into the community to meet its student and not the students who come to the university. Unless the university, without diverting its attention from higher goals of research and accumulation of knowledge, pays due attention to correspondence and continuing education, it is likely to end up as a study in decay. The University in essence is a living organism, and is inevitable subject to the principles of is a living organism, and is inevitable subject to the principles of evolution. It cannot remain static. To do so would be to perish.

In the USA, Carnegie Commission Reports (in thirteen volumes) suggest a blueprint for some fundamental academic reforms and reveal certain great new opportunities that lie before higher education. The major theme adumbrated therein relates to sufficient open access to opportunities for all who wish to have post-secondary education besides measures to overcome educational disadvantages due to race, sex, economic deprivation and inadequacies of prior schooling. Besides, the Open Door Community Colleges have been recommended to be spread across the nation with a view to providing for comprehensive type of education serving both academic and occupational interests. Stress has also been laid on encouraging the widespread use of the new educational technology to greatly enrich post-secondary education and to help people learn, as and when they wish, even beyond the traditional campus, to enable them to enhance their lives, professionally and academically. The new emphasis is on the development of individual human capabilities to enhance the quality of life in all its aspects and to enhance individual and social well-being.

What according to the Carnegie Commission Reports is good for U.S.A. is still better for India. An elementary proposition if the sociology of education suggests that education is an important channel to the social and economic rewards of society. It is essential to the economy and it is a large-scale and highly visible organisation. For these reasons education is controlled by the dominant groups of society so as to meet their definition of society's priorities.

It would not be far wrong to say that this is what exactly happened in the traditional system of education in India. At the university stage, more than 70 percent of the seats are taken by the top 5 percent of the social strata.

Educational development, particularly at the Secondary and higher stages, is benefiting the 'haves' more than 'have-nots'. This is a negation of social justice. The elitist bias in higher education has indeed been more marked in India than in the western countries. It was quite appropriate in the British India for educationists to think of a three-fold-significance of the work of the Universities - teaching, research and service to the society. However, the position has changed considerably since then and new pulls and pressures of an egalitarian society committed to the programme of social welfare have made it abundantly incumbent upon the universities to expand this programme. The elitist bias in higher education can indeed be minimised through universal education which should bring the university out of its ivory-tower isolation to the very door step of the student. The three-fold programme of the traditional university own includes a fourth goal - the goal of adult literacy, converting itself into continuing education for the adult in the course of time.

At present, a student at the undergraduate stage must either be admitted to a full-time basis or go without education altogether. This creates a great demand for full-time seats in colleges and leads to a deterioration of standards as the resources to provide all the seats needed are not available. Once solution to this is to keep full-time seats strictly limited on the basis of resources available and institute correspondence courses, part-time courses, evening courses etc. for those who aspire to a university degree but are not able to get admission to the regular courses. This device is being increasingly used in many countries such as the USA, the UK and Japan. The correspondence / distance education courses recently started by the many universities have proved to be a promising experiment and are producing satisfactory examination results.

Correspondence courses, in addition to the provision by Universities of regular part-time courses through evening colleges and other institutes, were visualised in the context of (a) an ever-growing number of students who want to seek higher education; (b) non-availability of seats in the existing colleges and university departments which have already reached a saturation point; (c) throwing open of opportunities of higher education to all who desire and deserve; (d) doing away with the need of opening institutions of higher education in remote corners, hilly areas and other places where a sufficient number of students may not be available and hence opening of colleges would be economically unwise; (e) providing dropouts a fresh start in their academic career if they have taken up jobs, and (f) relying mainly on the existing faculty of parent departments for designing courses and tailoring reading material for distant students thereby not adding considerably to the faculty strength.

At present, the parent universities which have established correspondence courses as multi-channel extension limbs have not taken into account the basic philosophical premise of correspondence education for giving them independence and autonomy from the inflexible course meant for regular students. There is a rigidity born of highbrow and stiff-collar attitudes. No attention has been paid, for example, to tailoring of new courses, flexible enough to have sufficient elbow room for academic reactivity, meant primarily for those 'academic orphans' who have failed to get seats in regular courses obviously on account of socio-economic compulsions. "The scope of correspondence education (in India) has remained narrow. It has got to be widened. For this purpose, new courses have to be designed keeping in mind the need of our society. Such courses should specially be linked to job requirements.

Though the aims of correspondence instruction and those of oral teaching are the same, the incitements, motives and methods differ. In oral teaching it is the established equation of the physical presence of the teacher and the taught in a given point in space and time which holds good only for that environment. In correspondence study, the equation of physical absence of oral communication makes it possible for the written and printed work to be employed as a vehicle for the dissemination of knowledge. Such a course of study transcends the physical limitations imposed on classroom teaching. It is with this end in view that governments and educational bodies have become increasingly aware of the possibilities offered by correspondence education and the record success of its programmes all over the world has strengthened the faith of educationists.

The traditional classroom teaching, as is evident, is a hang-over from the days of Plato and Aristotle. The golden age of Greek learning or the equally lustrous age of Indian scholarship in our hoary past conceptualised higher teaching as some thing fixed in the place where the wisdom-giver had his *ashrama* or his *academy*. The physical limitations of distance, scanty means of travel and lack of facilities for a number of students to work as in-scholars made it impossible for more than a selected few to sit at the feet of the master and learn. Nonetheless many flocked to the fountain-head to get wisdom. The very name *Upanishadas* (near sitting) symbolised the cadre of those who sat nearer to the wisdom-giver or the *guru* with their folded knees to imbibe his teaching. Suffice to say that but for the diligence of his pupils, the notes of Aristole's *Poetics* or Manu's code known as 'Manusmriti' and some other great works would have been lost to us. Education, throughout the intervening centuries, remained the prerogative and monopoly of those who could claim it by virtue of their higher birth or whole time life-long vocation. This indeed was true of the pre-Independence period because institutions of higher education were so few as to thwart the aspirations of many. But in spite of the great multiplication of the number of colleges as also their proliferation in the back belts of the known urban centres in India, the number of those who desire and deserve a seat in a higher study course has mounted manifold.

The socio-economic compulsions may thwart the aspirations of millions from higher education today. This particularly true of a big country like India with its large landmass and teeming population living in rural areas. As it is, universities and affiliated colleges can function only in towns and cities, away from the interior rural landscape, isolating the student community living in villages from the process of continuing education. Another socio-economic compulsion which cripples the aspirations of a large body of our youth is the seasonal employment or under-employment in a vocation which they have either inherited as their partimony (though a rigid caste-system which still holds its sway) or for the reason that they are compelled to eke out an existence solely because they are born at a certain place. Hill-folk in India, as sociologists will testify, still retain almost a racial compulsion to get their last rites at the place of their birth. The bulk of these under-employed, partly-employed or seasonally-employed young men and women cannot pursue a regular course of study in a college whereby they have to leave their village based life for a three-year sojourn in a city. It is befitting, therefore, that correspondence education should cater to this significant but ignored segment of humanity by reaching out to millions who work for their living and to those who do not have an institution in their geographical proximity.

A change in the educational technology, of which the introduction of correspondence or distance education is but a significant part, becomes imperative seen in the context of the education scene in India. This question has indeed received very little consideration at the hands of planners in the last fifty years and it was only with the advent of the nineties that a serious note was taken by policy-framers and planners to the central level while States which zealously guarded the realm of education as a State subject merely wasted time.

A typical class of one teacher attached to 60 or 80 students using textbooks is the prototype of the traditional classroom method. Absence of programmed learning though which teaching-learning apparatus could have been systematised leads to further pigmentation of an already hardened system in which formal education, apronstring-tied to degrees or diplomas linked with job-qualifications, rather than with job-requirements, become the *summum bonum* of education. Programmed learning within or on the periphery of the framework of a formal system can, by itself, reduce some of the burden. It can systematise learning considerably in many of its aspects and increase average class size of pupil-teacher ratio. Its requirements indeed would be highly professionalised manpower of programmes which would substitute for any very great improvement on the present formal education-intellectual competence of the teacher or the receptivity calibre of the pupils.

Education being a labour-intensive industry in the context of a developing country like India, a rapid technical change requires higher capital layout. Denied this, we have to fall back upon the home-made and indigenous systems which may come up to the modern level if they are given a fair deal of help and assistance. Whether it is the stress on productive work (earn while you learn - a cliche, but also a hard reality), or the fundamental change in the medium of teaching, the system has to be carried along in the changes of educational technology relevant to the Indian situation. But it is obvious that rapid technical change has to be carried out in education if, within the resources constraints that exist, much larger educational outcomes are sought to be achieved.

In a country of the magnitude of India, teacher's salaries alone amount to as much as 83.5% of the total educational outlay. Figures calculated reveal that consumption expenditure (teacher's salaries, scholarships etc.) and investment expenditure (buildings, equipment, library books, laboratories etc.) have a discordant ratio. It was found that the percentage of 'consumption expenditure' to the total university expenditure increased from about 41 in 1947-48 to 52 in 1965-66. It further jumped to 64 in 1971-72, 73 in 1974-75 and 83.5 in 1998-99, after the revision of the grades of university teachers.

Seen in real terms, the position is that idle children and idle adults who are eating and living at a level lower than the poverty line in most cases, have to be bunched together in order to bring them into the fold of education. It is, however, not they who finance education, for they obviously cannot, it is the state which has to do so. It has also been the time-honoured practice that higher the level of academic courses pursued, higher still is the public subsidy for the student trainee.

Judging from the scheme of social expenditure on education and training, a regular college student in a College of Arts or Science costs something like Rs. 401 per annum to the Government or the Management, without giving anything by way of return except that the gets a degree after completing a course and qualifying an examination. A correspondence student literally costs less than one-fourth to the Government or the Management. Since most of the institutions are run on a non-profit-no-loss basis (their surpluses are occasionally carried forward to the next year or become a source of general revenue for the University). There are normally no grants to meet deficit-on-account except where last years' surpluses are available. This position is, however, in for a welcome change in as much as many universities have now started meeting the on-account deficit of their correspondence course. A correspondence student, again, is not only not a liability on the state, but is a positive asset to the society.

However, while the fact remains that correspondence course can finance their own programmes from the revenue resources of fees from the students and do not become a dead burden on the sponsoring universities, it should not create an impression that such courses should eventually become commercial concerns running at a profit and constitute a permanent revenue source for the general budget of the university. Any part of its resources should at no time be regarded as surplus and utilised for purposes of the university unconnected with the correspondence courses institute. The surplus money should be diverted for more and more of developments and charitable purposes like earmarking substantial amounts for grant of fee concession or total exemption of fee or for scholarships to deserving but financially crippled sections of students of which there is a large number.

Correspondence distance education has come of age in India. However, no serious attempt has been made to evaluate the work and efficacy of the system in catering to the needs of thousands of students who cannot pursue a regular course of study. Institutes of Correspondence Education Centres of Distance Education have been working more or less as extension service agencies of universities which have created them. They not only teach the same courses of study but also use tools and skills which still retain their musky odour of the classroom system.

Since the examinations for regular students and correspondence students are one and the same, the students have to be given examination-oriented study programmes to make them show an equal rating with regular students. This forces designers of lessons and other reading material to fall back upon the time-honoured and time-abused system of written notes which some-times border on the realm of cheap 'digests' available in market. In some cases, even the question-answer form is used to give the correspondence students readymade material for use in the examination.

Evaluation of any educational programme which has successfully run for over a decade becomes one of the categorical imperatives of a system if the system has to look to the future needs of a changing situation. This applies to correspondence education as much as to the traditional modes of education. However, in the last decade U.G.C. committees on distance education on distance education have been able to review the working of only a few universities. Since no appreciable amount of data is available with the U.G.C. about the state of correspondence education in various universities (for the reason that the august body does not bother about a university unless funds are asked for a specific reason, and except for non-recurring investment expenditure, the universities do not hope to get anything for expansion of correspondence education), there has been no serious effort in evaluating the work of correspondence institutes. Occasional meetings and seminars or workshops organised by different universities have, however, given to the participants opportunities for exchanging views on various subjects. One thing that has emerged from this exchange of view and comparison of notes is the widespread belief that unless correspondence institutes are considered autonomous institutes, allowed to run their own courses to give their own degrees, they will continue to be looked down upon and considered 'poor relations' of their traditional counterparts. This is in spite of the fact that the system of degree linked jobs makes it imperative for a job-seeking individual to have the same degree either regular or though correspondence course of study. If an overhaul has to be done, it shall have to be done to the entire fabric of eduction. A built-in element of flexibility in course of study which can be given only through correspondence education is the need of the hour.

# 6

# Hunter Commission

In late 1881 William Hunter was appointed to conduct an Education Commission into the state of education in India. The Hunter Commission published its detailed report in 1884 and its focus was to explain the failure of Charles Wood's Education Dispatch of 1854 and to recommend reform. The principal objective of Wood's Dispatch had been to spread government and mission education to the broader population in India

However, by the early 1880s, Westminster had become concerned that this had not happened quickly enough and there was evidence that education departments in India were restricting earlier efforts of expansion. This was especially so concerning 'lower' schooling in rural areas and by the late 1870s most government funding was being directed to middle and upper schooling in the principal cities and towns of the subcontinent. Wood's clever administrative strategies had not worked well, largely because of the shock of the rebellion of 1857, government budget cuts in 1869-70 and Calcutta's policy of administrative 'decentralisation' in 1871.

By the 1880s it was clear further attempts at administrative fiat alone were not going to work. More information was needed by government from those closely involved in education in the field. This was especially so if primary education was to be rejuvenated and expanded. As a result Hunter and his commissioners embarked on a wide-ranging exercise in gathering evidence from indigenous, European and missionary stakeholders in 1882.

The hearings were conducted in the major cities across India and they lasted for two weeks in each province. A lengthy set of questions was asked of each witness and cross-examination by commissioners was permitted. Many petitions and memorials were also presented to the commissioners. This process represented the most thorough and possibly the most genuine attempt by the British in the nineteenth century to understand the failings of European education on the subcontinent.

The hearings in each province were meticulously recorded, bound and published. The separate final Hunter report of 640 pages, which draws together the information of the provincial reports, is reproduced on this site. The hand of the raj archivist is evident in the way the report is organised. The summary 'history' of education in each province before 1882 is mostly the European story and British constructs regarding caste and language pervade the report.

The powerful fiscal and legal regulation at work at the national and local level is also documented. Education for girls is discussed throughout and the dissenting views of commissioners. A second layer of recommendations targeted problems peculiar to each province. Each provincial Secretariat was then required to write a formal response about how it intended to implement reform and to report two years later about its implementation.

Hunter Commission officially known as the Indian Education Commission, 1882, was the first education commission in the history of modern India. Appointed by the Government of India, it was to review in depth, the state of education in India since wood's education despatch of 1854, and to recommend necessary measures for further progress. The other consideration, which prompted the Government to launch this enquiry, was the agitation of the missionaries, particularly in England, accusing lapses of the Government in implementing the provisions of the Despatch of 1854. Because of the great importance, which the Government attached to primary education, higher education was excluded from the Commission's purview and instead was directed to concentrate chiefly on primary education.

The Commission submitted its report in October 1883 and its thirty-six recommendations regarding primary education added a certain momentum in its slow advance. The Commission stated that 'while every branch of education can justly claim the fostering care of the State, it is desirable in the present circumstances of the country to declare the elementary education of the masses, its provision, extension and improvement, to be the part of the educational system to which the strenuous efforts of the State should now be directed in a still larger measure than herebefore'. It recommended that:

(1) 'primary education be regarded as the instruction of the masses through the vernacular in such subjects as will best fit them for their position in life, and be not necessarily regarded as a portion of instruction leading up to the University';

(2) 'an attempt should be made to secure the fullest possible provision for an extension of primary education by legislation 85';

(3) 'where indigenous schools exist, the principle of aiding and improving them be recognised as an important means of extending elementary education';

(4) 'primary education be declared to be that part of the whole system of public instruction which possesses an almost exclusive claim on local funds set apart for education, and a large claim on provincial revenues' and

(5) 'both Municipal and Local Self-Government Boards keep a separate school-fund'.

There were also recommendations for inspection and supervision, encouragement of night schools wherever possible, elasticity as regards attending hours to suit the needs of rural families, religious teaching etc. With its conviction that higher education is equally necessary for the balanced progress of a community the Hunter Commission made twenty-three recommendations regarding secondary education also. The Commission, however, recommended that while primary education should be provided without regard to the availability of local support, English Secondary Schools should ordinarily be supported on the availability of local co-operation.

## INTRODUCTION OF WESTERN EDUCATION IN INDIA

Introduced in the first half of the nineteenth century, and made the subject of a systematic policy by the colonial government from the second half, western education in India was attributed great significance and transformative powers- despite the small numbers affected by it. The colonial ruler who introduced this education anticipated all sorts of consequences, including the production of loyal brown sahibs, and the regeneration of a decayed civilization. The leaders of the Congress in its early years were fond of declaring that they and their movement were themselves outcomes of western education, and historians of nationalism have sometimes concurred, treating the rise of a nationalism as the unintended outcome of the introduction of Western education.

Education has also sometimes been attributed an important role in having widened the Hindu-Muslim divide. From the last third of the nineteenth century, the figure of the 'backward Muslim', falling behind his Hindu counterpart in educational attainments and hence in employment and influence, became a persistent theme and object of concern of the colonial government and of some Muslim organizations. Subsequently, he has figured as a controversial and contested explanation for the communal divide.

There is a certain plausibilty about attributing Hindu-Muslim divisions to educational and occupational disparities, because it accords neatly with the emergence and organizational expression of new interests and voices. One of the first Muslim organizations of the new and modern (voluntary and associational) type to be founded, the Muhammadan Educational Congress (later Conference) was founded to further the cause of Muslim education, and to some extent, as is well known, it presented itself as the Muslim counterpart and competitor to the Indian National Congress, founded the year before.

The Muslim League, founded in 1906, was the child of the Muhammadan Educational Conference, and for the first few years of its existence functioned as an adjunct to the latter. Given all this, it is tempting to explain communal separatism as partly arising out of educational inequality between the two communities; an inequality which translated into unequal access to the new sources of status and advancement, and the attempts to redress which (via organizational forms such as the Muhammadan association, and government policies treating Muslims as a distinct group) only exacerbated the communal divide.

The discourse of the backward Muslim created a new sociological category and a new identity, a new way of thinking of and being Muslim. The argument that identities such as this are 'constructed' is of course not novel, and nor is the idea that a colonial sociology was central to their construction.

### *Muslims and Education*

The conviction that Muslims were not being reached by the government sponsored western education introduced from 1835 on, and were consequently falling behind in the 'race of life', especially as measured by their representation in Government employment, was one which began to be increasingly voiced from the 1870s, though it had occasionally been heard before.

In 1871 W.W. Hunter's The Indian Musalmans was published, which stapled together three issues: alleged Muslim disaffection with British rule, a decline in the number of Muslims in government employment, and the failure of Muslims to partake of the government sponsored system of western education.

According to Hunter, Muslims were the least contented of Her Majesty's subjects. Whereas once they had been the rulers of the land, and even after being supplanted by the British, had continued to staff the courts and much of the ranks of the administration, more recently "The educated Muhammadan...sees himself practically excluded from the share of power and of the emoluments of Government which he hitherto had almost monopolized, and sees all the other advantages of life passed into the hands of the hated Hindu." Government employ had been delinked from those skills which Muslims had cultivated as part of their religion and their role as rulers of India, such as knowledge of Persian. Persian had been supplanted by the vernaculars and English as the language of courts in 1837, and more generally, western education was increasingly a requirement for government employ.

However, the secular education imparted in government and many government-aided schools and colleges, through the medium of vernaculars not known and/or despised by Muslims, and transmitted principally by Hindu teachers, was an education which according to Hunter was "opposed to the traditions, unsuited to the requirements, and hateful to the religion, of the Musalmans". Not surprisingly, Muslims had not taken to it readily or in great numbers; whereas the "pliant Hindu", who "knew no scruples" and was unperturbed by the non-religious character of the education imparted in western schools, took to western education with gusto.

The result was that Muslims ceased to supply much of the personnel for revenue collection, courts and police, as they had once done: instead, "The staff of Clerks attached to the various offices, the responsible posts in the Courts,, and even the higher offices in the Police, are recruited from the pushing

Hindu youth of the Government School". The backward Muslim was an idea which was to be embraced and articulated, in tandem with the government, by a section of the Muslim elites.

Thus Sayyid Ahmad Khan responded to Hunter's book by denying the idea that Muslims were a perpetually disaffected and potentially disloyal section of the population, but he endorsed the proposition that Muslims had fallen behind in education and hence in the 'race of life'. Indeed, this was to be the central premise behind his lifelong involvement in the Muhammadan Educational Conference and the Muhammadan Anlgo-Oriental College, both of which aimed at rectifying the situation through the voluntary efforts and labours of the Muslim community. It was the premise that underlay the 'Committee for the Better Diffusion and Advancement of Learning Among the Muhammadans of India' which Sir Sayyid helped to found in 1870, just before the publication of Hunter's book; and an essay prize competition which that Committee sponsored the following year set as its topic the reasons and remedies for the disproportionately small number of Muslim boys receiving a liberal English education, compared to Hindus.

The concern with Muslim backwardness was echoed by other Muslim organizations- in 1882 the Bengal based National Muhammadan Association presented a memorial to Ripon in which it complained that "while every community has thrived and flourished under British rule, the Muhammadans alone have declined and decayed." The idea of Muslim decline and backwardness was clung to with tenacity, as evidenced by the fact that whenever there was a suggestion that the gap was exaggerated, or alternatively that it was being closed, this was denied with some vehemence.

When a minority of the those who had submitted essays to the Select Committee denied that Muslims were in fact underrepresented in education, the Select Committee flatly declared their view to be erroneous, and pointed to the fact that "Government itself admits the fact and is in search of a remedy." The Government had indeed gave official endorsement to the idea that Muslims were falling behind in education. Mayo observed in a Viceregal Note that "There is no doubt that as regards the Muhammadan population, our present system of education is, to a great extent, a failure."

This understanding lay behind a resolution of the Government of India of August 1871, which observed that in most provinces Muslims were not availing themselves of educational opportunity in proportion to other communities, and called upon provincial administrations to suggest ways and means of redressing this imbalance. Not all the provincial administrations, then or later, concurred that there was a serious problem to be redressed, but at the highest levels the 'fact' and 'problem' of Muslim educational backwardness had been constituted as one to to which the government must seek remedies, and it was to retain this status for the next fifty years and more.

After 1871, no major enquiry into education did not address the question of the educational needs, and difficulties of Muslims; and from time to time, special enquiries were established to investigate Muslim educational backwardness. On the recommendation of the Indian Education Commission, appointed in 1883 and chaired by Hunter, all annual reports of education compiled by provincial governments were required to treat the subject of Muslim education separately, in some detail. And a series of measures were adopted at different times and in different provinces to address the problem, depending upon how it was diagnosed.

If Muslims were 'backward' (the main measure of this being their numbers in government employ), and if this was because they were backward in western education in particular, why had Muslims been tardy in embracing western education? Many explanations were offered. The Hunter Commission discussed Muslim educational backwardness at some length, and made a large number of recommendations directed at alleviating it. It also summarized many of the explanations commonly given by Muslims, before advancing its own, immensely influential, explanation:

> "some held that the absence of instruction in the tenets of their faith, and still more the injurious effects of English education in creating a disbelief in religion, were the main obstacles...Some contended that the system of education prevailing in Government Schools and Colleges corrupted the morals and manners of the pupils, and that for this reason the better classes would not subject their sons to dangerous contact. The small proportion of Muhammadan teachers in Government institutions; the unwillingness of Government educational officers to accept the counsel and co-operation of Muhammadans; numerous minor faults in the Departmental system, the comparatively small progress in real learning...the absence of friendly intercourse between Muhammadans and Englishmen; the unwillingness felt by the better born to associate with those lower in the social scale; the poverty nearly general among Muhammadans; the coldness of Government towards the race....these and a variety of other causes have been put forward at different times by members of the Muhammadan community to account for the scant appreciation which an English education has received at their hands...but a candid Muhammadan would probably admit that the most powerful factors are to be found in pride of race, a memory of bygone superiority, religious fears, and a not unnatural attachment to the learning of Islam"

According to this explanation Muslims had not become reconciled to no longer being the ruling 'race', and were therefore suspicious of the new qualifications demanded of them if they were to continue occupying even a subordinate place in the administration of the land. This reluctance was reinforced by the decline in importance of Persian and Arabic, the langauges Muslims valued for their religious and cultural significance; and by the secular nature of the education imparted in Government and Government aided schools, anathema to a community for whom an education disasscoiated from religion was to be regarded with suspicion.

Both the question of language and the secular nature of Governmental education were indeed often invoked as explanations by Muslims lamenting and explaining their backwardness. Azizul Huque traced the decline of Muslim fortunes to the introduction of a system of education in which Persian and Arabic no longer had a privileged place. "Mahomedans, fresh with the memory of the past, could not reconcile themselves to the system of liberal education"'; and once having fallen behind, "continued to be steeped in ignorance", so that, "poor in education, backward in general advancement and culture, [they]found themselves hopelessly lost in the battle for life." A "Memorial of the Central National Muhammadan Association" to Montagu and Chelmsford dated the decline from 1837, when Persian ceased to be the language of law- "

The English-educated Hindus...poured forth into every office, and completely edged the Musalmans out year by year...Before they had quite awakened to the necessity of learninmg English, they were shut out from Government employment. Thenceforth their political influence dwindled..". It was also sometimes claimed that vernacular education disadvantaged Muslims, for whom Urdu was their mother tongue, though the claim that Urdu was the vernacular of all Muslims was hotly disputed.

That the secular character of instruction in Government schools- the policy of the British government of 'religious neutrality', which disallowed religious instruction in government schools and colleges- was the cause of Muslim disinterest in western education was a reason very widely advanced. Most of the essayists and almost all the judges in the essay competition sponsored by the Select Committee, for instance, agreed that the disassociation of learning from religion in the government sponsored system was a major reason for Muslims staying away from it. The quinquennial report on education for 1927-32 attributed Muslim educational backwardness to "loyalty to their traditional learning and religion"

A Government of Bengal resolution on the question of Muslim education concluded that "The primary cause of educational backwardness has been the suspicion with which a conservative people, anxious to preserve their distinctive beliefs and customs, have hitherto regarded the general secular schools." The report of the Hornell Committee, appointed by the Bengal government to investigate Muslim educational backwardness in 1914, concluded similarly that one reason why Muslims "failed to take their proper share in the public life of Bengal" was that "They were at one time afraid that education given through the medium of English and the Vernaculars would sap the principles of Islam and for a long time they refused to take any part in the educational system of Government, thereby failing to profit by the opportunities of which the Hindus took full advantage."

### *Muslim backwardness*

Why was the question of Muslim backwardness foregrounded in this way? For, as David Lelyveld points out, "One could just as easily say that poor Bengali cultivators, who were mostly Muslim, were behind the Kayasths and Brahmins of Calcutta; that upper India was behind Bengal; that the sons of landlords lagged behind the sons of government employees." That these comparisons were not widely made was partly due, no doubt, to colonial policies of 'divide and rule', but also, according to Lelyveld, because they did "not lend themselves to ready statistical analysis".

The importance of statistics stands out, for the discourse of the 'backward Muslim' was made possible by numbers, conducted through numbers, and indeed obsessed with numbers. The issue of Muslim educational backwardness first became a public concern around the time of the first Indian census. This was in part reflected in how figures were collected for the census, and of course the census made it possible to pursue, and seek to prove or disprove, Muslim backwardness.

Religion appeared as a fundamental category in the census, one which was crosstabulated against a number of others - sex, marital status, occupation (after 1881), and education. Numbers on Muslim backwardness proliferated, as concern occasioned by it soon generated further figures.

The Hunter Commission, confirming the fact of Muslim backwardness, had recommended that in order to keep track of it and the efficacy of measures to remedy it, the annual reports on progress in education have a section specially devoted to Muslims. A Government of India resolution of July 1885 mandated this, specifically requiring information on "the position and advancement of the Muhammadan community, not merely as a whole, but with reference to local variations, in order that the Government of India may be kept fully informed as to the state and progress of this important section of the community."

It is perhaps more than a coincidence that W.W. Hunter, who was so frequent and important a contributor to the discourse of Muslim backwardness, was also, as Director General of Statistics, the compiler of many of the statistics he mobilized. It was soon after completing his labours compiling the Imperial Gazetteer that Hunter took on the role of Chairman of the Indian Education Commission. The importance of information, and of figures in particular, was not a fact recognized only by government.

The 'Aims and Objectives' of the Muhammadan Educational Congress, drafted by Sir Sayyid in 1886, observed that "people in one district...know little about the state of education of Mahomedans in other districts; they do not know whether their co-religionists outside their own local circle are going forward or backward, and what are the causes of the same." It was to enable Muslims from various parts to gain an overall picture of the state of Muslim education, and to allow them to "meet together to converse on the subject of national education, and think over the means by which it may be advanced", that an annual meeting was necessary. At this meeting, Sir Sayyid suggested, delegates from districts should "read before the meeting a statistical report of the condition of Musalmans in their districts", which would cover, among other topics, the number and type (urban and rural) of Muslims in the district, their general condition, the number and types of schools and colleges, the kind of education imparted in them, and the number of Muslims being educated in them.

The annual sessions of the Muhammadan Educational Conference did function, among other things, as an occasion to hear reports about educational status of Muslims, sometimes in mind-numbing detail. The original text of what later became an ample-sized book on the history of western education in India, and especially of the education of Muslims, was delivered as a lecture in two parts by Syed Mahmood at the eighth and ninth annual sessions at Aligarh, in 1893 and 1894; each lecture lasted five hours. The importance of collecting numbers in addition to the official statistics was stressed- in 1893 Theodore Beck, Principal of MAO College, launched a 'Mahomedan Educational Census', seeking to mobilize 'public spirited Mahomedans' to go door to door to the house of every Muslim in their locality to collect information of a type and at a level of detail not covered by the census.

This 'avalanche of numbers', to borrow a phrase from Ian Hacking, should make us wary of the idea that from the 1870s statistics simply helped to document the fact of Muslim educational backwardness. Statistics and the categories which they presuppose also sometimes 'create' reality, as historians of science remind us; and the categories of a colonial sociology, as has been observed and documented, sometimes help to constitute the phenomena which they so meticulously catalogue. The category of 'Muslim', deployed by a colonial sociology in a way which now contained within this overarching category all the differences between sharif and plebian culture, between regions and languages, helped to create an identity to be inhabited.

As Kenneth Jones writes, "the census reports provide a new conceptualization of religion as a community, an aggregate of individuals united by a formal definition and given characteristics...Religions become communities mapped, counted, and above all compared with other religious communities...each decennial census measured changes for good or ill in the state of the community and might even reshape a community through a new definition. The census thus created a concept of religious community more detailed and more exact than any existing prior to the creation of the census...created a new way of thinking about religion..."

Another feature of the discourse of Muslim backwardness worth noting was the often densely literary and charged character of its depiction and explanation of that backwardness. Hunter Commission's summary of the explanations circulating to explain this backwardness, and its own conclusion, namely that "the most powerful factors are to be found in pride of race, a memory of bygone superiority, religious fears, and a not unnatural attachment to the learning of Islam."

This explanation of the reasons for Muslim educational backwardness, with all its imagery of a ruling race fallen upon hard times, nostalgic for the past and reluctant to adapt to the new realities- the idea that "Muslims were now laggards, all sulking in their tents, dreaming of lost empires and reciting decadent poetry"- was to have a long life. The image was sometimes elaborated upon, as by a senior educational official who wrote, some twenty years after the Hunter Commission, that "the most powerful factors which have up to now held them back will probably be found in their pride of race, memory of by-gone superiority, religious fears, a deep-rooted attachment to the religion of Islam, and the question of language...When the control of the country passed from the Muhammadan conquerors to the British...[Muslims] sat apart, wrapped in the memory of their traditions and in the contemplation of their ancient literature and bygone systems of science".

Some thirty years later again, a deputation of the UP Muhammadan Educational Conference to the Governor of that province declared that a major reason why "our community has not been able to keep pace with the sister communities of the country in assimilating and profiting by the new education" was the "conservatism inherent in a community which has had an illustrious past".

The idea that the Muslim was 'conservative', in part because he was more proud of his past and less willing to compromise it in pursuit of worldly success than the opportunist Hindu was a theme popular both to government and to other writers on the subject. In a prize winning essay on education in India in 1890, F.W. Thomas attributed the reluctance of Muslims to participate in Western education "to pique", and even more so "to the character of their own instruction, which is exclusively religious." "The Muhammadan", explained Thomas, "in contrast to the supple Hindu, is extremely tenacious of the memory, the customs, and the religion of his forefathers."

An Assistant Inspector of Schools in Bengal (appointed to one of two positions especially created for Muslims as part of the ongoing experiments designed to promote Muslim education), opined that when Persian was replaced as the language of courts in 1837, "Our utilitarian fellow-countrymen, the Hindus, quick to perceive the immense advantage which a knowledge of English literature and science would give them, early devoted themselves to Western studies." By contrast, the Muslim middle classes regarded English education "as a step towards conversion to Christianity", a risk they- unlike the Hindus- were not willing to countenance.

The Calcutta University Commission similarly attributed Muslim resistance to western education when it was first introduced to India, when the main sources of English education were missionary schools, to the fact that Muslims "were less willing than the Hindus to expose their sons to missionary influences. Their pride and their religious loyalty revolted..." There is more going on here than simply the presentation of the 'fact' of Muslim backwardness. The seemingly 'empirical' issue of Muslim backwardness has in fact acquired all the density and dramaturgical possibilities of a well-rehearsed and much elaborated trope, one of a ruling race now fallen upon hard times, because of changed circumstances and their own proud and unyielding inflexibility.

The image of the backward but proud Muslim was to be repeatedly reproduced, paraphrased and elaborated, taking on a life and vitality of its own. The Muslim was in the process of being created here; a colonial statistical sociology and an imaginative trope combined to produce the 'proud but backward Muslim', a category which was available for habitation. Muslim became available as an identity in a new sort of way, a way less local and tied up with relationships of obligation, duty and affect, less tied up with a particular mileau, and a way which was defined and measured vis-a-vis other 'religious communities', particularly the Hindu.

## EDUCATION, GOVERNMENTALITY, IDENTITY

Why is it that education was an important site- not the only one, of course-where the 'backward Muslim' came to be discursively constituted? And what does it mean to say that Muslim became available as an identity in a new way, given that no one, presumably, would willingly embrace an identity as the backward Muslim?

Many Muslims, we know, received 'instruction' of different types and in different settings- maktabs, madrassas, patshalas, learning to recite quranic verses from a learned man in the mosque, and so on. These forms of instruction were a feature of Indian society up to and after the introduction of modern, western education. It was often, though not always, an explicit object of this instruction to pass on and reproduce the values and norms of communities characterized, amongst other things, by their adherence to Islam. Indeed, if 'Muslim' and 'education' are to be juxtaposed, they were more meaningfully juxtaposed here than in the education system authorised by the British.

However, the problem of 'Muslim backwardness' could not be posed from within this system of instruction. Why not? Because although the madrassa and the maktab did indeed contain a conception of Muslim as transcending the limits of class and region, it did not easily imagine this as a subset of a wider social field, one where measurements of 'backwardness' were meaningful, let alone necessary. 'Education' in pre-modern society was not predicated upon a conception of society as a horizontal field, as a population, but rather as a series of segmented and hierarchically organized domains with correspondingly different needs and practices.

Consequently, 'education' was not conceived of as the transmission of a unitary body of knowledge, but rather as different knowledges and different forms of instructions for different social groups- tols and maktabs and madrassas, maulvis teaching recitation of Quranic verses in the mosque, village patshalas providing some very basic skills, specialized patshalas providing instruction for certain professions and castes, and so on. Sometimes the same individual could be exposed to different forms of learning at different times.

An Indian official in the UP Educational Service describes the various types of instruction he underwent before joining a government school- he was taught at home by a maulvi, attended the local village patshala where he learnt to read and write Hindi, attended a mahajani patshala in Allahabad where he learnt the mahajani script, bookkeeping, drawing up bills of exchange, and writing business letters; and from there to a guru to learn Sanskrit grammar, recite the vedas and acquire other skills appropriate to a moderately well-to-do Brahmin.

There was a great variety of instruction in pre-modern India, and it is not, in fact, useful to think of all this as 'education', precisely because that can make us miss both the newness of modern education and misread, through modern lenses, the character and function of the learning which went in the home, in the maktab, tol, madrassa, pyal 'school' and patshala, and in the mosque. Within this learning, the unified social field which makes judgements about backwardness and forwardness possible, and which makes it possible to conceive of Muslim in a way which fundamentally abstracts from class, status and community and yet inserts this into a wider social field of which 'Muslim' is but a part, were lacking.

These became possible with the emergence of an education which was closely articulated with the state: which viewed the social field from the vantage point of the state, and which presupposed and sought to instantiate the new regime of power represented by the modern state. It was from the viewpoint of the modern state that the social field became conceived as a horizontal expanse, as a 'population' rather than as segmentary and hierarchically organized. This did not mean that this population was seen as homogeneous- on the contrary, it was important for the state to distinguish the different groups and elements within it, for such distinctions could be all-important to the efficacy of its policies.

It was thus from the perspective of the modern state, which governed its population rather than simply ruled over it, and therefore sought knowledge of it through statistics and the like, that it became possible to think of 'Muslim' in a new way . And it is from the standpoint of this state, concerned with questions of political and social order, national wealth, and the management of populations, that the 'backwardness' and progress of the groups it had identified, and of society as a whole, could be measured, mapped and sometimes conceived as a problem needing remedy.

Modern education was an important aspect of the emergence and functioning of this modern state. It reflected as well as articulated the states' perspective on society and on knowledge. It reflected it in that knowledge was no longer conceived as plural, as so many knowledges and arts specific to different social groups, but as a unitary body, differentiated only as to complexity and level (and thus a vertical system of education, from primary to secondary to tertiary), in principle accessible to all members of the population. It articulated it in that the practices and institutions which constitute modern schooling- a specialized place of instruction, a concern with 'order' in the classroom, the inculcation of self-discipline- were aspects of a new mode and regime of power, closely linked to the emergence of the state and new modes of governance.

From this viewpoint, the old pedagogy appeared ineffective and inefficient. The simultaneous talking of many students, collective recitation and the resultant 'babel' of voices and 'din' were frequent complaints. The complaint that indigenous education only trained the memory was standard. Lack of order and control- the inadequacies of the techniques or technology of this pedagogy- were a central element in the critique of it. Lt T.B. Jervis of the Statistical Survey complained that at indigenous schools he had observed in Bombay Presidency attendance was unpunctual and irregular, and "their holidays exceedingly numerous"; and when the pupils were in attendance, "they sit without order, or distinction into classes and leave their work when called for to assist their young companions, thereby occasioning much confusion and hindrance to others."

The Secretary to the Bengal Council of Education described his visit to an indigenous school, where the students "were squatting upon the clay floor, without order or regularity", and where it was evident that their learning was "a mere laborious effort of memory, without any attempt to expand the intellect". By contrast, a government established vernacular school across the way held its classes "in a neat, open, small puckah building", and in the activities of the students "there was an order, regularity and earnestness...not to be seen in the old indigenous schools." In these critiques we find not one set of 'educational doctrines' being opposed to another, but rather very different conceptions of knowledge, and different ways of conceiving power and order and discipline.

The critique of 'indigenous education' from the vantage point of the state and associated technologies of disciplining and producing modern subjects, could see in other forms of learning only the absence of guiding principles and order.

For this historically new form of power, one associated with the administrative territorial state and successive transformations which saw the emergence of 'population' as the subject of power, schooling was at once a means and a site, a technique and a locale, for the disciplining and regulating of population. Governmentality was about both a 'bio-politics of the population' ("propagation, births and mortality, the level of health, life expectancy and longevity...") and also new 'technologies of the self', was about the governing of people and things, and the governing of self. Education was an important aspect of governmentality because it was connected both with the production of skills and competences and other aspects of the regulation of population, and also with individual disciplining and shaping; indeed, it was where the regulation of population occurred in part precisely via the production and disciplining of subjectivities.

As such, it was also the site and the object of desire. Frequent and flowery encomiums to western education from English educated Indians, including (often especially) nationalists, were an expression of this. Surendranath Banerjea told the Congress in 1902, "The three great boons which we have received from the British Government are High Education, the gift of a Free Press and local Self-Government...But high education is the most prized, the most deeply cherished of them all."

It was the most prized, Banerjea went on to explain, because it was due to education that local self-government and a free press had been a success; or as the Deccan Sabha told Sir Montagu and Lord Chelmsford, education was the "greatest gift" of British rule because it "has helped us to avail of and assimilate the civilizing elements which accompany and distinguish your rule". If education was valued even more than rule of law, good government and all the other frequently enumerated blessings of British rule, it was recognition of the fact that education produced the subject capable of inhabiting and operating these new public spaces, and capable of deriving reward and pleasure from doing so; and expressed the desire to be that sort of subject.

A later nationalist discourse would be far more critical of British rule and also of the education system it operated. This critique too was an expression of desire, the desire for a nationalist but still modern self (one more likely, it argued, to be produced through 'national education' or the like, rather than the existing colonial pedagogy), which would be capable of inhabiting the newly opened spaces and institutions of an independent India.

Backward Muslim was the product of a colonial sociology, and that education was an important site for his production because it was tied up with the state and practices of governmentality. For a category to be produced in no way, however, guarantees that it will be embraced. Not, of course, that the backward Muslim became an object of desire; but rather that his emergence as a sociological 'fact', capable of being measured and made the subject of remedial action, generated as an object of desire the 'forward' Muslim. This 'modern' Muslim, capable of inhabiting and successfully negotiating the new world of colonial law courts, assemblies, hospitals, voluntary associations, offices and schools and colleges, was the very negation of the category of backward Muslim. He was to be all that the backward Muslim was not; conversely, the shortcomings attributed to the backward Muslim were an expression of all that was desired of and for his opposite.

However, whereas the backward Muslim was singular, the modern Muslim came in many versions, and with many projects for his founding. Sayyid Ahmad Khan desired a "new generation of Muslims who would have the knowledge, skills and values necessary to qualify them for public leadership.", and hoped that the Muslim Anglo-Oriental College would be the crucible in which this could be forged. Maulana Azad, as Congress nationalist and then as Education Minister of independent India, sought a Muslim identity which would securely anchored in Islam and Indianness, and would combine these, in part, by being 'modern'. Jinnah, himself very much the modern Muslim, had his own visions of what the Muslim who was not backward, but master of his own fortunes, needed to be like; and so on. Indeed, it was the heterogeneity of the desires, and the variety of projects which this produced, which ensured that the figure of the 'backward Muslim', whether he 'in fact' existed or not, proved to have real and lasting historical consequences.

# 7

# Sadler Commission

Calcutta University Commission, was appointed by the Government of India in 1917 to conduct an investigation into the problems connected with the university of calcutta, and to make recommendations on the question of the proposed University. Presided over by ME Sadler, Vice-Chancellor of the University of Leeds, the Commission had other distinguished members like JW Gregory, pj hartog, Professor Ramsay Muir, Sir asutosh mookerjee, WW Hornwell (the then DPI of Bengal) and Ziauddin Ahmad (a teacher of Aligarh College). G Anderson (Assistant Education Secretary of India) was to act as the Secretary of the Commission.

The Sadler Commission (as it was called) assembled during the first week of November 1917. On the advice of the President, the members toured India extensively, visiting most of the educational centres, colleges and schools and presented a monumental report to the government of India on 18 March 1919.

The report of the Commission was not unanimous; two of its members - Ziauddin Ahmad and JW Gregory - submitting their own note of dissent. Obviously, the main recommendations of the Commission dealt with almost all aspects of education covering the whole spectrum of Bengal education above the primary level. The Commission was of the opinion that no satisfactory reorganisation of the University system of Bengal would be possible unless a radical reconstruction of secondary education, upon which the University's work was dependent, could be carried into effect.

The Calcutta University Commission proposed that the duty of providing training at the intermediate stage should be transferred to the intermediate colleges. The Commission recommended the creation of a Board of Secondary and Intermediate Education empowered to appoint advisory and other committees. It opined that the majority of the Board should consist of non-official members, but would allow special representation to Hindu and Muslim interests. The Board would have a salaried President appointed by the government. The Director of Public Instruction would act as an ex-officio member.

The Commission suggested several important remedies for the eradication of the shortcomings that plagued the existing University system. It proposed the creation of a real teaching University for Calcutta and for the immediate execution of the project of establishing a University at Dhaka [Dacca]. For the proposed University at Dhaka, the Commission overturned the recommendations of the nathan commission of 1912, which practically amounted to a state institution -almost a special branch of the administration.

The Commission recommended an almost autonomous University, making it responsible for its internal administration, finance and all formal teaching. As for the lower tier of higher education, the Commission maintained that no satisfactory reorganisation of the University system of Bengal would be possible without radically reorganising secondary education system. The role of the Calcutta University would predominantly be that of a teaching University consisting of incorporated and constituent colleges. Incorporated colleges would be those which would be owned and managed by the University. The conditions of admission to the rank and privileges of a constituent college would be defined by the University statutes. The presidency college would play its role as the best equipped in the University, at least ten chairs would be held by teachers of this college and would be known as Presidency Chairs.

Among its other important recommendations were the formation of an Islamia College for Muslim students to which University Chairs or Lectureships for Arabic, Persian and Islamic History were to be attached. An orthodox Hindu College based on the Degree Department of the sanskrit college holding University Chairs or Readerships in Sanskrit and Pali was also proposed.

The Commission suggested vital reforms regarding the mofussil colleges scattered throughout Bengal. It foresaw the necessity of creating new Universities in the mofussil areas. The Commission envisaged a three-year honours course and the appointment of Professors and Readers by special Selection Committees including external experts.

For the promotion of students' health and welfare the post of a Director of Physical Training holding the rank and salary of a Professor and the formation of a Board of students' Welfare also featured in the proposals. The Commission, with a view to addressing itself to women's education urged the establishment of a special Board of Women's Education in Calcutta University. The need for professional and vocational training also received considerable attention of the Commission. The formation of the Department for Oriental Studies was the outcome. As regards medicine, the Commission recommended that the calcutta medical college and the Belgachia Medical College form constituent colleges of the teaching university. The establishment of a Dental College was also in its proposals.

The Commission recommended that the Civil Engineering College at Sibpur should form a constituent college of the University and would not only provide training in Civil Engineering but also in Electrical and Mechanical Engineering, Mining and Architecture. In order to broaden the options of commercial careers the creation of a School of Agriculture was proposed. The importance of the scientific study of vernaculars also received the attention of the Commission. Separate departments of Education were to be formed in the Universities of Dhaka and Calcutta and Education included as a subject in the Intermediate, BA and MA degree examinations. Finally the Commission stressed the need for training of manpower for the industrial development of the country. In effect, the recommendations of the Sadler Commission turned out to be crucial not only for the University of Calcutta but also in the evolution of the teaching Universities of India as a whole

In 1846 England became the first major industrial country to end its centuries-old protectionist policies against imports from other nations. This was a revolutionary move. Free trade was much more than an economic policy. It reflected the philosophy of justice and limited government. Breaking down barriers to trade helped break down the barriers of class and the obstacles to civil liberty.

For 85 years free trade reigned as England's national policy, influencing all the commercial nations of the world. Most of the credit for this radical change has gone to Richard Cobden, John Bright, and their Anti-Corn Law League based in Manchester. They spent nearly a decade of zealous effort smashing those outdated trade obstacles.

Yet there was a lesser-known advocate of free trade who made an impact: Dr. Andrew Ure (1778–1857), a lonely pioneer who promoted the great advantages of international free trade and its corollary, unregulated internal industry. Ure was a medical doctor and a chemist. He was also a passionate advocate of the factory system and its new steam-driven machines. This led him to become an important inventor. Textile mills needed a constant temperature to produce uniform goods, but this was difficult to achieve, and so the quality of products fluctuated. Ure patented the thermostat, which automatically regulated the temperature and greatly advanced the standardization of textiles.

In the 1830s Ure wrote two remarkable books, The Philosophy of Manufactures (1835) and The Cotton Manufacture of Great Britain (1836). His books drew an inescapable conclusion: by repealing protectionism, England would become vastly wealthier, benefiting all her citizens and bettering relations with her European neighbors and the United States. In contrast, protectionism caused antagonisms that often led to war. Aimed at Britain's legislators, the books were filled with charts and data on the industrial productivity of nations, wages, profits, and more. Also included were blueprints of the astonishing new machines that were creating this wealth. Ure's purpose was to make it as easy as possible for Parliament to deregulate commerce.

"Foreign competition should always be permitted, to urge on, like an impelling spring, the movements of our own industry," Ure wrote. "Free trade consists in the entire absence of restrictions of any kind on the export or import of merchandise."

Protectionism, on the other hand, was "necessarily very complex, being entangled with numberless springs and counterchecks." Encouraging one industry, like wool, he believed, put the cotton, silk, and linen manufacturers at a competitive disadvantage. This forced each branch to fight one another in Parliament for government subsidies, regulatory aid, or higher tariffs. Since human intelligence could never reconcile these opposing interests by government control, justice required that trade be left free until that "liberty be proved dangerous to others."

Free trade benefited working people dramatically by lowering the cost of consumer products. Ure gave a graphic example. When the tariff on printed calicos was repealed, it caused a tremendous celebration in Manchester, the center of the industrial revolution. The two delegates who helped push the repeal bill through Parliament were greeted like heroes with a seven-mile long procession and an inscribed silver cup.

"Repeal enables the consumer to get the articles from thirty to forty percent cheaper and females of the lower ranks to clothe themselves in handsome, comfortable dresses," Ure wrote. Repeal also freed business from the espionage of tax collectors who previously could be bribed to steal trade secrets.

## ARKWRIGHT AND COLUMBUS: VOLUNTARY AID VS. STATE GRANTS

Ure greatly admired Richard Arkwright, one of the major early innovators of the industrial revolution. His "water frame" spinning jenny, patented in 1769, was a big step toward the mass production of textiles. Ure saw Arkwright as a revolutionary, another Isaac Newton.

To demonstrate the advantages of the free market over government subsidy, Ure pointed to Arkwright's struggle to invent the water frame and Christopher Columbus's begging for funds from the Spanish throne. "It required a man of Napoleonic nerve and ambition," Ure wrote, to overcome the irregular work habits of the early mill hands and the "prejudice, passion and envy" of his rivals. Ure added that "with the cooperation of two or three spirited citizens, he [Arkwright] advanced with unfaltering energy toward his object, living in affluence and dying in honor." Arkwright, concluded Ure, "has forever affixed his name to a great era in the annals of mankind." Columbus, on the other hand, wasted years pleading with kings before obtaining only paltry equipment for his heroic expedition, Ure said. The explorer's compensation was "disgrace, poverty and prison."

Before Ure's time, most European countries had erected high trade barriers. In the seventeenth century, France's King Louis XIV wished to aggrandize commerce through royal patronage. His minister, Jean Baptiste Colbert, carried out the policy. Ure described the intent of their self-destructive folly: "Colbert's avowed purpose was to render France as much mistress of the civilized world in manufacturing as he thought her to be in military glory." To make France independent of other nations, Colbert subsidized any adventurer who would advance his scheme. Industry flourished first, then withered and died, unable to be sustained by the artificial channels scooped out by the government.

To show the degree of havoc that Colbert generated, Ure produced statistics revealing that France, in the half century between 1787 and 1830, had nearly doubled its population but its gross national product remained static.

Ure saw that the misguided policy of protection created a natural antidote: smuggling. "Governments may, indeed, enact absurd laws, but they cannot compel mankind to obey them," he wrote. "The smuggler becomes the corrector of faulty legislation, and the vindicator of human rights."

Switzerland, the only other free-trade country in Europe, verified this principle by reaping the benefits through a black-market policy by which her people received goods cheaply and then "smuggled them with advantage into the territories of her neighbors."

### *Protectionists Falsely Charge Business*

In the nineteenth century the factories were condemned as "satanic mills." The outside world was informed that the workers labored under dangerous, inhuman conditions and contracted fatal diseases. Mostly this is false. It was the propaganda of threatened aristocrats, who used any tactic, fair or foul, to thwart free-trade legislation. Ure focused on the reason for their falsehoods when he said that the hatred of factories proceeded "more from the envy of one ancient and powerful order of the Commonwealth [the aristocrats] toward another suddenly grown into political importance [the industrialists]."

The famous Sadler Commission was the main source of the fabrications. It conducted hearings in London in 1832 and produced 600 pages of damning testimony against the cotton-mill owners. The data was used by Parliament to enact the first major industrial regulations, which later led to the nationalization of some British industries.

Ure was one of the few who had the courage and insight to see the consequences of the Sadler Commission and publicly state that the charges were lies. "Of 89 witnesses, only 3 came from Manchester, although it is the largest manufacturing town . . . . [O]ne was a convicted rapist. Another would not take the oath." When the regulatory bills were debated in Parliament, Ure called them "worthy of the darkest ages."

Countering the Sadler Commission's charge of widespread disease among mill employees, Ure reproduced a letter by E. Carbutt, the physician to the Royal Manchester Infirmary, which stated that most of the doctors who testified before the commission had neither been inside a mill nor examined a factory worker. The doctors attributed scrofula (tuberculosis of the lymph nodes) and cholera epidemics to industrial labor. But this was untrue. Because of the controlled environment of the factories, Carbutt wrote, "the mill workers enjoyed a remarkable immunity."

### *Misleading Charges of Child-Labor Abuse*

The Sadler Commission concentrated its attention on child labor, knowing that the charge of abuse by "heartless capitalists" would provoke such a public outrage that restrictive legislation would be easier to pass. The commission alleged that children were beaten by the factory supervisors or owners as they worked at the "Slubbing Billy," a machine used in wool mills to reduce rolls of wool into a continuous cord. The children were called "pieceners" because they pieced together the porous rolls. Ure pointed out that the pieceners did not work for the factories but rather for independent contractors called "slubbers," or overseers. Moreover, the slubbers were often the fathers of the pieceners. Later, the pieceners' work was automated, eliminating the need for the children and hence the potential for abuse.

The commission claimed that the owners employed mostly children in the "dangerous, disease-ridden" factories; again the charge was an attempt to promote legislation to control private enterprise. And once again, Ure shattered the charge. Using data from an impartial study of 43 major cotton mills in Manchester, he demonstrated that children constituted an insignificant portion of the work force. Only 1.7 percent of mill workers were between 9 and 10 years old; 3.2 percent were 10 to 12. Together this represented a small percent of all those employed. As automation increased, these numbers declined further.

Andrew Ure performed a great service for his countrymen. Though his accomplishments have been widely ignored, it should be noted that one German exile in nineteenth-century London found Ure's work utterly distasteful. None other than Karl Marx chided Ure for his "apotheosis of large-scale industry.

# 8

# Basic Education

Basic education in schools, propagated initially by Gandhi and later modified by Gandhian educationists, its vicissitudes after independence up to its latest reincarnations in the form of work-experience and socially useful productive work (SUPW). Its attempt to introduce craftwork also failed, and for the same reasons. The same has been the fate of work-experience and SUPW, which are now largely neglected. Work-experience or SUPW can succeed only in a society that is either rapidly industrializing itself or where industrialization is largely achieved. Even in such a context, the contents must be reviewed periodically to adapt to changes taking place in production processes.

The real reason for the failure of all these ideas in India is that the Indian reality was never the (rural) society, which Gandhi had advocated, nor the socialist society that launches industrialization in a determined manner as socialized production. Advocates of basic education or its later variants appear to have realized this basic incongruity. Harking back to pre-capitalist or an incipient capitalist era, as did Gandhi and Gandhians, or borrowing uncritically from foreign models do not help in the reality of India

## PRIVATE AND PUBLIC SCHOOLING IN RURAL INDIA

In a majority of locations, it is found, private schools do not fill a "demand gap" created by the absence of a public sector school; rather, private schools are found in locations where public schools already exist. Instead of meeting unmet (quantity) demand, private schools meet "differentiated" (quality) demand, attracting children from higher-income groups or from advantaged social groups; parental educational background, too, influences schooling choice. The authors conclude that private schools "may strengthen the forces of inequity further."

## PRIVATE SCHOOLS IN BASIC EDUCATION

Schools in India come in three basic forms – Government schools, Private Aided (PA) schools (almost fully government financed but privately managed), and Private Unaided (PUA) schools. A very large increase in the number of and enrollment in PUA schools at the primary school level has been noted in recent years. This is in stark contrast to earlier trends, where PUA schools were important only at the secondary education level.

A deterioration of the "public" school system has caused PUA schools to emerge even in areas that already had government of PA schools. Citing a number of recent case studies, the authors find that in a vast majority of States, there is a deep and widespread dissatisfaction with government and PA schools. Despite the growth of the PUA sector, the enrollment in government schools, particularly in rural areas, has not changed significantly; this rules out the possibility that PUA schools are supplanting the public sector. Instead, the paper finds that enrollment in PUA schools – which tend to be very expensive relative to other types of schools – is largely confined to higher income groups.

There are also, however, found to be enormous variations in PUA fees, which enables some poor households to send at least one of their children to such schools. After reviewing a number of aspects of school quality and finances, the chapter concludes that much more research is needed to determine whether, in fact, PUA schools are, on net, more cost effective, operationally efficient, or qualitatively better than the public sector schools.

### *Household Expenditure on School Education in Rural India*

The results of NCAER's 1994 Human Development in India (HDI) survey, begins by noting that the existing literature on household expenditures on education in India is very limited, and that research on the determinants of household expenditure is "virtually non-existent."

Attempting to partially fill this research gap, there are three broad areas: the extent of household expenditure on education by different groups; the elasticity of household expenditure on education to changes in both household income and government expenditure on education; and the determinants of household expenditure on education.

### *Several important results emerge.*

- It is found, there is a complete absence of "free education" in India: regardless of a household's socio-economic background, spending on education is very substantial even at the primary school level.
- "Indirect" costs, such as books, uniforms and examination fees, are very high, even in government-run schools, including at the primary level.
- Given the absence of a well-developed credit market for education, expenditure on education is highly (and positively) correlated with income.
- Willingness to pay and "compulsion to pay" (i.e., the need to compensate for a shortage of government spending on education) are both important factors.
- Government spending and household spending on education are not substitutes, but complements: an increase

in government spending is associated with an increase in household spending (due to an "enthusiasm effect" resulting from improvements in school facilities, number of teachers, etc.); conversely, a reduction in government expenditure leads to a decline in household spending on education.

— It is found that the provision of schooling in rural habitations, or the provision of such school incentives as mid-day meals, uniforms, textbooks, etc., are both associated with increased household demand for education.

Looking at the determinants of household expenditure, Tilak finds, as might be expected, that income levels, demographic factors, occupation types, school type, and the level of village development, are all important factors.

### *What should be taught in schools? How should we teach it?*

Gardner says while there is a consensus on the importance of education there is no comparable agreement about:

The first dilemma, what should be taught? What should be highlighted: facts, information? data? If so, which of the countless facts that exist? Subject matters and disciplines—if so, which ones? Which science, which history? Should we nurture creativity, critical thinking? If there is to be an additional focus, should it be arts, technology, a social focus, a moral focus? If you try to have all of these foci, you would break the backs of students and teachers, even given a demanding elementary and secondary school curriculum. If knowledge doubles every year or two, we certainly cannot multiply the number of hours or teach twice as quickly. Some choice, some decisions about what can be omitted, is essential or the second dilemma, how should we teach? Even if we could agree on which emphases should be adopted, one must still determine whether to teach all subjects or all students the same way, or to individualize the curriculum for each student or groups of students. How much emphasis should there be on computers, distance education, various media? What should be the role of home, school, the church, the media, or extra-curricular activities? How much responsibility should be placed on teachers, students, peers, parents, the wider community? Issues of pedagogy/instruction turn out to be as vexed as issues of curriculum/content.

Gardner argues that in making these two decisions, we should depend primarily on two foundations or bases: the science of learning, and our own values as human beings living in communities, and suggests ways in which we can build on both.

### *Why do our schools stifle curiousity and kill motivation to learn?*

The government presented the free and compulsory education for children bill in the winter session, and we are celebrating as though we had beaten Australia in cricket. We should hail it as a great blow against the curse and shame of child labour. But we are not, and for good reason — we have lost faith in the state's ability to run schools. We accepted capitalism and the liberal reforms in 1991 because we thought that as the state withdrew from running businesses, it would pay attention to education. Having abandoned the socialist ideal of the equality of result, we now hoped for greater equality of opportunity, as so many capitalist societies in the West and the Far East have achieved. But this did not happen. Government schools remain unreformed, the gap persists, and a sense of betrayal mocks us. Gurcharan Das refers to an article titled Primary Education in Rural Areas published in the Economic & Political Weekly a few months ago which proposed a model that is cost-effective, self-sustaining and has reduced scope for corruption, designed mainly for rural India. The model suggests the following:

— State will provide 'free and compulsory educaiton' to all children subject to the limits of its economic capacity;

— Competition ensures better service at lower cost;

— Human beings per se are not avers to learning;

— In other words, given the proper environment, every child yearns to learn;

— The prime objective of primary level education is to help the child acquire the ability to read and write;

— The state will build schoolrooms around a playground and lease them out to qualified teacher entrepreneurs to run primary schools from standard I to IV according to the curriculum designed and approved by the state;

— The state will continue to support primary education by giving education vouchers to all eligible children which can be used to pay fees in any school of their choice run by the teacher entrepreneurs;

School vouchers were first mooted in Prime Minister Vajpayee's Economic Advisory Council in 2000. They have been tried in many countries with varying degrees of success, as a World Bank report brings out. In India, primary schools are in such distress that we owe it to ourselves to test this idea in at least one district, perhaps in Rajasthan, which is home to the best innovations in education. Through the test we will gain conviction before expanding vouchers nationwide.

We should also be prepared for opposition from vested interests — teachers, bureaucrats, and politicians don't want to become accountable. But if the test succeeds, it might revolutionise primary education just as the STD booth revolutionised telecommunication.

## A NEW MODEL FOR SCHOOLS

One area of education seems to have gotten little attention in India - the business of schooling. In contrast to the debates on the curriculum, the methods of teaching and the like, there seems to be very little debate or discussion on innovative models for schools. If we are to make any headway in providing education opportunities for everyone , we need to come up with school models that are affordable, high quality (effective) sustainable (operationally profitable) and replicable.

*What will the Local Unites (LU) do?*

The LUs will

— function like a "school" but without necessarily having to be affiliated to any board of education. They will take in students from Kindergarten through Class XII, and have the freedom to decide on their own syllabus/curriculum, educational agenda and methodologies to help children learn.

— remain small in size with a maximum of around 50students and around 8-10 staff per LU

— aim to prepare the students so that they are able to take the Class X and Class XII exams through the National Open School (or the State board exams or the ICSE exams depending on the student's choice) as private candidates and prepare them well so they can crack the exams with high scores. All LU students who pass the Open School exams can then enter the mainstream (for admission to Classes XI and XII in a conventional school if they so desire and for admission to undergraduate courses in colleges and universities as well).

— have a small computing facility with always-on broadband internet connectivity.

— get the students to create and publish local information on an ongoing basis to address the information needs of the locality. This activity will be woven around the day-to-day learning activities of the students.

— organise an educational trip each, at least once a year for students to visit another LU in another part of the country to learn about that part of the country and likewise also host some other LU's students when they visit.

The LUs should aim to be self-sustaining (i.e. not rely on grants) and generate income to meet all operational costs through:

— student fees

— information services provided to the local community by the LU's students

— returns from endowments generated through local community fund-raising

The LUs will not itself invest in infrastructure like a library, laboratories and other facilities requiring large investments. The LUs could get started with initial capital investment coming from the Center Unit (CU) or from other local sources and government funds.

*What will the CU do?*

The CU will

— function as the hub for all LUs within a geographical radius of say 10-20 km.

— invest in setting up an infrastructure facility with a well-stocked library, well equipped laboratories, teaching and learning aids and other infrastructure.

— consolidate the function of purchasing to meet the basic supply needs of all the LUs nearby to exploit economies of scale

— provide administrative support services for all LUs

— help the LUs in starting up, recruiting staff and training them on an ongoing basis and facilitate interaction between the various LUs

— provide the LUs with some basic direction on interfacing with local education authorities where/when required and helping the LUs maintain consistent quality levels.

— integrate the local information resources that each of the LUs generate into an umbrella database and commercialise the information and in turn funnel a share of the revenues back to the LUs

The LUs can book time slots at the CU to access the various facilities operated by the CU and all the LUs can make use of the CU's library. In return they will pay a monthly per student service charge to the CU. The CU-LU relationship is loosely patterned on the Central Franchisor Organisation's relationship with a franchisee outlet like in the case of an education franchise like NIIT or a restaurant franchise like McDonald's. The difference from a typical franchise model is that here the LUs will have full operational autonomy. The CU will basically provide only a supporting role.

The Central Franchisor Organisation can be set up as Trust but in practice work like a profit making company and aim to maximise revenues by providing services to the LU for a compensation and also commercialising the information resources generated by the LUs. This should help the CU remain operationally profitable and also generate some surplus to invest in better/more facilities.

*The Benefits*

— Each LU with its autonomy can innovate and experiment with different educational methodologies and practices to constantly improve the effectiveness of the educational methodologies practices. Not being affiliated to any board of education also provides the freedom to set its own curriculum and agenda.

— With the multitude of innovations and experimentation going on across all the LUs, each of the LUs can learn from the successes and the failures of the others.

— All students will be able to get into the mainstream at Class X or Class XII level - a major worry taken care of.

— A small group of about 50 students and about 8-10 staff will keep both start-up and operating costs low and also allow for small units such as this to get started quickly with minimal set-up costs.

— The students build up a local information resource as part of their education and learn much more than just the curricular content, apart from adding value to the community

— The key idea in this model is for the LUs to also generate some revenue from its activities to offset the operational costs, by providing services to the local neighbourhood

— The CUs can generate revenues for the LUs by leveraging the information resources created by the LUs at minimal cost as part of the educational activities.

— The model can work in both urban as well as rural areas

One of the most important requirements is for a whole lot of innovation and experimentation at the classroom level to constantly improve the effectiveness of the education process. The autonomy of the LUs will allow them to experiment with different educational methodologies and practices and the successful ones can emerge and proliferate with the unsuccessful ones falling by the way side. All LUs can learn from each others' successes as well as failures. This is more of a statement of an ideal without much thought having gone into the practicalty. Is this a reasonable model? Can it be made to work? Should the government be involved in something like this (by providing grants/subsidies to set up the CUs) or should it be left entirely to the private sector?

### *Not sending a child to school is now a cognisable offence in Himachal Pradesh*

Education upto class VIII has been made compulsory for all

children in Himachal Pradesh. Primary education is already compulsory in HP and HP will be the second state in North India, after Punjab, to make elementary education compulsory. Education Department sources said it would be the responsibility of both the government and parents/guardians to ensure children are educated up to Class VIII. A draft legislation has been prepared by a three-member committee comprising state Principal Secretary, Education, Law Secretary and Rural Development Secretary. The Law Department has already approved the proposed legislation.

As per the draft, a person who does not send his child to school, even after repeated persuasion, will be punished. Powers to punish the offender would vest with the village panchayat and the panchayat can impose a fine of up to Rs 500. If the child is not sent to school even after the fine, the panchayat has been empowered to refer the matter to the executive magistrate who would issue a showcause notice to immediately send the child to school. The magistrate can also impose a fine of up to Rs 2,000. And if this fails as well, the Bill allows imprisonment of one month to the offender.

Does HP have enough number of schools and teachers to be able to handle all the children in HP below 13 years of age? It's one thing to make education compulsory, but meaningless if the infrastructure is not in place to handle it. How many other states in India have made elementary education compulsory? What are their experiences? Would be interesting to find out.

### *Programme for Universal Elementary Education in India*

Basic education is a prerequisite for building a just and equitable society. It is also an established fact that basic education improves the level of human well being-especially with regard to life expectancy, infant mortality and nutritional status. Studies have shown that universal basic education is an important factor in economic growth. The Indian Constitution states: The State shall endeavour to provide, within a period of ten years from the commencement of this Constitution, for free and compulsory education to all children until they complete the age of 14 years.

In accordance with the Constitutional commitment, provision of universal elementary education has been a salient feature of national policy since independence. This resolve has been spelt out emphatically in the National Policy of Education (NPE), 1986, and Programme of Action (POA), 1992. A number of schemes and programmes were launched in pursuance of the aims embodied in the NPE and the POA. These included the Operation Blackboard, Non-formal Education, Teacher Education, Mahila Samakhya, and a number of state-specific programmes.

### *Status of Elementary Education*

India has made enormous progress in terms of increase in institutions, teachers, and students in elementary education. The number of schools in the country has increased four-fold-from 2,31,000 in 1950-51 to 9,30,000 in 1998-99, while enrolment in primary schools has jumped about six times from 19.2 million to 110 million. At the upper primary stage, the increase in the enrolment during the period was 13 times, while the enrolment of girls recorded a huge rise of 32 times. The gross enrolment ratio (GER) at the primary stage has exceeded 100 percent. Access to schools is no longer a major problem. At the primary stage, 94 percent of the country's rural population has schooling facilities within one kilometre and at the upper primary stage, it is 84 percent.

Most Children are curious, they want to know; but their eager enquiry is dulled by our pontifical assertion, our superior impatience and our casual brushing aside of their curiosity.

However, the flip side is that out of the 200 million children in the age group of 6-14 years, 59 million are not attending school. Of this, 35 million are girls. There are problems relating to dropout rates, low levels of learning achievement and low participation of girls, tribals and other disadvantaged groups. There are still at least one lakh habitations in the country without schooling facility within one kilometre. Coupled with this are various systemic issues like inadequate school infrastructure, poorly functioning schools, high teacher absenteeism, large number of teacher vacancies, poor quality of education and inadequate funds.

The central and state governments will together implement the SSA in partnership with the local governments and the community. To signify the priority attached to this programme, a National Sarva Shiksha Abhiyan Mission has been set up, with the Prime Minister and Human Resource Development Minister as the chairperson and vice-chairperson. The states have been asked to form implementation societies for UEE under the chief ministers and education ministers-many states have already done this.

The SSA will not disturb existing structures in states and districts but would only try to bring convergence in all these efforts. Functional decentralisation down to the school level will be ensured to maximise community participation. Besides recognising PRIs/ Tribal Councils in Scheduled Areas, including the Gram Sabha, the states would be encouraged to enlarge the accountability framework by involving NGOs, teachers, activists, and women's organisations.StrategiesStrategies central to the SSA include:

— Institutional reforms in the states' education systems;

— Sustainable financing through partnership between central and state governments;

— Improving mainstream educational administration through institutional development;

— Community-based monitoring with full transparency and accountability;

— Focus on girls, SC/ST, religious and linguistic minorities, disabled, and other disadvantaged groups;

— Focus on the development needs of teachers;

— Thrust on quality through improved curriculum and effective teaching methods;

— Elementary education plans in each district to reflect all investments being made in the elementary education sector.

## *Sarva Shiksha Abhiyan*

The Sarva Shiksha Abhiyan (SSA) is a historic stride towards achieving the long-cherished goal of Universalisation of Elementary Education (UEE) through a time-bound integrated approach, in partnership with the states. It aims to change the face of elementary education in the country by providing useful and quality elementary education to all children in the age-group of 6-14 years by 2010.

*Girls' Education:* A lifeline to developmentEducation is one of the most critical factors in the empowerment of women, as both the Cairo and Beijing conferences affirmed. It is also an area that offers some of the clearest examples of discrimination women suffer. Among children not attending school there are twice as many girls as boys, and among illiterate adults there are twice as many women as men.Offering girls basic education is one sure way of giving them much greater power, enabling them to make genuine choices regarding their lives. This is not a luxury.

The Convention on the Rights of the Child and the Convention on the Elimination of All Forms of Discrimination against Women establish it as a basic human right.That women might have the chance of a healthier and happier life should be reason enough for promoting girls' education. However, there are also important benefits for society as a whole. An educated woman has the skills, information and self-confidence that she needs to be a better parent, worker and citizen.An educated woman is, for example, likely to marry at a later age and have fewer children.

Cross-country studies show that an extra year of schooling for girls reduces fertility rates by 5 to 10 per cent. And the children of an educated mother are more likely to survive. In India, for example, the infant mortality rate of babies whose mothers have received primary education is half that of children whose mothers are illiterate.An educated woman will also be more productive at work and better paid. Indeed, the dividend for educational investment is often higher for women than for men. Studies from a number of countries suggest that an extra year of schooling will increase a woman's future earnings by about 15 per cent, compared to 11 per cent for a man.

The recent decades have seen significant progress in girls' education. Between 1970 and 1992, combined primary and secondary enrolment for girls in developing countries rose from 38 per cent to 68 per cent, with particularly high rates in East Asia (83 per cent) and Latin America (87 per cent). But there is still some way to go. In the least developed countries, enrolment rates are only 47 per cent at the primary level and 12 per cent at the secondary level.What would it take to improve girls' access to education? Experiences in scores of countries show the importance, among other things, of:

— Parental and community involvementFamilies and communities must be important partners of schools in developing curriculum and managing children's education.

— Low cost and flexible timetablesBasic education should be free or cost very little. Wherever possible, there should be stipends and scholarships to compensate families for the loss of girls' household labour. Also, school hours should be flexible so that children can help at home and still attend classes.

— Schools close to home, with women teachersMany parents worry about girls travelling long distances on their own. Many parents also prefer to have daughters taught by women.

— Preparation for schoolGirls do best when they receive early childhood care, which enhances their self-esteem and prepares them for school.

— Relevant curriculaLearning materials should be relevant to the girl's background and be in the local language. They should also avoid reproducing gender stereotypes.

## BASIC EDUCATION-ENSURING OPPORTUNITY FOR ALL

Canada's Official Development Assistance (CIDA), program supports sustainable development in developing countries in order to reduce poverty and to contribute to a more secure, equitable, and prosperous world. In a world of increasing interdependence, this mandate is more important than ever. Canadians recognize that their economic prosperity, the state of their environment, and their security as individuals depends on developing effective responses to the daunting challenges faced by the developing world.

For a development agency like the CIDA, responding to the challenges of global interdependence means we must work on several fronts. We need to work with developing countries to help them participate more fully in issues dealing with trade and the environment, where effective international institutions and agreements are fundamental to our self-interest. We need to strengthen our capacity to affect the policy positions adopted by the Canadian government, so that the perspectives of the developing world are brought more effectively to the table. We need to expand our cooperation with other departments to advance Canada's leadership in human security and strengthen our approach to conflict resolution, peacebuilding, and the protection of civilians.

We need to build stronger partnerships to tap into the world-class expertise within Canadian society-in non-governmental organizations, in business, and in universities and colleges-to respond to development challenges. Above all, we need to find ways of engaging developing countries more effectively as equal partners in resolving these broad global issues. Meeting these global challenges won't be possible in a world where too many countries are faced first and foremost with the reality of widespread poverty. This is why, as a first priority, we must increase our focus on providing for basic human needs. Healthy, well-nourished, and educated people are the basis of prosperous economies and stable states. Without them, development is impossible. The broader community recognizes the need to focus on responding to basic human needs. Through agreements reached at several United Nations conferences and summarized in the Organization for Economic Cooperation and Development (OECD) report, Shaping the 21st Century, there is an international consensus on the priority development challenges.

Ambitious but realizable targets have been adopted for reducing extreme poverty, providing universal primary education, eliminating gender disparity in education, reducing mortality rates for infants and mothers, providing universal access to reproductive health services, and developing strategies for sustainable development. CIDA's Social Development Priorities: A Framework for Action announces a strengthening of resources devoted to basic education, health and nutrition, HIV/AIDS, and child protection, with gender equality as an integral part of all these priority areas.

As Minister responsible for the Canadian International Development Agency, determined in the first instance to focus more of our resources on some key priority areas of social development which respond to this international consensus and meet developing country needs. CIDA's Social Development Priorities: A Framework for Action announces a strengthening of resources devoted to basic education, health and nutrition, HIV/AIDS, and child protection, with gender equality as an integral part of all these priority areas. The first three areas fall within the basic human needs category, while the fourth is part of our contribution to Canada's human-rights and human-security agenda.

## CIDA'S SOCIAL DEVELOPMENT PRIORITIES

The primary goal of the Canadian International Development Agency (CIDA) is to reduce poverty. This goal is the foundation of CIDA's policies and programming in diverse areas that range from providing for basic human needs to developing the private sector. While some believe that global poverty is only getting worse and there is very little that can be done, the experience of the past 30 years suggests otherwise.

— Between 1970 and 1997, the average life expectancy at birth for all developing countries rose from 55 to 65 years.

— Over the same period, the percentage of adults in developing countries considered literate rose from just under 50 percent to just under 70 percent, with the gap between women and men and girls and boys beginning to narrow.

— About 70 percent of the population of the developing world has access to safe water, compared to 30 percent in 1970.

— Between 1983 and 1997, the percentage of children under 12 months old who were immunized for diphtheria, pertussis, and tetanus rose from 37 to 80 percent.

While progress has been made, poverty remains the daunting challenge. Of the planet's six billion people, half live on an income of under US$2 per day, and 1.3 billion live in extreme poverty on less than US$1 per day. Most of the credit for this progress must go to developing countries themselves. However, development assistance has played a key role. Canada has made a significant international contribution to reducing the number of children born with iodine-deficiency disorders. UNICEF has credited the work of the Ottawa-based Micronutrient Initiative-funded by CIDA-with the fact that over 7 million children have been born without the mental impairments that accompany iodine deficiency. Canada's efforts to combat vitamin-A deficiency have also met with success, winning the praise of the World Health Organization. Improvements in agriculture-leading to a 20-percent rise in per-capita food production and consumption-and declining birth rates, improved basic infrastructure, and a diminished prevalence of disease can all be attributed in part to international cooperation and the assistance provided by countries like Canada.

While progress has been made, poverty remains the daunting challenge. Of the planet's six billion people, half live on an income of under US$2 per day, and 1.3 billion live in extreme poverty on less than US$1 per day. Seventy countries have average incomes below their 1980 levels. The poorest 20 percent of the world's people receive only 1.2 percent of world income. Over 30,000 children die each day from largely preventable diseases.

Poor nutrition contributes to over half these deaths. Little progress has been made in maternal health, with over half a million women dying each year of pregnancy-related causes. Over 20 percent of school-aged children are still out of school. Of this number, two-thirds are girls. AIDS is now killing more people than any other infectious disease, and HIV is outstripping efforts to contain it. Already, there are about 33 million people infected worldwide. Some 13.7 million Africans have already been claimed by the virus, leaving behind about 11 million orphans. In some countries, HIV/AIDS is reversing hard-won development progress. Perhaps most disturbing of all is the fact that children make up over half the world's poor. Within this group are tens of millions of children further marginalized by armed conflict, sexual exploitation, hazardous labour, the impact of HIV/AIDS, or life on the streets.

Over 30,000 children die each day from largely preventable diseases. Poor nutrition contributes to over half these deaths. In summary, in a world of ever-increasing wealth and technological advances, there are still far too many children who begin life malnourished, in poor health, vulnerable to preventable diseases, and without access to even basic education. In short, they never get the chance to live a productive life and rise out of poverty.

### *The need for international goals*

After 50 years of development cooperation, the international community-both developed and developing countries-agreed to and set measurable international development goals. The goals are based on agreements reached at several global United Nations conferences and summits held during the 1990s, and are outlined in the OECD's document Shaping the 21st Century. The consensus among donors and developing countries is that these targets, while ambitious, are achievable. These goals, which Canada has endorsed, are as follows:

— a reduction by one-half in the proportion of people living in extreme poverty by 2015;

— universal primary education in all countries by 2015;

— demonstrated progress towards gender equality and the empowerment of women by eliminating gender disparity in primary and secondary education by 2005;

— a reduction by two-thirds in the mortality rates for infants and children younger than five years old, and a reduction by three-quarters in maternal mortality, all by 2015;

— access through the primary health-care system to reproductive health services for all individuals of appropriate ages as soon as possible and no later than 2015; and

— the implementation of national strategies for sustainable development in all countries by 2005, to ensure that current trends in the loss of environmental resources are effectively reversed at both global and national levels by 2015.

Reaching these goals depends on the level and quality of effort by developing countries and donors themselves. A recent World Bank assessment indicates that, although progress is being made, accelerated efforts will be needed if the goals are to be achieved.

### *A need for CIDA to focus*

CIDA's current policy framework for Official Development Assistance was introduced in 1995, and appears in the foreign policy statement Canada in the World. It lists six program priorities:

— basic human needs;
— gender equality;
— infrastructure services;
— human rights, democracy, and good governance;
— private-sector development; and
— the environment.

After 50 years of development cooperation, the international community-both developed and developing countries-agreed to and set measurable international development goals... Reaching these goals depends on the level and quality of effort by developing countries and donors themselves. These priorities are in keeping with internationally agreed-upon objectives and consensus in the areas most important to development success. These priorities will therefore continue to guide CIDA programming.

However, given the enormity of poverty in the world today and the limited resources available to tackle urgent development needs, it is imperative that CIDA bring greater focus to its priorities. CIDA must strengthen its programming and focus the public's resources where the needs are the greatest, and where CIDA's assistance can make the biggest difference.

### *CIDA's Social Development Priorities*

One area that clearly meets these two criteria is basic social development-essentially, health and education. There is strong evidence that sound investments in basic health and nutrition and basic education can significantly outweigh the return on investments in other areas of programming.2 Returns are both immediate and long term. A healthy, well-nourished, and literate society can improve its members' lives and help spur broad economic growth, which in turn contributes to poverty reduction and a better future for society as a whole.

Among the many health matters that developing countries face, there is one that stands out as a challenge with far-reaching development impacts across all society: the HIV/AIDS pandemic. Despite its relative youth, AIDS is killing more people than any other infectious disease. In some countries, it threatens to overwhelm development gains and has led to a decline in life-expectancy rates.

Despite its relative youth, AIDS is killing more people than any other infectious disease. In some countries, it threatens to overwhelm development gains and has led to a decline in life-expectancy rates. Social development must reach all members of society, especially the children. Many girls and boys in the developing world are deprived of their basic rights to health and education.

Some, however, are confronted with additional challenges, such as exploitative labour, the loss of family members, sexual exploitation, life on the streets, and, in societies torn apart by war, recruitment into armed forces to fight as soldiers or to work in supportive roles. These children often exhibit great resilience in coping with the many challenges they face. However, they often lack access to health services or to appropriate forms of education. They may also experience other forms of discrimination and exploitation. For these reasons, CIDA will expand and strengthen its programming in four priority areas:

— basic education;

— basic health and nutrition;

— HIV/AIDS; and

— child protection.

CIDA will strategically invest to make a stronger contribution to human well-being, and to accelerate progress toward achieving the international development goals and strengthening the development impact of Canadians' aid investments.

CIDA will emphasize new approaches to development cooperation that will help increase the effectiveness of Canada's aid program. It will use an integrative approach to ensure that programming in one priority area also contributes to work in the other priority areas. For example, because there are clear links between HIV/AIDS and other health issues, such as tuberculosis and child health, CIDA will look for every opportunity to ensure that its programming in both these areas is mutually reinforcing and works toward complementary goals.

Education has clear impacts on health, the spread of HIV/AIDS, and the welfare of children. Educated people are better able to make sound choices on issues that affect their health and the welfare of their children. This is especially true for women and girls; education is one way of helping them overcome traditions that put them more at risk of HIV/AIDS infection. CIDA will shape its support for education in ways that contribute more broadly to the well-being of individuals and families in the developing world. By incorporating these kinds of integrated approaches, Canada will get the maximum impact from its aid dollars, and make the greatest possible contribution to social and economic progress in its partner countries.

The heart of the Framework is poverty reduction. This overarching objective will be supported by investments in other areas-not the least of which is achieving broad-based sustainable and equitable economic growth in developing countries. However, without investments in the priority areas of social development, economic growth will not reduce poverty, and many hundreds of millions of people will continue to be left behind.

### *Gender equality is a central issue*

Gender equality is essential. Women and girls typically face inadequate and unequal access to primary health care-especially reproductive health care-and to the food and nourishment they need for a healthy life. In fact, the greatest disparity between indicators of human well-being for developing countries and industrial countries is in maternal mortality rates, which are still shockingly high in many developing countries. Education is another area of gender disparity. In the developing world, male primary-school enrolment rates are double those of females.

Gender power relations and social stigma are major barriers to the control of HIV/AIDS. Among children requiring special protection, gender-based discrimination contributes to specific problems for girls, including sexual exploitation and violence. For boys in war-affected countries, problems include forced recruitment into armed forces. CIDA will ensure a strong focus on gender equality in each of the four priority areas. Specifically, it will base its work on sound gender analysis, building on opportunities to empower women and men, promote respect for human rights, and help close gender gaps that block or slow human development.

### *Human security*

For the poorest and most vulnerable members of society, poverty and lack of security are linked in a vicious circle. Breaking that cycle requires measures to promote human development through access to reliable social services. People have a right to education and health services. They have a right to live in an environment free from the deadliest diseases, exploitation, and abuse. CIDA's Social Development Priorities will help to underpin and thus bolster the Government's human-security agenda. The Framework is but one way in which CIDA can contribute to the human-security agenda. Other dimensions of CIDA's ongoing contribution include its support for governance reform, post-conflict peacebuilding, mine action, the promotion of human rights, the protection and management of environmental resources, the promotion of food security, and the promotion of gender equality.

### *Health and nutrition*

Good health is crucial to human well-being, and a healthy population is essential for development. Relatively modest investments in proper nutrition, primary health care, and water and sanitation can make enormous strides in reducing poverty and improving the quality of life. Canada has world-class expertise to offer. The Micronutrient Initiative, which is helping improve the lives of millions of children, is based in Ottawa. CIDA will build on its knowledge and strengthen its reputation in this field through a series of new initiatives. CIDA has developed a Leadership Initiative in Health and Nutrition, and is currently elaborating a health and nutrition action plan.

Relatively modest investments in proper nutrition, primary health care, and water and sanitation can make enormous strides in reducing poverty and improving the quality of life. CIDA will expand its support for international health initiatives launched by the United Nations and the World Bank, including the Roll Back Malaria campaign, the Global Stop Tuberculosis Initiative, and the Global Alliance for Vaccines and Immunization. The impact of these initiatives will be substantial. Over the next 12 months, these efforts will contribute to the eradication of polio, a significant achievement in the struggle to prevent disability. CIDA will increase its support for reproductive health care and safe- motherhood programs in ways that complement and support its increased investment in HIV/AIDS prevention. As part of the health and nutrition action plan, CIDA will also develop a water and sanitation plan that sets out cost-effective ways to accelerate access to clean water and adequate sanitation for the poor.

Despite it being a fundamental human right, millions of children, especially girls, are denied a basic education. Rapid population growth, increased poverty, persistent conflicts, and the devastating impact of the HIV/AIDS epidemic are worsening the situation and leaving an increasing number of children out of school. To help remedy this situation, CIDA will develop and implement a basic education strategy and action plan to guide its investments and programming. CIDA will also develop a Leadership Initiative for Canada in Closing the Gender Gap in Primary Education, which will build on its well-established strengths in girls' education as well as its commitment to gender equality. As part of its action plan, CIDA will also support the development and reform of the basic education sector in selected countries, strengthen the integration of locally driven education efforts within the formal education system, and improve the quality of basic education. It will also look at ways in which education can be used to help prevent the spread of HIV/AIDS.

### *Child protection*

Canada is a signatory to and leading participant in international agreements on children, the most important of which are the 1989 Convention on the Rights of the Child and the Convention on the Worst Forms of Child Labour, which Canada ratified on June 6, 2000. The Convention on the Rights of the Child lists a range of rights related to protecting girls and boys, and calls upon states to honour their obligations to uphold these rights. In the past, although children had benefited from CIDA programs in many ways, few of the programs were explicitly aimed at child protection. As CIDA expands its child-protection programming, it will focus on two specific areas: war-affected children and exploitative child labour. CIDA is now developing a child protection action plan.

CIDA will develop a multidimensional program on war-affected children that focuses on priority areas like basic education and education that empowers young people to prevent and resolve conflicts, as well as the rehabilitation of children, including access to basic health and psychosocial services. CIDA, in partnership with the Department of Foreign Affairs and International Trade, is hosting an international conference on war-affected children in September 2000 to explore strategic alliances with key partners.

CIDA will develop a multidimensional program on war-affected children that focuses on priority areas like basic education and education that empowers young people to prevent and resolve conflicts, as well as the rehabilitation of children, including access to basic health and psychosocial services. CIDA will also promote opportunities to engage youth as full participants in developing policy and programming for war-affected boys and girls.

Concerning child labour, CIDA will expand its policy dialogue with developing countries, particularly those where exploitative child labour is a serious problem. CIDA's approach to child labour is based on a distinction between hazardous work, which threatens a child's health and physical and psychosocial development, and work that is not hazardous and allows for educational opportunities. CIDA's priorities in these areas will include identifying strategies to remove children from the worst forms of child labour and prevent their being employed in these conditions in the first place, while also enhancing access to and improving education for children who continue to work in safe conditions. CIDA will also support innovative research initiatives in new areas, such as how small- and micro-enterprise development can become part of the solution to exploitative child labour at the local level.

## HEALTH AND NUTRITION - MAKING STRIDES TO IMPROVE HUMAN WELL-BEING

### *The challenge*

Good health care and proper nutrition are rights that many people in developing countries do not enjoy. According to

UNICEF, 12 million children die from preventable diseases and malnutrition each year, and about 55 million children are deficient in vitamin A, risking measles, diarrhea, blindness, or death. The number of women who die in childbirth far exceeds the number of men killed in armed conflict. Each year, some 600,000 women die giving birth, while another 15 million suffer painful, debilitating, and often permanent injuries. The number of women who die in childbirth far exceeds the number of men killed in armed conflict. Each year, some 600,000 women die giving birth, while another 15 million suffer painful, debilitating, and often permanent injuries.

Access to clean water and proper sanitation is key to improving global health. More than two decades after the 1977 UN Water Conference declared that access to safe water is a universal right, approximately 1.4 billion people still do not have it, and 2.9 billion lack adequate sanitation. Proper nutrition is an equal challenge. More than two billion people are deficient in key micronutrients, such as iron, vitamin A, and iodine. Our bodies need only small amounts of these micronutrients, but without them people are more susceptible to blindness, reduced immunity, mental impairment, and death. Poor health care and nutrition are fundamental obstacles to development and progress, but they need not be. Relatively modest investments in good health systems and proper nutrition can help improve human well-being, reduce poverty, and support sustainable economic growth.

Like the other key areas of CIDA's Social Development Priorities, health and nutrition are reflected in the international development goals outlined in the OECD's Shaping the 21st Century:

— to achieve a two-thirds reduction in the mortality rates for infants and children younger than five years old and a reduction by three-quarters in maternal mortality, all by 2015; and

— to provide access through the primary health-care system to reproductive health services for all individuals of appropriate ages as soon as possible and no later than 2015.

Access to clean water and proper sanitation is key to improving global health. More than two decades after the 1977 UN Water Conference declared that access to safe water is a universal right,approximately 1.4 billion people still do not have it,and 2.9 billion lack adequate sanitation.

The OECD has also articulated several supporting objectives:

— the eradication of polio by 2005;

— a reduction of iron-deficiency anemia in women by one-third of 1990 levels;

— the virtual elimination of iodine and vitamin-A deficiency disorders;

— a one-half reduction in the number of undernourished people by 2015;

— a reduction in measles deaths by 95 percent by 2005; and

— a 95-percent reduction in deaths due to malaria by 2005.

Quality basic education is a fundamental human right. However, many continue to be denied this right and the opportunity to enjoy its many benefits: better health, reduced fertility, higher productivity, increased family income, and the chance to live and work in dignity and make informed decisions about one's life.

In 1990, representatives of 155 governments met in Jomtien, Thailand, and committed to "meeting the basic learning needs of all." These challenges are formidable:

— More than 150 million children start primary school but drop out before they have completed five years of education and acquired basic literacy and life skills. The vast majority of these dropouts are girls.

— 125 million children of primary-school age are not in school. Two-thirds of them are girls.

— One in four adults in the developing world-nearly a billion people-are unable to read or write, and these numbers are increasing. Most are women.

Giving girls and boys in Egypt an equal chance at education In some 200 communities throughout Upper Egypt, development partners are addressing the critical problem of illiteracy among rural girls. New 'girl-friendly' community schools-built and managed by parents-are overcoming the cultural barriers that have prevented girls from attending classes taught by male teachers and located outside their villages. This innovative project is supported by the Egyptian government, CIDA, and UNICEF, as well as Canadian and Egyptian non-governmental organizations. The Toronto-based Foundation for International Training provides technical and management expertise. As a result, 4,500 girls and about 2,000 boys attend new community schools. Of the 450 pupils who have graduated so far, 400 have gone on to further education.

Poverty is the key contributing factor to educational disadvantage. Poor families must focus on survival rather than getting their children into schools. Child labour, rather than child schooling, is often an economic necessity. In cases of extreme poverty, children may contribute up to half of their family's income. Instead of being in school, poor children often enter the informal economy, working the streets as bonded labourers or in illegal, exploitative work such as prostitution.

The spread of HIV/AIDS has also forced many children out of school. Many more children are becoming orphaned-11 million in Africa-and dropping out of school. HIV/AIDS also threatens to reinforce gender disparities in education, since girls in affected households are more likely than boys to remain at home to care for the family. HIV/AIDS is also devastating the teaching profession, as teachers die or fall ill. This has profound impacts on the overall quality of educational systems. Conflict and natural disasters also have significant impacts. Schools and educational institutions have been destroyed. Costs to rebuild are often beyond the capacities of the state and civil society, leading to more children dropping out of school.

Three challenges are especially critical:

— There is limited and unequal access to educational opportunities-particularly between girls and boys. While poverty excludes both from school, girls are especially affected because "cost" is a matter of perception, and the perceived value of educating girls is often low. Many factors work against parents' natural inclination to educate their daughters. These include the high dowry costs for educated girls, the expectation that girls should care for siblings and perform domestic chores, marriage preparations and puberty rites, as well as the limited promise of future earning potential in societies where men are still seen as the principal breadwinners.

— It is not enough that children attend school. The quality of the school environment, teaching, and learning is critical. This means that it is essential to tackle the complex set of factors that contribute to the low quality of education in many developing countries: poor teacher training and lack of motivation; inadequate, unavailable, or irrelevant learning materials; unsafe, unhealthy, and unfriendly schools; and poorly planned and managed educational systems.

— Investments in education must be appropriately targeted. In many countries with the worst education indicators, education spending is directed more towards the upper levels, where participation is low and dominated by high-income groups. Often, there is weak political commitment and institutional capacity within governments to develop and implement education strategies that focus on the poor. If education systems are to be sustainable, existing resources must be effectively focused. This means investing in basic education.

Bangladesh's education miracle In Bangladesh,more than 34,000 thatched-roof schoolhouses with earthen floors and simple teaching materials have sprung up in rural villages since 1985. Established by Bangladesh 's largest non-governmental organization, the Bangladesh Rural Advancement Committee (BRAC), these schools are helping more than one million girls and boys enjoy a better life. More than 70 percent of the students enrolled are girls.Along with the Aga Khan Foundation Canada, CIDA has supported this program for 10 years. BRAC 's goal is to reach 2.4 million children by 2004.

## BASIC EDUCATION ACT 628/1998

Basic education is general education provided free of charge for entire age groups. Basic education is governed by the Basic Education Act of 1998. According to the act, comprehensive school lasts nine years and is intended for children between 7 and 16 years of age. Children are summoned to school in the year that they become seven years of age. Within certain limits, pupils are free to choose the comprehensive school of their preference. If it is impossible for a pupil to attend school for medical or other reasons, the municipality of residence is obligated to arrange corresponding instruction in some other form. The network of comprehensive schools covers the entire country. Schools offering instruction in the first six forms are particularly close-set in order to avoid unreasonably long school journeys. For school journeys exceeding five kilometres, transportation is provided free of charge.

All children permanently resident in Finland are subject to compulsory education for a period of ten years starting in the year of their seventh birthday. Compulsory education ends when the pupil reaches the age of 17 or when he or she has completed the comprehensive school syllabus, whichever occurs first. Compulsory education does not entail an obligation to attend school, but pupils may also acquire the equivalent knowledge and skills in some other way. In practice, however, almost all Finns go to nine-year comprehensive school. Teaching groups in basic education are formed according to year classes, i.e. forms. During the first six years, instruction is usually given by the class teacher, who teaches all or most subjects. Instruction in the three highest forms is usually in the form of subject teaching, where different subjects are taught by subject teachers. Basic education also includes pupil counselling and, if necessary, special education.

The basic education syllabus includes at least the following subjects: mother tongue and literature (Finnish or Swedish), the other national language (Swedish or Finnish), foreign languages, environmental studies, civics, religion or ethics, history, social studies, mathematics, physics, chemistry, biology, geography, physical education, music, visual arts, craft and home economics. The broad national objectives and the allocation of teaching time to instruction in different subjects and subject groups and to pupil counselling are decided by the Government. The National Board of Education decides on the objectives and core contents of instruction by confirming the core curriculum. Based on these, each provider of education prepares the local basic education curriculum.

### *Features of basic education*

- no admission requirements
- no charges
- a nine-year comprehensive school
- may include voluntary one-year pre-school education and voluntary one-year additional education (10th form)
- instruction arranged in schools near the home
- no official qualification; final certificate granted for acceptable completion of the syllabus
- provides eligibility for all upper secondary education
- almost all Finnish children complete comprehensive school

— interruption and repeating a form is rare

— compulsory education is fulfilled by completing the basic education syllabus

### *Development of Skills and Attitudes in Basic Education*

Popular basic education is becoming more and more elusive. This unattainability is reflected in its failure to encompass the mass of people, in its inability to offer a meaningful pedagogy and in its inability to offer to the people a satisfying instrument. It is amazing that not only a populous country such as India, or a less populous but perhaps poorer country as one would find in Africa, have failed in providing for education; but also the richer countries that boast of statistics of 'literate' populace sadly lack an educated mass of people. As a result the edifice of 'public space', built up through literacy or informative institutions of popular education and on which the pillars of democracy were mounted, is now crumbling. Ironically, neither 'science' nor 'democracy' appears to be in a position to confront this fear of death.

Naturally, for some proponents of science, it is time to redefine and rechart their enterprise. It is equally so for the proponents of democracy or of the 'public sphere'. Such a strategy may pay some dividends to those who want to save their own houses. However, it is unlikely to better the lives of the millions. Surely our central inquiry cannot set aside the question of conducting a good life - a life that can satisfy its desires through undertaking enlightened actions. If this is our concern, how the millions can be enabled to live a good life, then surely the other concerns regarding democracy, science, theory or literacy will have to abide by this centrality or will have to be given up. Is it not legitimate to pay central attention to this question of basic education, how the people can be enabled to conduct a life which assures satisfaction?

Let us begin by asking the simple question, what is primary education for? Is it in order to inculcate the 'spirit' or 'ideology' of a civilisation (compare with the bildung concept), or to empower with liberationist ideals, or to make each child 'literate'? May we, in contrast, conceive of primary education as the inculcation of an attitude (of truth) and the drilling of the student through an engagement with a productive skill? Our exploration is of this latter kind.

In basic education we argue for two basic elements. The first is drilling in a productive engagement, following authoritative rules, such that the student may acquire a skill. Second is the inculcation of an attitude of aesthetics or of truth so that the student may engage with the world later in life, fearlessly, in order to know and enjoy and also in order to secure the good for which she/he has acted. We also argue that the characteristic feature of basic education is that it is non-theoretical. The goal of non-theoretical basic education is to enable the student to undertake independent action.

Basic education is derived from two sources. The first is the tradition of imparting basic education in India. The second is some distinctive features of the Indian theoretical tradition that provide the ground and the content of basic education. This tradition of conducting basic education is rather old. We shall, however, not refer to the history of this business. We shall instead refer mostly to some necessary elements of the theoretical tradition.

### *Divides in Education*

What is the legitimate and appropriate basis of divisions in education? A 'primary' education is normally defined as the first tier of a segmented educational system. A segmented educational system is not only the result of historical evolution in Western Europe, but also cannot be defined either on grounds of epistemology or on grounds of practical reasoning or pragmatic concerns. As a result, 'primary' education, as existing in this segmented system of education, can neither lead the student to higher and more abstract levels of epistemic concerns nor can it lead the student to practical concerns of achieving the good in life.

There is now a likelihood of dividing the educational system in terms of its exposure to information and its ability to process information. The primary aim of this approach, it appears, is to replace skill and knowledge with an allegedly 'objective' status describable in terms of information. With the advent of new technologies of handling information, and also with the growing disintegration of society, this informational basis of education is gaining ground. As of now, the educational system cannot be divided on this ground; however, there remains a distinct trend in that direction. Contemporary slogans around literacy are largely reducible to such a classification. Exposure to information and logical operations on that constitute the basis of divisions. Instead of going into debates, it may be briefly pointed out that a load of information is not knowledge; neither is a skill information processing capacity.

Moreover, non-numeric information has to be described or literally narrated. Finally, a wish or a desire cannot be reduced to information. As a result, primary education cannot be defined on the basis of its exposure to information. Sadly, however, the latest pedagogy is being reduced to the provision of structured information. Organised money, a politics of hegemony and a group of opportunist ideologues are doing their best to enforce on the child this information-derived pedagogy, which cannot be justified on grounds of rationality and aesthetics.

This first tier of education can also not be defined by the primacy of a set of certain text-books. Proponents of such a view define segmentation in terms of interpretive capability. In fact, the literacy view of education also proposes this iconic relevance of textual signs. 'Texts' and 'text-books' assume a major significance. 'Connotations of civilisation' (bildung), 'conscience' and morality too are attached to this view. However, by being limited to interpretation, education here limits its capacity for inferential reasoning, its materiality and its activities on transforming the material. Moreover, such a view attaches undue importance to teleology and culture. Hence this basis of education and educational segmentation is also not acceptable.

Significantly, Indian educational practice is very different from these groups. However, in contemporary India, especially in urban areas, we have a significant presence of the institutions of these three above groups. Governmental activities are largely reducible to these practices. In contrast, the history of educational practice in India and the debates and practices on education since the middle of the nineteenth century to the middle of this one, especially the practice and thinking of Gandhi, Tagore, Bankim, Vinoba and others do provide a strikingly different alternative.

### *Basic Education is not Primary*

In this tradition of educational practice, education is divided according to whether it is theoretical or non-theoretical. Since such a division does not refer to a hierarchy, Gandhi and Tagore preferred the use of the term basic education. A non-theoretical education is basic. The goal of a basic education is to enable a student to acquire the desired fruit through his or her own actions. Basic education not only enables a person, by imparting a skill, to undertake the right action, but also provides for the meaning or the acquisition of the fruit of that action. Moreover, in case the skill fails the person's reasoning, basic education provides for the inculcation of an attitude of truth.

Non-basic or higher education is primarily theoretical. Its emphases are on inferencing, theory-defending and theory-refuting. This emphasis on theory is due to the presence of a situation of discourse. The goal of higher education is conceptualisation, defending one's own concept and refuting the opponent's concept. The instrument of these activities is theory. Basic education, in contrast, is not engaged in building, defending or refuting theories. It is therefore not in a situation of discourse. The defining characteristic of basic education is skill formation and attitude development in a non-discourse situation. This education is aimed at the conducting of a good practical life. It is thus not primary. It can be provided to any age group or to anyone having the desire to conduct a practical and pragmatic life.

Basic education too is describable in four sentences. In basic education too we require a source of injunction (the guru), an injunction (on what not to undertake), a causal description in the form of a theory, a set of names of the terms for which the action has been undertaken, and a set of rule-based integrated practices or action orientation. Indian practice in basic education puts great emphasis on some of these four types. Basic education has the goal of imparting a vidya. A vidya offers a realisable good. It is attained and maintained in a non-discourse environment.

As a result, skilled practice receives its nourishment from advances in science. The student trainee becomes responsible to others in society. In short, this approach leads to an enlightened society. What is relevant socially and politically is that education becomes widespread, nourished by the material availability in its locale; it is maintained and nurtured by the local people, trained by local skill masters. It must be mentioned that this is most environment friendly as well. Such a basic education does not ideologise young minds into a civilisational mould, nor does it moralise (through freeing the conscience) or simply inform and attempt only to make students literate. In contrast, this basic non-theoretical education skills the population, nurtures aesthetic and an attitude of truth and of cooperative work.

## IMPROVING THE EDUCATION SYSTEM

The Indian Education system is in great trouble. These are some of the faults in the current education system.

— Several children do not even get a basic elementary education.

— The rich and upper middle class in cities find decent quality private schools to send their children to. Even in these schools, getting a pass in the exams is the priority, not learning. Even these schools fail in teaching various arts, and in particular common sense to children.

— Both the private and government schools in smaller towns and villages are uniformly pathetic.

— Even if a student graduates from a higher secondary school, there are not enough colleges. The only hope left to most high school graduates is correspondence education. It is not clear to me whether one can be motivated enough to study through the correspondence course material sitting at home.

— Even if one graduates from college, the graduates are mostly unemployable, because of poor quality course material and teaching in the colleges. I have myself seen a number of such people while interviewing them for various posts in my organization.

Despite all this, several thousand young men and women have been leading our nation forward. On just about all counts of economic indicators including the foreign exchange reserves, "India is Shining". Just imagine where we can be if only we resolved our education related problems? Here are some of ideas:

1. *Compulsory free education should be made available till Class XII :* The state and central governments should completely absorb the cost of providing free education till 12th standard to every child, irrespective of caste, religion and economic status. This should cover not just school fees, but also free books, food if necessary, uniform clothing and even a place to stay if the parents cannot afford that to their children. Those with money can always opt for their favourite private school, and feed their own children.

Alternately, some rich may decide to send their children to the govt. schools.

2. *Govt. schools should be run by private entities/ entrepreneurs.* It is very doubtful if the government can manage hiring qualified teachers and provide quality education to children. Like in the USA, the government can opt for building the schools and make them available to private companies on a long-term lease, based on auction . The organization that comes up with the lowest bid and agrees to maintain the best quality education would be chosen to run each school in each locality.

We need to introduce a concept of 'education credit '. It is an amount equal to the average cost incurred in teaching a child in the privately run Govt. schools. This education credit is made available to every child. The child can either avail of the education by exchanging this credit in the Govt. owned and private operated school, or cash this portion against the fees and other costs incurred by them in a completely private school. This way, the tax payer does not have to feel miffed that his her money is used only to train OTHER children. Panchayat and municipalities must own and manage the school premises and oversee the operation of the private entities running the school.

3. All education above higher secondary school level should be primarily dealt with by private entities: If some state governments wish, they can run colleges, but it should be unnecessary. Students should be offered lenient education loans at very low interest rates.These loans are liable to be paid only after the students finish their education and find a job of their own.

That is, free education until higher secondary; but paid-for education after that. Those who can't afford to pay for this higher education get low-cost and lenient loans. This kind of comfortable educational loans are made available to students in USA.

4. *Alternate education must be promoted :* It appears to me that there is no need to teach anyone for more than 3 hours a day till the secondary school. Therefore, the available education infrastructure can be used more effectively through the shift system. Three normal shifts can be run between 0700-1000, 1100-1400 and 1500-1800 hours. An hour gap in between for the children to leave the school and the next set to walk in. In the late nights - from 1900-2200, the facility can be used to provide education to old and unlettered. Facilities such as the building, furniture, library, computer centre, laboratories and play fields can be used very efficiently in this manner.

Further, individual teachers wanting to run their own curriculum can be entertained to use the nearby school facilities including the building, furniture, library, computer centre and laboratories. Like the 'Gurukula' method, a single teacher can lead a group of about 20 children from 1st to 12th standard. The students can write their 10th and 12th standard examination under the National Institute of Open Schooling. Nothing stops those who graduate through this system from joining the available colleges. Through the 'education credit', each student can pay his teacher. This helps the teacher earn a reasonable income and the student is also guaranteed quality infrastructure.

5. *College education through correspondence system to be increased :* In each town, "Tutorial" colleges can be set up by individuals who enroll their students in a correspondence course run by authorised universities. The day-to-day training is provided by these Tutorial colleges. The timings can be flexible, allowing for the students to also find a part-time work during the day.

6. *Impediments in the way of setting up for-profit private colleges to be removed :* Today, only a charitable trust can set up educational institutions. Therefore, honest entrepreneurs interested in making profits will not get involved in spending their time and setting up quality educational institutions. The result is that only criminals

who plunder money illegally in the name of "charitable trusts" get involved in providing education, and make money through capitation fees. To stop this, the government should allow for for-profit companies to set up educational institutions.

This move will result in considerable capital flowing into the education sector. These colleges so set up will still come under the purview of the education ministries around the country, and so the government can still regulate the fees charges for providing the education. This is akin to regulating the distribution of power in Mumbai and Delhi. The government regulator only decides the upper limit cost per unit of power. Similar regulation now exists in telecom. Therefore it is perfectly possible to bring about the same in education as well.

1. Buy up the following equipment and infrastructure that every school requires and lease it to the schools

— laboratory equipment

— library books

— educational software and tools

— transport vehicles

2. Provide support services to help schools

— take care of payroll and other paperwork

— purchase any supplies and other equipment that they need, that can't be leased

— collect applications of students for public examinations and and interface between the schools and the Boards to register the applications

— train their staff

— organise extracurricular activities

— in renting out the school premises to third parties during non-school hours thereby generating some revenue for the schools

— purchase text books, note books and other supplies in bulk at discounted prices

— develop educational software and tools

— run career awareness seminars

— run various community service activities

— set up and operate school websites and share knowledge and information

IETS has completely ignored the first part, and focussed on some of the things listed in the second part above. One of the biggest challenges for a school today is to find the capital investment required for a school. The school after investing in buying some of the infrastructure often make use of what they've bought for a small fraction of the time. We think it makes a lot of sense for an educational infrastructure company to look at buying in bulk and then leasing out infrastructure to schools so that the schools don't need huge capital investment. The company can also claim depreciation benefits on the capital investment in equipment and infrastructure.

The capital expenditure costs and even many of the recurring expenditure costs can now be amortised over a larger number of students across multiple schools instead of just one school, thereby bringing in economies of scale. The infrastructure company will also be able to upgrade its equipment and facilities on a regular basis to make sure that they are contemporary and state of the art instead of being very old legacy ones.

### *Global Education Management Systems (GEMS)*

Global Education Management Systems (GEMS ), a Dubai-based school education company run by the Varkey Group plan to set up 100 schools in India and have set up an office in India. They are also expanding into the UK.

GEMS advertised in the Times of India (October 20, 2004, page XI of the recrutiment supplement) for Principals/Heads of Schools and Heads of Primary.

To complement GEMS' launch into India, we are seeking qualified education professionals to lead the development of GEMS schools; innovative individuals who are committed to high quality processes and a fresh approach to child-centric education. In return, GEMS offers professional development opportunities and attractive remuneration packages including accommodation and other benefits commensurate with an international organisation. The following positions are open for January 2005 and June 2005 for premium, international style GEMS schools that will open in April and September 2005 respectively.

# 9

# EDUCATION FOR ALL IN INDIA

The World Conference on Education for All held in March 1990 in Jomtien, Thailand, adopted a Declaration calling upon all member states and international agencies to take effective steps for achieving EFA by the year 2000. The ultimate goal affirmed by the World Declaration on Education for All is to meet the basic learning needs of all children, youth and adults. These needs were further specified as consisting of:

— Essential learning tools such as literacy, oral expression, numeracy and problem solving; and

— The basic learning content such as knowledge, skills, values and attitudes.

Towards fulfillment of these learning needs, the Declaration of EFA took a broadened vision of basic education as consisting of formal schooling, non-formal education programmes as well as open learning systems which together attempt to reach basic education to all children as well as adults. India was a signatory to the Jomtien Declaration and began working towards the EFA commitments forthwith. The World Declaration on Education For All and the 'Framework for Action to meet Basic Learning Needs' were considered by the Central Advisory Board of Education (CABE) which is the highest education policy making body in the country, in 1991 and 1992. The CABE recognized that the World Declaration on EFA was, from the national point of view, a reaffirmation of the policy orientation given to elementary education in the National Policy on Education (NPE) in 1986.

The CABE endorsed the Declaration and called for further strengthening of the processes initiated through the NPE -1986. The CABE highlighted the need for increased financial inputs to achieve the goals of EFA and formulated a broad operational framework for receiving financial assistance from international agencies for undertaking large-scale projects to achieve the goals of EFA. Further, the CABE emphasized that the additional resources generated through external assistance should be utilized for educational reconstruction, which should go beyond the conventional measures such as opening new schools, construction of school building and appointing teachers.

The goals, targets and strategies enunciated in the National Policy on Education and endorsed by the CABE have then been incorporated into successive Five Year Plan proposals. The goals were pursued during the Eighth Five Year Plan which also involved the launching of major projects supported by external funding and the literacy campaigns under the auspices of the National Literacy Mission. They are further being followed up during the current Ninth Five-Year Plan operating from 1997 to 2002. Thus, the goals of EFA have been incorporated into the national plan framework which in turn guides all developmental actions at the state level.

**ECCE**

Early childhood care and education (ECCE) is considered a significant input to compensate for early environmental deprivations at home by providing a stimulating environment to the children. While on one hand, it is expected to provide the necessary maturational and experiential readiness to the child for meeting the demands of the primary curriculum, it also affects positively the enrolment and retention of girls in primary schools by providing substitute care facility for younger siblings. Envisaged as a holistic input fostering health, psychological and nutritional development, the policy emphasized the significance of making it play based while cautioning against the danger of reducing it to the teaching of three R's i.e., reading, writing and arithmetic. The holistic and integrated concept of ECCE clearly represents this spirit.

Though programmes of early childhood care have been under implementation on a large scale though the programme of Integrated Child Development Scheme (ICDS), efforts to integrate early childhood education into activities of these centres and to extend institutionalised educational facilities for children in the pre-school age group have begun only during recent years. Pre-school education in urban areas which is fairly wide spread and is continuously expanding is largely in the hands of the private sector without much supervison or support from the government. Considering the magnitude of resources needed to reach out to all children in this age group, the target set for the sector has been modest. It is envisaged that the network of early childhood centres would expand to two million centres and cover about 70 per cent children in the pre-school age group by the year 2000.

## UNIVERSALISATION OF ELEMENTARY EDUCATION (UEE)

Universalisation of elementary education (UEE) has been accepted as a national goal since 1950. The Directive Principles of the Constitution of India envisage provision of free and compulsory elementary education to all children upto the age of 14 years. The overall goal in this regard is to provide free and compulsory education of satisfactory quality to all children. It is significant to note that the National Policy on Education defines universal elementary education in a broad framework. It made a significant in emphasis from enrollment to participation and retention. The goal of universal elementary education was enlarged to include provision of education of a satisfactory quality to all children.

The Elementary Education system in India is one of the largest in the world. There has been massive expansion of Elementary Education (EE) during the post- independence period, however, the goal of Universalisation of Elementary Education (UEE) is yet to be achieved. Though considerable progress has been made towards achieving the target of EFA as indicated by the overall figures, more rigorous and sustained efforts are required to universalize elementary education. A major bottleneck in this direction has been the persistence of regional and sectional disparities. The policy goal, therefore, has been to intensify the efforts to reach primary education to such deprived sections of population. Specifically, the goals of EFA with respect to universal access focus on:

- Universal enrolment of all children including girls, disabled children and children belonging to SC and ST in primary classes and provision of upper primary education for them.
- Provision of NFE for school drop-outs, working children and girls who cannot attend formal schools.

The country has made significant progress in terms of provision of access to basic education. Recent surveys show that more than 95 per cent population has access to primary education within a distance of one km. Overall enrollment figures have also shown a massive increase. However, the number of children who participate in schooling regularly and complete the first cycle of education still needs to be improved substantially. For a number of reasons, many children initially enrolled in the school do not complete their primary schooling. Here again, there are wide disparities among different states; for instance, while almost all children enrolled in the initial classes of the primary school complete at least 4-5 years of schooling in the states of Kerala, Goa and Mizoram, the figures of school dropout in certain other states continue to be very high. Thus, the policies have reiterated reduction in the number of dropouts as an important goal:

> Reduction of drop-out rates between classes I-V and classes I-VIII from the existing rate of 36.3 per cent and 56.5 per cent in 1994 to 20 per cent and 40 per cent respectively. These rates were set as targets to be achieved during the Ninth Five-Year Plan period (1997-2002).

Universal access, universal retention and universal achievements are broad parameters to achieve UEE. Considering the magnitude and the complexity of the problem, meticulously formulated strategies have been adopted in the form of Operation Blackboard (OB), Non-Formal Education (NFE), Teacher Education (TE). District Primary Education Programme (DPEP) to address the specific problem areas, gender and regional disparities. Special focus has been laid on the access to education for millions of girls and working children, who cannot participate in the school system on account of socio-economic compulsions. These segments largely constitute girls, SCs/STs and the other deprived sections of the society.

Unattractive school environment, unsatisfactory conditions of buildings and insufficiency of instructional material acting as major demotivating factors for enrolment and retention of children in primary schools called for a drive called Operation Blackboard for substantial improvement in the infrastructural facilities at the primary stage. The physical targets for the Eighth Plan were achieved with remarkable success. The scheme has been expanded to cover upper primary schools as well. A national evaluation of the scheme has been entrusted to NIEPA recently. A large and systematic programme of Non-Formal Education (NFE), which is an integral component of the strategies to achieve UEE has been taken up to cover children who cannot attend formal school due to socio-economic compulsions.

Girls, working children, dropouts and those belonging to SC/ST and deprived sections of the society stand to benefit from this approach. NFE has enough flexibility to provide education at their doorsteps to enable them to learn at their own pace and convenience. The major challenge is for NFE to maintain quality comparable with the formal system. The National Programme of Nutritional Support to Primary Education is intended to boost enrolment, attendance and retention in primary schools and also to supplement nutritional requirements of children.

The scheme covers the children studying in primary classes in the Government, local body and Government- aided schools throughout the country. Total beneficiaries are estimated to be 9.75 crores in nearly 6.88 lakh primary schools in the country during the period under report. The District Primary Education Programme provides special thrust to achieve Universalisation of Primary Education (UPE) through decentralised planning and management, disaggregated target setting, community mobilisation, district and population specific planning.

The programme mainly aims at providing access to primary education for all children, reducing dropout rates to less than 10 per cent, increasing level of achievements of primary students by at least 25 per cent and reducing the gap among gender social groups to less than 5 per cent catering to the needs of special target groups like tribals, SCs, women and other marginalised sections. The Teacher Education scheme envisages setting up of DIETs in each district to provide academic and resource support to elementary education teachers and non-formal and adult education instructors. It also envisages establishment of CTEs/IASEs to organise preservice and in-service training for secondary teachers and provide extension and resource support service to secondary schools.

IASEs are expected to conduct programmes for preparation of elementary teacher educators-, conduct in-service training for elementary and secondary teacher educators and Principals of secondary schools; engage in advanced level fundamental and applied research especially of inter-disciplinary nature; and provide academic guidance to DIETs and support services to CTEs. 448 DIETs, 76 CTEs and 34 IASEs have been established under the scheme till the end of January 1999. Some area-specific externally aided projects in the field of primary education are also being implemented. Shiksha Karmi Project (SKP) aims at universalisation and qualitative improvement to primary education in remote and socioeconomic backward villages of Rajasthan with focus on girls. It identifies teacher absenteeism as a major problem in primary schools and in inaccessible areas.

Mobilisation and participation of the community to improve primary schools is an important feature of the project. Lok jumbish is an innovative people's movement for education. Bihar Education Project (BEP) is meant to provide education for all through people's mobilisation and participation. It is a basic education project which aims at bringing out qualitative improvement in the educational system and overall socio-cultural situation in Bihar.

Although special programmes have been taken up to improve upon specific deficiencies in the educational system, no strategies can succeed in achieving UEE without specifically addressing its gender and regional dimensions. Gender disparities are conspicuous in India. Recognising this gender bias, most programmes have specific components for ameliorating the condition of the girl child.

## IMPACT OF NATIONAL POLICY ON EDUCATION

The National Policy on Education - 1986 emphasizes the importance of giving special attention to quality aspects of primary education. Several policy guidelines have been formulated for this purpose.

Improved quality of school provision: With the expansion of the school system, a systematic exercise has been carried out to determine basic norms for provision - physical, human as well as academic, in each school. It is envisaged that this should help improve the quality of provisions significantly. These norms act as the guiding principle for creating additional schooling facilities for primary education.

*Focus on learning outcomes*: Alongside provision of improved facilities in the school policy makers have also focussed their attention on the learning levels attained by children who attend schools. A National Committee of experts set up by the Government of India in early nineties evolved a framework of "Minimum Levels of Learning"" to be attained by every student undergoing primary education. It is envisaged that this would act as a guide for the teachers in ensuring that the teaching-learning process is effective and that expected learning levels are attained by all children.

*Teacher Capacity Building*: Critical role of the teachers in ensuring quality education has also come into sharper focus. As in case of infrastructure, massive expansion of the system has also influenced the quality of teachers and the support system available for guiding them in their work. One of the major policy interventions in the last decade is to make institutional arrangements at district and sub-district levels for inservice education of primary teachers. The emphasis is on decentralizing the training arrangement and providing guidance and support to teachers on a continuous basis.

### Secondary education

Secondary Education which serves as a bridge between primary and higher education serves a step towards preparation for higher and professional education. Socio-economic imperatives and initiatives taken during the Eighth Plan to provide learning facilities to school- going children up to elementary stage, has necessitated that the perspective for Secondary Education Sector in the Ninth Plan would be, besides vocationalisation, substantial expansion of infrastructure, innovation in harnessing technology for improved teaching/ learning and quality upgradation.

This visualises the maximum expansion requirements of the secondary education infrastructure during the Ninth Plan without diluting the quality. The schemes initiated during the

Eighth Plan such as Vocationalisation, Improvement of Science Education, Computer Literacy, Educational Technology, special interventions for girls, Integrated Education of Disabled Children, etc. have been made fully functional during the Ninth Plan. Besides, applications of available communication technology to promote school education at all levels and in all areas figure prominently in the deficient and remote areas. For this, open learning system (Distance Education) has been emphasised.

The key issues in Secondary Education apart from access are quality, relevance, modernisation and diversification. The norms developed by the NCERT for standards of minimum facilities for schools are being provided. The concept of Minimum Levels of Learning is being extended to the secondary stage as well. Emphasis has been laid on programme in Value Education, Population Education and various newly emerging concerns such as Human Rights, Adolescence Education. Greater diversification and flexibility, proper education materials, capacity building in the schools to gradually eliminate the domination exercised by the public examinations are some of the aspects of modernisation of curriculum.

The NCERT continues to play a nodal role in evaluation of textbooks from the standpoint of national integration and incorporation of core elements outlined in the National Policy on Education (NPE). More transparency and authenticity is being visualised as a part of examination reforms. Teacher Education is being strengthened to provide quality pre-service and in-service training to secondary school teachers to update their competency and professional skills. The thrust on Vocational Education is continuing to meet the increasing demand of skilled manpower in the context of changing economic environment with globalisation and consequent induction of new and emerging technologies.

Given the complexity and magnitude of the task a multi-pronged strategy has been adopted with multiple entry and exit options to vocational students. Almost 35 per cent of children drop out before reaching Class V and over 50 per cent reach Class VIII Finally, only about 6 per cent reach the degree level and hence, intervention at each stage in the form of vocational education is necessary to enable the potential dropouts with some skills. The programme is being strengthened and expanded. Kendriya Vidyalayas and Navodaya Vidyalayas are promoting excellence in education with a national identity throughout the country. Navodaya Vidyalayas have an added objective to provide opportunities to talented rural children particularly girls of deprived sections of the society. These schools are intended to become pace-setters of a nationwide programme of school improvement with innovation and experimentation.

The National Open School has been providing flexible life-related education through distance education mode to deprived and socio-economically backward sections of the society in the remotest parts of the country. It designs, develops and offers flexible courses at secondary/ senior secondary stage and is equipped to meet the growing demand of those who find it difficult to attend full time school and the working people, who could not complete secondary stage. The major beneficiaries are women, SCs/STs; and other deprived sections of the society. The technological advancement has increased its potential substantially.

The National Council of Educational Research and Training (NCERT) continues to provide major resource support to school education in the form of various experimental innovative programmes; to diversify and make qualitative improvements in secondary education and also reducing the burden of school bag. The NCERT textbooks have the unique distinction of being attractive and inexpensive.

### *Vocational education*

The National Policy on Education (NPE), 1986 accords high priority to vocationalisation of education at the secondary stage. The NPE as revised in 1992 set the target of achieving diversion of 10 per cent of the students at the +2 level to the vocational stream in 1995 and 25 per cent by 2000 A.D. Accordingly, a Centrally-sponsored scheme of Vocationalisation of Secondary Education was launched in February 1998. Under the scheme, substantial financial assistance is provided to states/UTs for introduction of vocational courses in classes XI and XII of the school system.

So far, all states/UTs except Lakshadweep have joined the programme. In all 18,719 vocational courses have been sanctioned in 6,486 schools all over the country thereby creating capacity for diversion of about 9.35 lakh students to the vocational stream which is 11 per cent of the enrolment at the +2 stage.

About 150 vocational courses have been introduced in six major areas, *i.e.*, agriculture, business and commerce, engineering and technology, health and paramedical, home science, humanities and others and 94 vocational courses have been notified under the Apprenticeship Act.

Collaborative arrangement has been made with National Institute of Fashion Technology (NIFT) for introducing of courses in Fashion and Garment making in three, identified schools at Ludhiana (Punjab), Vizag (AP) and Indore (MP). Students have also been admitted to the courses in these schools. Under the scheme 75 voluntary organisations have also been provided assistance so far for conducting innovative and non-formal programmes of vocational education.

A centrally sponsored Scheme of pre-vocational education was launched in 1993-94 with the objective of imparting simple marketable skills to the students of classes IX and X. So far assistance has been provided to 11 states/UTs for introduction of pre-vocational courses in 652 schools.

A joint Council for Vocational Education (JCVE) was set up in April 1990 for policy formulation and coordination at the national level. A Standing Committee of JCVE was also set up in April 1990 to follow up on the decisions taken by the

JCVE. A Central Institute of Vocational Education (CIVE) was set up at Bhopal in July 1993 to provide technical and academic support to the vocational education programme in the country. The Institute has also been identified as a UNEVOC Centre and considerable network has been established with other countries of the region.

During the Ninth Plan it is proposed to start a pilot project in collaboration with CBSE and FICCI/CII which is to be entirely industry driven. To start with 100 schools across the country are to be covered in a phased manner.

### *Education for disabled children*

The scheme of Integrated Education for Disabled Children (IEDC) was launched in 1974 to provide educational opportunities for disabled children in the general school system so as to facilitate their retention and integration in the system. Under the scheme 100 Per cent financial assistance is provided for education of disabled children which includes assistance towards books and stationery uniforms, transport allowance, readers allowance for blind children, escort allowance for severely handicapped children, boarding and lodging charges for disabled children residing in hostels.

Besides this, assistance is given for setting up and equipping resource rooms with aids and assistive devices, salary of resource teachers, salary of helpers/attendants, funds for survey to identify disabled children, assessment of these children, purchase and production of instructional material, training and orientation of resource teachers, funds for making modifications in the school buildings and the toilets and salary of an Administrative Cell at the State level to implement and monitor the programme.

At present, the IEDC scheme is being implemented in 26 States/UTs through 14,905 schools. With the coming into force (w.e.f. 7 February 1996) of the Persons with Disabilities Act, 1995, there is now a statutory responsibility on the Central and

State government to ensure that all disabled children receive free education in an appropriate environment till the age of 18 years.

Against the allocation of Rs. 21.20 crore, expenditure during the Eighth Plan was Rs 26.12 crore. For the Ninth Plan period (1997-2002), the scheme of IEDC has projected a budget of Rs 100 crore with Rs 13 crore each for the year 1997-98 and 1998-99. The population of disabled children was estimated at 16.15 million whereas the coverage is low. A concerted and coordinated effort is proposed during the Ninth Plan to strengthen the outreach, impact and coverage under the IEDC programme.

### *Boarding and hostel facilities for girl students*

In order to implement the recommendations in POA-1992 for formulating a special enabling plan to ensure increase in enrolment of girls in secondary education and the NPE directive for encouraging NGO participation in education, the scheme for strengthening of boarding and hostel facilities for girl students of secondary and higher secondary schools was launched during the Eighth Plan period. Under the scheme, financial assistance is given to the eligible voluntary organisations, to improve the enrolment of adolescent girls belonging to rural areas and weaker sections in the secondary and higher secondary schools as under:

— A one-time grant at the rate of Rs 1,500 per girl boarder for purchase of furniture (including beds) and utensils and provision of basic recreational aids, particularly material for sports and games, reading room equipments and books; and

— Rs 5,000 per annum per girl boarder for food and salary of cook and warden if the hostel/boarding house accommodate at least 25 girl boarders who are students of classes IX-XII of recognised schools subject to an overall number of 50 boarders.

The eligibility condition for giving financial assistance under the scheme is that the voluntary organisations, societies, public trust and non-profit making bodies should be registered for at least three years and should have at least 25 girls studying in classes IX-XII staying in the hostel/boarding houses in recognised schools, subject to an overall number of 50 girl boarders.

### *Computer Education in schools*

A pilot project on Computer Literacy and Studies in Schools (Class) was initiated in 1984-85 in collaboration with Department of Electronics. The broad objectives of the pilot project included demystification of computer and to provide 'Hands on' experience. The project has been continued up to 1992-93 on ad hoc basis and funds to the tune of Rs 4 to 5 crore were provided on year to year basic. In all 2,598 schools were covered up to 1992-93. The scheme has been modified and is being implemented as a Centrally-sponsored scheme from 1993-94. To be eligible for assistance under the modified scheme, the following conditions are to be satisfied by the state/ UTs :

— The coverage of the scheme for new schools will be restricted to senior secondary schools;

— In selected schools, instructions in Computer Literacy will be compulsory for all students of classes XI and XII. These instructions will be part of the school timetable with the evaluation in the subject taking place with/without formal examination and;

— Infrastructure such as a *pucca* room with electricity and other fittings will have to be made in the school to be covered under the project by the State Government concerned, before taking the project.

The National Steering Committee under the Chairmanship of Education Secretary is responsible for monitoring and supervision, etc. At State/UT levels, Cells set up for the purpose, will discharge the dual responsibility of monitoring and actual implementation of the scheme in the schools and of releasing the -funds to the implementing agencies. During the Eighth Five Year Plan 2,371 schools were covered under the revised scheme besides the 2,598 schools already covered under the pre-revised scheme.

### *Environmental education*

The National Policy on Education 1986, provides that the protection of environment is a value which along with certain other values, must form an integral part of curricula at all stages of education. Operationalisation of this noble objective required that the mind and intellect of the students must be sensitised to the hazards inherent in the utter disregard and over exploitation of the bounties of nature. This step intends to inculcate awareness and respect among the students for the basis concepts relating to conservation of the environment. To this end a Centrally-sponsored scheme, Environmental Orientation to School Education was initiated in 1998-98 to assist state governments/UT administrations and voluntary agencies. The voluntary agencies are assisted for the conduct of experimental and innovative programmes aimed at promoting integration of educational programme in schools with local environmental conditions.

### *Science Education*

To improve the quality of science education and promote scientific temper, as envisaged in the National Policy on education, 1986 a Centrally Sponsored Scheme. "Improvement of Science Education in Schools" was initiated during 1987-88. Under the Scheme, financial assistance is provided to state governments /union territory administrations and voluntary agencies. While voluntary agencies are provided assistance for conducting experimental and innovative programmes, States/ UTs, are assisted for provision of science kits to upper primary schools; upgradation and strengthening of science laboratories in secondary/senior secondary schools, supply of books on science related subjects in secondary and senior secondary schools; and training of science and mathematics teachers. One of the important components of this scheme is participation of Indian students at school level in the International Mathematical Olympiad (IMO) as well as International Physics Olympiad (IPO). Indian students have been participating in IMO since 1989 and in the IPO from 1998.

### *National open school*

The National Open School (NOS) was established in November 1989, as an autonomous organisation in pursuance of the National Policy on Education, 1986 by the Ministry of Human Resource Development, Government of India to provide education to school drop outs and those who cannot attend the regular classes. The Open School of the Central Board of Secondary Education established in July 1979 was subsumed in the NOS. Open schooling is a significant innovation for complementing formal education.

The mission of NOS is universalisation of education, enhancing social equity and justice and creating a learning society. The marginalised groups, namely, rural youths, girls and women, scheduled castes and scheduled tribes, handicapped, ex-servicemen are priorities for NOS. With about 40,000 students in 1990, NOS has a student strength of more than three lakh students literally from each state and UT. NOS network of study centres consists of around 667 accredited Vocational Institutions (AVIS) for vocational courses all over the country. NOS makes provision of teachers, for tutoring and also counselling the students, at the accredited institutions.

It also encourages setting up of the State Open Schools. Such Schools have started functioning with the support of NOS in the states of Haryana, Madhya Pradesh, Karnataka and West Bengal. Punjab, Rajasthan, Andhra Pradesh, and Tamil Nadu have also State Open Schools. State Centres for Open Schooling have also been set up in Meghalaya, and Himachal Pradesh.

Negotiations are on for setting up of State Centre for Open Schooling in Manipur. During Ninth Five Year Plan period, 15 State Open Schools are planned to be established.

### *Navodaya vidyalaya*

The Government of India launched in 1985-86 a scheme to establish *Navodaya* Vidyalayas on an average of one in each district to provide good quality modern education to the talented children predominantly from the rural areas. The admission to *Navodaya* Vidyalayas is at the level of class VI based on an admission test conducted by NCERT. The medium of test is the mother tongue or regional language of the children.

The Vidyalayas are fully residential and co-educational to which admission to the children from urban areas is generally restricted to 25 per cent of the seats. Efforts are made to ensure that at least one-third of the students in each Vidyalaya are girls. Reservation of seats in favour of children belonging to SCs and STs is provided in proportion of their population in the concerned district provided that in no district such reservation is less than the national level. The Vidyalayas provide education in the streams of Humanities, Commerce, Science and Vocational up to +2 level and are affiliated to CBSE. There are at present 389 sanctioned Vidyalayas in the country operating in 30 states/UTs.

### *Kendriya vidyalaya*

The scheme for establishment of Central Schools was approved by the Government of India in 1962 and its implementation was started by the Ministry of Education in 1963 when 20 regimental schools run by the Ministry of Defence were taken over and converted into Central Schools or Kendriya Vidyalayas. Later on the Kendriya Vidyalaya Sangathan, an autonomous body was set up by the Ministry of Education and was registered as a Society in December 1965. During the academic year

1997-98 there are 877 Kendriya Vidyalayas with a student population of approximately 7.5 lakh. There are two Vidyalayas abroad one each in Kathmandu and Moscow.

Kendriya Vidyalayas are opened in Defence establishments on the recommendation of the Ministry of Defence and in the civil sector on the recommendation of the various ministries/ departments of the Central Government, state governments or the Central Government Employees Welfare Association. The sponsoring agency has to provide a piece of land measuring 15 acres for the construction of permanent building for Kendriya Vidyalaya.

The Kendriya Vidyalayas are opened in the campuses of public sector undertakings if they are ready to bear all the recurring and non-recurring expenditure on the proposed Kendriya Vidyalaya. The children of the employees of such undertakings get priority for admission to Kendriya Vidyalayas.

However, for admission in Kendriya Vidyalayas under civil and defence sectors the transferable Central Government employees including defence personnel get the priority. The reservation of 15 per cent and 7-1/2 per cent of fresh admissions is available in all Kendriya Vidyalayas for the children of SCs and STs respectively. All Kendriya Vidyalayas follow the same textbooks and medium of instruction which is in Hindi and English. Introductory computer science has been introduced as an elective subject in Kendriya Vidyalayas from this year for the XI and XII class students.

### *National council of educational research and training*

The National Council of Educational Research and Training (NCERT) was established in September 1961 in New Delhi as an autonomous body. Qualitative improvement and excellence in school education and teacher education are some of its major objectives. It develops curricula, syllabi and prepares textbooks for classes I-XII which form the basis for prescription of schemes of studies by Central Board of Secondary Education (CBSE) for the schools affiliated to the Board. It also develops instructional material for childhood education and training packages for teacher educators and supervisory personnel.

It provides technical assistance for national population education programmes designed to introduce population education in the formal education system. NCERT also provides its expertise to states/UTs. It also designs courses and material, generates software systems and sets up resource centres for computer literacy and studies in school projects.

NCERT organises Jawaharlal Nehru Science Exhibition every year in which a large number of school students from all over the country participate. It prepares comprehensive guidelines for curriculum evaluation of teachers on vocationalisation of education. Training courses for the officials involved in the Integrated Education Programme for Disabled Children are also conducted. Major projects entrusted to NCERT includes Sixth All India Education Survey, assistance in implementing the District Primary Education Programme (School and Non-Formal Education) etc. There are four regional institutes under NCERT at Ajmer, Bhopal, Mysore and Bhubaneswar. The North-Eastern Regional Institute at Shillong has also started functioning from the academic session 1996-97.

The NCERT under its National Talent Search Scheme (NTSS) awards 750 scholarships including 70 scholarships for SC/ST candidates each year. The purpose of this scheme is to identify brilliant students at the end of class-X and give them financial assistance towards getting good education. The selection for the award is done in two stages. The first stage selection is done by the state/union Territories through written examination conducted usually between October and December. The second stage selection involves both a written examination and an interview amongst the candidates recommended for second level test for the selection of the requisite number of awardees.

These awards were instituted in 1958. Initially, these were given away on convenient dates. From mid-60s, 5 September came to be the date of investiture. Twenty of the awards are reserved exclusively for teachers of Sanskrit, Persian and Arabic teaching in traditional institutions. For general teachers there are two categories (a) Primary Teachers (Class I to VIII) and (b) Secondary Teachers (Class IX to XII). Each State/UT has an earmarked quota based on teacher population, with the quota for secondary being half that of the primary; for smaller UTs, however, the quota is one each for both the categories. In order to be eligible the teacher should have put in 15 years of continuous service on the date of consideration of his claim by the State Level Selection Committee. For principals and headmasters the eligibility period is 20 years.

Selection is made by State level Selection Committee presided over by Director (Education) with State Coordinator of NCERT also as a member. The Committee considers recommendations received from districts. Committee's recommendations are forwarded by the State Government to Government of India without the authority to change the order of merit. State Government is competent to delete names after recording reasons for such deletion. The Government of India makes final selections strictly in order of merit on a scrutiny of the bio-data and service record, only ineligible are weeded out. Each award consists of a certificate of merit, silver medal and a cash prize of Rs 10,000. The awards are conferred each year on 5 September at a function specially held to honour the awardee teachers. In the award year 1997, 324 teachers / scholars have been conferred the National Award.

### *Technical education*

Technical Education which includes Management Education as well, is the main vehicle of social and economic transformation in the country. It is one of the most vital and significant components of the human resource development spectrum with great potential for adding value to products and services, for contributing to the national economy and for improving the quality of life of the common man. It has also been instrumental in making significant contribution to India's economic development by way of manpower production and relevant activities suiting to the needs of the industry and society and adapting to the vast changes in the global economy.

The rapid industrialisation during the post-independence period witnessed phenomenal growth of technical education facilities in the country. The first three Five Year Plans were devoted to expansion of technical education to meet the growing demands for technical personnel at Diploma, Degree and P.G. levels. From the Fourth Five Year Plan onwards, emphasis was on the improvement of quality and standards of technical education.

Apart from the Government Sector, involvement of private and voluntary organisations in setting up of Technical and Management Institutes helped in the expansion of the system. From 43 Polytechnics with an intake of 3,400 students at the time of Independence, the number has grown to 1, 128 Polytechnics with the intake of 1.90 lakh students in 1997.

Similarly, the number of Degree level institutions and the corresponding intake figure rose from 38 and 2940 in 1947 to 552 and 1.36 lakh in 1997. 185 institutions today conduct P.G. courses in Engineering and Technology with an annual intake capacity of 16,800. Facilities for Doctoral Studies in Engineering, Technology and Applied Sciences have also been created in a number of Technical Institutions.

This quantitative increase had its repercussion on the quality of technical education. A mushroom growth of self-financing private Engineering Colleges /Technical Institutions in the country, particularly in the southern region was causing concern to the policy makers, throwing to the winds all norms and standards for ensuring quality technical education.

Accordingly, AICTE which was an advisory body since 1945, was given statutory status with the introduction of AICTE

ACT, 1987 with a view to the proper planning and co-ordinated development of technical education system throughout the country. The AICTE issued Regulations in October 1994 relating to grant of approval for starting new technical institutions, introduction of courses or programmes and approval of intake capacity of seats for the courses for programmes. These were subsequently amended in May 1997. The technical education system was to enhance its coverage and accessibility suiting to the needs of organised as well as unorganised and rural sectors with its relevance to productivity.

Several initiatives were taken to revamp the technical education system by modernising the laboratories, etc. in technical institutions, promoting industry-institution interaction, providing continuing education for upgrading the skill and knowledge of technical personnel working in industry and services sector, transfer of technology to the rural sector and setting up of Technology Development Missions to meet the emerging challenges in the field of engineering and technology with active participation of industries. A major project was undertaken with the assistance of the World Bank to upgrade the technician education system for enabling the Polytechnics to improve their capacity, quality and efficiency.

The scheme of Community Polytechnics was launched that aims at sustainable community development without environmental degradation by way of science and technology applications for socio-economic uplift and improvement in the quality of life of the common man through micro-level planning and people's participation at the grassroot level. The scheme lays stress on poverty alleviation, employment generation and removal of drudgery for the women through location- culture specific non-formal need-based short term training in skill oriented technical /vocational trades.

To upgrade the Technician Education System in the Polytechnics, in the terms of capacity, quality and efficiency, a massive World Bank aided State Sector Project was launched in two phases starting 1990. The fall-out of the project created increase in women's participation in Technician Education from 12 per cent to 27 per cent through establishment of new Women's Polytechnics and Women's Wings in the existing Polytechnics. To render the benefits of techno-economic advances in Technical Education towards rural/community development, the scheme of Community Polytechnics with Extension Centres are functioning all over the country today including hilly, desert, coastal, remote, difficult and minority concentrated areas.

Meaningful and relevant Apprenticeship Training is being provided under the apprentice Act, 1961 (amended) to a large number of Engineering Degree, Diploma and 10+2 (Vocational) Pass-outs to bridge the gap between the world of Academics and the Industry and to help them achieve better employment prospects. Development of appropriate technical manpower with assured quality in technology and management areas, was sought to be achieved through establishment of six Indian Institutes of Technology and six Indian Institutes of Management at different places in the country.

Two specialised institutes with flexible academic design and non-conventional modular courses at Certificate, Diploma and Degree levels in Engineering /Technology/ Applied Sciences, viz. (i) North Eastern Regional Institute of Science and Technology (NERIST), Itanagar, Arunachal Pradesh and (ii) Sant Longowal Institute of Engineering and Technology at Village Longowal, Sangrur, Punjab were also set up for appropriate manpower development in technical areas. An Institute for Information Technology and Management for development of specified technical manpower in the emerging area of Information technology has also been set up at Gwalior.

It may thus be seen that India has a large infrastructure of technical institutions spread all over the country which qualitatively and quantitatively can compete with the best available facilities in the world. The Indian -Institutes of Technology (IITs) are premier centres of education and training in engineering and applied sciences at under-graduate level and provide facilities for post-graduate studies and research.

Indian Institutes of Management (IIMs) have been functioning as centres of excellence with the objective of providing education, training, research and consultancy in management. Indian Institute of Science, Bangalore has earned recognition as centre of research in basic and engineering sciences and allied fields. Excellence and creativity in research and development and learning programmes have characterised academic activity of the Institute. The Institute has also set up Super Computer with an Internet Hook-up. The National Policy on Education has laid emphasis on modernisation and removal of obsolescence of laboratories and workshops of engineering colleges and polytechnics in order to enhance functional efficiency. The scheme covers IITs and Regional Engineering Colleges (RECs) and other Engineering Colleges, Technical Faculties of Universities and Polytechnics.

Priority is being given to bring industrial commercial system and institutions closer. Technology missions in seven identified generic areas of strategic significance have been set up on the basis of their relevance to the Indian economy through IITs and IISc. These missions have earned wide acceptance and confidence among industries for development and know-how transfer of various technologies/ products by them and as such a unique example of industry-institute partnership has been established. The technical education system is vibrant even in the remote areas of North East (including Sikkim), Andaman & Nicobar Islands, Jammu & Kashmir and the Union Territories of, inter alia, Daman and Dadra & Nagar Haveli.

Towards promotion of overall societal development in such areas through technological inputs, expansion of technical education facilities is always encouraged through establishment of newer technical institutions and strengthening of the existing ones through all sorts of academic, technical and managerial support, co-operation and guidance. As such, while we have higher level technical institutions like (i) I.I.T, Guwahati, (ii)

NERIST, Itanagar, (iii) R.E.C., Silchar and scores of Diploma level Polytechnics in the North East, the Union Territories of Delhi, Chandigarh and Pondicherry offer high quality technical education through Degree and higher level technical institutions as well as Diploma level Polytechnics which are there even in the other UTs of A&N Islands, Daman and Dadra & Nagar Haveli.

The State of J&K does not lag too far behind with one Regional Engineering College at Srinagar, one Government College of Engineering and Technology at Jammu and a large number of Polytechnics in the State. In spite of this massive and cumulative build-up of a diverse infrastructural base, technological capability and institutional growth stand threatened from the sudden and complex change in the industrial base of the country and the advent of global competition in the wake of economic liberalisation.To face new challenges the thrust during the Ninth Plan is envisaged on the following four dimensions:

— Sustaining and consolidating the infrastructures and initiative with visible gains developed during the Eighth Plan and expanding the scope of such infrastructures for additional gains.

— Strengthening system of management and governance at all levels, networking between institutions and developing effective new linkages.

— Introducing new and innovative schemes which shall enhance the vibrancy of the system and help it conform to the emerging demands of industrial growth and societal development in terms of new technologies as well as quality enhancement.

— Expanding the research base amongst technical institutions to effectively tackle the industrial problems related to product, process and technology developments and also the manpower need.

### *Higher education*

Higher Education has a crucial role to play in the process of progress and modernisation. There has been considerable expansion of higher education with its role for economic and social development. The expansion of the system has been affecting the quality to a great extent. The Government, during the year, has tried to focus upon the initiatives to address the quality issues in higher education. There has been consistent efforts to improve upon the salaries and service conditions of University and College teachers so as to attract talents in the teaching profession.

Accordingly, the recommendations of the Fifth Central Pay Commission were extended to the University and College teachers with further improvement and modifications in the scales suggested by the committee earlier set up by the UGC for this purpose. As a result, the expenditure on account of the salaries to Central University teachers increased over Rs 300 crores during the year 1998-99. The Government also agreed to meet 80 per cent of the expenditure incurred by the State Government towards implementation of the improved pay scales, for a period of five years. The country made significant contribution to setting up the world agenda for higher education in the twenty-first century.

A high power delegation led by the Minister for Human Resource Development attended the UNESCO World Conference on Higher Education held at Paris between 5-9 October 1999. India's amendments to the World Declaration on Higher Education were highly appreciated by the Conference. One such accepted amendment. Ultimately, higher education should aim at the creation of a new society—non-violent and non-exploitative—consisting of highly cultivated, motivated and integrated individuals, inspired by love for humanity and guided by wisdom.

The Government took concrete measures to reform Higher Education and initiated steps for restructuring the UGC to achieve the purpose, during the year. A Task Force, headed by Prof. Amrik Singh submitted its report and has recommended amendments in the UGC Act so as to provide for wholetime members in the Commission, increase the penalty for running fake universities and awarding unrecognised degrees and make the laws more stringent, regulate the operation of foreign universities, encourage the setting up of self-financing institutions that could award degrees also and allow colleges and universities to determine the tuition fees within a broad policy framework and guidelines.

By the end of Ninth Plan it is expected that at the rate of 5.5 per cent compound rate of present growth there will be 8.5 per cent million students, and 10,000 colleges. Innovative initiatives have been taken up in the form of distance education to cater to the unprecedented expansion. It is expected that reforms initiated in Higher Education during the year would go a long way to meet the needs and challenges of the system in terms of quantity as well as quality.

Higher Education is imparted through 214 universities in the country. Of these, there are 16 Central universities and the remaining are functioning under the State Acts. Total number of colleges in the country is 9,703. There are 38 institutions declared Deemed-to-be Universities under the University Grants Commission Act, 1956. The enrolment of students is 67.55 lakh while the number of teachers is 3.21 lakh.

Coordination and determination of standards in higher education is a subject of the Union List and hence a special responsibility of the Central government. This responsibility is discharged mainly through University Grants Commission (UGC) which was established in 1956 under an Act of Parliament to take measures for promotion and coordination of university education and determination and maintenance of standards in teaching, examination and research in universities.

To fulfil its objectives, the Commission can enquire among other things into financial needs of the universities; allocate and disburse grants to them; establish and maintain common services and facilities; recommend measures for improvement of university education and give advice on allocation of grants and establishment of new universities. UGC has approved 119 colleges for autonomous status, 19 in Andhra Pradesh-, 44 in Tamil Nadu, 38 in Madhya Pradesh, five each in Orissa and Himachal Pradesh, three in Uttar Pradesh and two each in Maharashtra and Gujarat.

*Indian Council of Historical Research*

Indian Council of Historical Research, New Delhi, set up in 1972 enunciates and implements a national policy on historical research and encourages scientific writing of history. It operates research projects, finances research projects by individual scholars, awards fellowships and undertakes publication and translation work. Indian Council of Philosophical Research, which started functioning from 1981 with offices in New Delhi and Lucknow, reviews the progress, sponsors or assists projects and programmes of research in philosophy, gives financial assistance to institutions and individuals to conduct research in philosophy and allied disciplines.

Indian Institute of Advanced Study, Shimla set up in 1965 is a residential centre for advanced research on humanities, social sciences and natural sciences. It is a community of scholars engaged in exploring new frontiers of knowledge aimed at conceptual development and offering interdisciplinary perspectives on questions of contemporary relevance. Indian Council of Social Science Research, New Delhi, is an autonomous body for promoting and coordinating social science research. Its main functions are to review the progress of social science research, give advice on research activities in government or outside, sponsor research programmes and give grants to institutions and individuals for research in social sciences.

*National council of rural institutes (1995)*

The National Council of Rural Institutes was set up on 19 October 1995 as an autonomous organisation fully funded by the Central government to promote rural higher education on the lines of Mahatma Gandhi's revolutionary ideas on education, consolidate network and develop educational institutions and voluntary agencies in accordance with Gandhian philosophy of education and promote research as a tool for social and rural development.

*Indira Gandi National Open University*

Indira Gandhi National Open University (IGNOU) was established by an Act of Parliament in September 1985 for the introduction and promotion of open university and distance education system in the educational pattern of the country and for the coordination and determination of standards in such systems.

The major objectives of the university include widening access to higher education to larger segments of the population, organising programmes of continuing education and initiating special programmer, of higher education for specific target groups like women, people living in backward regions, hilly areas, etc.

The IGNOU provides an innovative system of university level education, flexible and open in regard to methods and pace of learning, combination of courses, eligibility for enrolment, age of entry, methods of evaluation, etc.

The University has adopted an integrated multimedia instructional strategy consisting of printed materials and audio-video aids, supported by counselling sessions at a network of study centres throughout the country. It conducts both continuous evaluation as well as term-end examinations.

The IGNOU introduced its programmes in 1987 and has so far launched 39 programmes consisting of 486 courses.

During 1997 over 1.63 lakh students have been registered for various programmes of study. The University has established an extensive student support services network consisting of 18 regional centres and 315 study centres situated in different part of the country.

A Distance Education Council (DEC) established by the University as a statutory authority is an apex body for coordination and determination of standards in distance education Doordarshan commenced telecast of IGNOU's programmes in May 1991 while the Mumbai and Hyderabd stations of All India Radio started broadcasting selected audio programme of the IGNOU from early 1992.

At present there are eight other open universities in the country, viz., B.R. Ambedkar Open University, Hyderabad (Andhra Pradesh), Kota Open University, Kota (Rajasthan), Nalanda Open University (Bihar), Yashwant Rao Chavan Maharashtra Open University, Nasik (Maharashtra), Madhya Pradesh Bhoj Open University, Bhopal (Madhya Pradesh), Ambedkar Open University, Ahmadad (Gujarat), Karnataka State Open University, Mysore (Karnataka) and Netaji Subhas Open University, Calcutta (West Bengal).

### *Women's Education*

The National Policy for Education document made a strong commitment to 'a well conceived edge in favour of women' as 'an act of faith and social engineering'. These commitments have been translated into concrete guidelines, and have resulted in a number of interventions which focus on the empowerment of women as the critical precondition for their participation in the educational process. The impact of these programmes is reflected in the decennial growth rate in female literacy of 9.54 per cent (Census 1991) which is significantly higher than the corresponding figure for males (7-76 per cent).

The following special provisions for women have been incorporated in the existing schemes :

— Operation Blackboard scheme now provides that at least 50 per cent of the teachers recruited in the future should be women. Out of the 1.27 lakh posts of the teachers filled under the scheme, 47 per cent are by women;

— An innovative approach taken up in Rajasthan to improve access to education is the Shiksha Karmi Project. It envisaged substitution of the primary school teacher in single teacher schools by a team of two locally resident educational workers called Shiksha Karmis, of whom 10 per cent are women;

— Under the scheme of Non-Formal Education, 90 per cent assistance is given for NFE centres exclusively for girls. The scheme has recently been revised so as to provide more facilities for educating girls by increasing the ratio of NFE centres exclusively for girls from 25 per cent to 40 per cent of the total;

— Efforts are being made to ensure that at least one-third of the students in each Navodaya Vidayalayas are girls. In Navodaya Vidayalayas and Kendriya Vidyalayas, free education is imparted to girls up to Class XII;

— Free education is provided to girls up to class VIII in Punjab (Government schools), Manipur, Rajasthan (Government schools), UP, Delhi, Meghalaya and Chandigarh and up to secondary stage in Andhra Pradesh, Assam, Bihar (Government schools), Himachal Pradesh (Government schools) ' Karnataka, Tamil Nadu (Government schools), Mizoram and Lakshadweep and up to senior secondary stage Class XII in the states of Arunachal Pradesh, Goa, J and K, Kerala, Sikkim (Government schools), Tripura, West Bengal, A and N Islands, D and N Haveli, Daman and Diu, Pondicherry, Gujarat and Madhya Pradesh;

— Under the Centrally-sponsored programme, at+2 level vocational programmes with emphasis on entrepreneurship are being designed to cater to the needs of girls who drop out of schools. Efforts are also on to consciously encourage participation of girls in the non-traditional and emergent technologies;

— Women's education at the -university and college levels have been diversified and re-oriented in tune with the changing requirement of society, industry and trade. The number of women enrolled institutions of higher education increased from 40,000 in 1950-51 to about 20,65,000 in 1995-96, an increase of more than 51 times over the 44 year period;

— The enrolment of women students at the beginning of the year 1993-94 was 15.90 lakh, as against 15.12 lakh in the previous year. At the postgraduate level the enrolment of women was 34.09 per cent of the total enrolment;

— The UGC has been providing assistance to universities for undertaking research projects in women's studies; a number of research projects have been approved for assistance. Also assistance has been provided to 22 universities and 11 colleges for setting up women's studies/cells. The UGC has also created 40 positions of part-time research associateships for women candidates; and

— The participation of women in technical and professional streams has also shown a marked increase from a little over 6,000 in 1950-51 to 1.46 lakh in 1986-87, an increase of 23 times. There was also noticeable growth in the number of women students in the engineering and technology streams (in IITs and Polytechnics). As against 40 women students in 1950-51 (0.3 per cent) it rose to 16.67 thousand in 1986-87 (7.7 per cent) and 78.3 thousand in 1993-94 (13.1 per cent).

*Mahila samakhya programme*

*Mahila Samakhya* programme is a women's empowerment project which aims at creating an environment for women to seek knowledge and information with a view to bringing about a change in their perception about themselves and that of the society. Mahila Samakhya launched in 1989 is being implemented in about 5,500 villages spread over 38 districts of Uttar Pradesh, Gujarat, Karnataka, Andhra Pradesh, Bihar, Assam and Madhya Pradesh. The programme has been able to lay the foundations for women's empowerment at the grass-root level and make strategic interventions to support education of adolescent girls and adult women.

### *Education for Minorities*

In pursuance of the revised Programme of Action (POIA) 1992, two new Centrally sponsored schemes i.e. (i) Scheme of Area Intensive Programme for Educationally Backward Minotrities and (ii) Scheme of Financial Assistance for Modernisation of *Madrasa* Education were launched during 1993-94. The objective of scheme of Area Intensive Programme for Educationally Backward Minorities is to provide basic educational infrastructure and facilities in areas of concentration of educationally backward minorities which do not have adequate provision for elementary and secondary schools.

The scheme of Financial Assistance for Modernisation of *Madrasa Education* is being implemented with a view to encouraging traditional institutions like *Madrasa* and *Maktabs* to introduce science, mathematics, social studies, Hindi and English in their curriculum. Under this scheme, cent per cent assistance is given to such institutions for appointment of qualified teachers for teaching the new subjects to be introduced. The University Grants Commission introduced in 1984 a coaching scheme to prepare students belonging to educationally backward minorities for various competitive examinations. As part of implementation of the 15 point programme by the end of financial year 1990-91, 41 minority concentration districts have been covered by community polytechnics or their extension centres.

According to the 1991 census Scheduled Castes and Scheduled Tribes population in India was 13.82 crore and 6.8 crore forming 16.33 per cent and 8.01 per cent respectively of the total population of the country. As against the national average of 52.21 per cent the literacy rate among SCs and STs was 37.41 per cent and 29.60 per cent respectively. The National policy on education (NPE) 1986 as updated in 1992 lays special emphasis on removal of disparities and equalisation of educational opportunities attending to the specific needs of those who have been denied equality, particularly scheduled castes, scheduled tribes and educationally backward minorities. Some of the important programmes of the Department of Education are:

— Norms of opening of primary school has been relaxed to have a primary school within one kilometer walking distance from habitations of 200 population instead of habitations of 300 population;

— Abolition of tuition fee in all states in government schools at least up to Upper Primary level. Most of the states have abolished tuition fee for SC/ST students up to senior secondary level and also provide incentives like textbooks, uniforms school bags, etc. to these students;

— The major programmes of the Department of Education like Universalisation of Elementary Education, Operation Blackboard, Non-Formal Education, District Primary Education Programme, etc., accord priority to areas of concentration of scheduled castes and scheduled tribes. Lok *Jumbish* and *Shiksha* Karmi projects which are community based non-formal education projects have a specific focus on SC/ST inhabited areas;

— Reservation of seats for SCs and STs in Central government institutions of higher education including IITs, Regional Engineering Colleges, Central Universities, Kendriya Vidyalayas and *Navodya* Vidyalayas, etc., Reservation in universities and colleges apart from relaxation in the minimum qualifying cut off stages. UGC has established

SC/ST Cells in 98 universities including central universities with a view to ensuring proper implementation of the reservation policy;

— In order to improve the academic skills and linguistic proficiency of students in various subjects and raising their level of comprehension, remedial and special coaching is provided for SC and ST students. IITs have a scheme under which SC/ST students who marginally fail in the entrance examination are provided one year training and then admitted to the First Year of B. Tech. Course.

— Out of 43,000 scholarships, 13,000 scholarships are provided to SC/ST students under the scheme of National Scholarship at the secondary stage for talented children from rural areas.

— Junior Research Fellowship (50), scholarships (25), Research Associateship (20), and Fellowships (50) are awarded by UGC exclusively to SC/ST students;

— Central Institute of Indian Languages (CIIL) Mysore, prepares textbooks, primer's grammar books, dictionaries, bilingual text books facilitating translation from regional languages, etc. into tribal languages.

— The NCERT has prepared /developed/ published 10 textbooks in tribal dialects and prepared teaching learning material in 15 tribal dialects.

### *Literacy Programmes and Adult Education*

Adult education and literacy programmes have been transformed under the auspices of the National Literacy Mission (NLM) into a mass campaign leading towards a people's movement for total literacy and a new awakening for education. The goal of NLM is to attain full literacy. NLM envisages that focussing on imparting of functional literacy to non-literates in the 15-35 age group would help achieve this goal. This age group has been selected because they are in the productive as well as the reproductive period of life.

NLM seeks to bring non-literates to a level of self-reliance in the three R's. It also provides them facilities for skill development to improve their economic status and well being. It enables them to imbibe values of national integration, conservation of the environment, women's equality and observance of small family norms. And finally, it facilitates their participation in the development process. Functional literacy, encompassing all of the above, is the overall goal of NLM.

The success of the campaign mode in the Ernakulam district of Kerala laid the foundations of the campaign approach. While developing a national strategy for the country, the National Literacy Mission was fully aware of the need for diversity of approaches, given the inter-regional variations in the country. It was also aware that in many parts, participation of women and disadvantaged sections would require an intensive environment building process.

In this context, efforts of NLM represent a major initiative for bringing together civil society to actively participate in a people's movement for achieving literacy in time bound fashion. Recognising the fragile nature of literacy levels achieved in a campaign mode and the need to create a learning society, the NLM provides for a Post Literacy Campaign where the gains of literacy are consolidated and an effort is made to link learning skills with life skills. Similarly, in order to sustain the learning process in the community, NLM supports the establishment of Continuing Education Centres that provide a package of life-linked services for neo-literates.

*Total Literacy Campaign (TLC)*

The Total Literacy Campaign (TLC) is the principal strategy adopted by NLM for eradication of illiteracy in the country. The Literacy Campaigns are area-specific, time-bound, delivered through voluntarism, cost effective and outcome- oriented. After completion of the TLC in a distruct, Post Literacy Programme (PLP) is launched to mop up the leftover illiterates and also to consolidate the gains accrued during TLC. This enables the neo-literates to develop abilities for self-learning and skill upgradation. A total of 450 districts have been covered by TLCs. Of these, 250 districts have moved into the Post Literacy phase. The ultimate objective is to carry forward the literacy programmes in the district to the third phase of life-long learning which is conceived under the scheme of Continuing Education.

The Continuing Education Centres would aim to create a learning environment in the villages and habitation which they serve. There would be opportunities here for addressing the residual non-literates and for providing neo-literates with Equivalency Programmes, Income Generation Programmes, Quality of Life Improvement Programmes, and Individual Interest Promotion Programmes.

The NLM takes special care to emphasise linkages between literacy and life and in so doing provides enhanced opportunities for skill development and improved income generation. This attempt is operationalised through the scheme of Shramik Vidyapeeths. The basic idea behind the multi -dimensional or polyvalent education approach to the education of urban working community in Shramik Vidyapeeth is to meet the various inter-related needs of target groups which mainly constitute the socially and economically deprived sections of worker communities with specifically tailored programmes. This provides knowledge and imparts vocational and technical skills in an integrated manner. The programme helps in enhancing employment opportunities and supplementing their income.

The NLM also lays emphasis on involving voluntary agencies. Several of them have been provided with assistance to take up innovative programmes on adult education in various parts of the country. The NLM also has set up 25 State Resource Centres which provide academic input, improved training practices and opportunities for creation of imaginative literature for neo-literates. Under Adult Education Programmes 72.56 million persons have been made literate so far, 60 per cent of them are women: 22.40 per cent are SCs and 13.20 per cent belong to STs. The NLM has a system of concurrent and external evaluation of literacy campaigns and post-literacy programmes by reputed research agencies in the field of social sciences.

According to the National Sample Survey Organisation (NSSO) the percentage of literacy has increased from 52 in 1991 to 62 in 1997 and projected at 64 for 1998. The quantum jump of 10 percent between 1991 and 1997 and 12 per cent between 1991 and 1998 thus compares extraordinarily favourable with the decadal trends of previous years which are at an average of 8.5 per cent since Independence. The urban-rural differential in literacy rates has also shown a marked decline of 4 per cent, this is faster than in any previous decade. The rise in female literacy between 1991 and 1997 has been 11 per cent whereas the male literacy rate has risen by 9 per cent. This is a tribute to the special emphasis laid by NLM on women's participation. With annual rate of literary growth of 2 per cent revealed by NSSO survey, India could be expected to touch sustainable threshold level of 75 per cent by 2005.

Although the literacy campaigns are being implemented with varying degrees of success, it is certain that remarkable progress has been achieved. The focus is now on the four low literacy Hindi-speaking States which together account for nearly 50 per cent of the total number of illiterates in the country. Now that the process has begun in these States as well, the goal of universal literacy appears closer. Some of the spin-offs of TLCs have been improved enrolment at primary level; social empowerment of women; improvement in immunisation and acceptance of the small family norms and organised correction of superstitions and social evils. This has generated a great demand for adult education projects throughout the country.

The National Literacy Mission has undertaken a number of new initiatives in adult education. These include rigorous system of monitoring of literacy campaigns; transparent and more effective evaluations; sensitising Panchayati Raj representatives to ensure mass participation in literacy programmes and decentralising of financial and administrative powers to State Literacy Mission Authorities.

### *Teacher Education*

As envisaged in NPE and POA—1986, the Centrally-sponsored scheme of Restructuring and Reorganisation of Teacher Education was taken up in 1987 to create a viable institutional infrastructure, and academic and technical resources base for orientation/ training and continuous upgradation to knowledge, competence and pedagogic skills of elementary education teachers in the country. The Scheme envisaged setting up of DIETs in each District to provide academic and resource support to elementary education teachers and NFE/AE Instructors. It also envisaged upgradation of selected Secondary Teacher Education Institutions (STEIs) into CTEs and IASEs to organise pre-service and in-service training for secondary teachers and to provide extension and resource support services to secondary schools.

IASEs were expected to conduct programmes for preparation of elementary teacher educators; to conduct in-service training for elementary and secondary teacher educators and principals of secondary schools; to engage in advanced level fundamental and applied research especially of interdisciplinary nature, and to provide academic guidelines to DIETs and support services to CTEs. Till the end of 1997-98, 444 DIETs have been sanctioned, 76 CTEs and 34 IASEs have been upgraded and 19 SCERTs have been strengthened.

### *NCTE*

The National Council for Teacher Education (NCTE) has been established under the National Council for Teacher Education Act, 1993 as a statutory body with effect from August 17 1995, with the objectives of achieving planned and co-ordinated development of teacher education system, regulation and proper maintenance of norms and standards of teacher education and for matters connected therewith. As per provisions of the Act four Regional Committees for the northern, southern, eastern and western regions have been set up at Jaipur, Bangalore, Bhubaneswar and Bhopal respectively. These Committees consider the applications of institutions of teacher education for recognitions of institutions of teacher education for recognition /permission in accordance with the provision of the NCTE Act.

The Council has laid down norms and standards for pre-primary, elementary, secondary level teacher education institutions and for B.Ed. through correspondence/distance education mode. During the year 1997-98 the NCTE has held a number of seminars, workshops, symposia, awareness meeting etc. The NCTE have also taken up a number of projects and studies for the development of teacher education in the country.

## *INC*

India has been a member of the United Nations Educational, Scientific and Cultural Organisation (UNESCO), a specialised agency of the United Nations, since its inception in 1946. The Government of India, set up an Interim Indian National Commission for Cooperation with UNESCO (INC) in 1949 which was later put on a permanent footing in 1951. The composition of the Commission is reviewed from time to time to make it more effective in the discharge of its assigned functions in relation to the scope and content of UNESCO's programmes. The Commission has been last reconstituted in June 1997. The Commission consists of five Sub-Commissions, namely, Education; Natural Sciences; Social Sciences; Culture and Communication. The main objectives of the Commission are to contribute to the maintenance of peace and security and the common welfare of mankind by participating in the activities of UNESCO and to play an ever increasing role in UNESCO's work particularly in the formulation and execution of its programmes.

of non-Hindi speaking states study in Hindi and scholarships to enable talented rural children to continue secondary education. These programmes are administered through the state governments/Union Territories. Scholarships for advanced or specialised studies are offered under the provisions of cultural Exchange programme, bilateral agreements, Commonwealth scholarships/ fellowship plan and ad-hoc scholarship offers received from different countries.

# INDEX